THE RISE AND RISE OF

THE BLACK EYED PEAS

LET'S GET IT STARTED

D0547687

THE RISE AND RISE OF

THE BLACK
EYED PEAS

LET'S GET IT
STARTED

DARYL EASLEA

**OMNIBUS PRESS**

London / New York / Paris / Sydney / Copenhagen / Berlin / Madrid / Tokyo

Cover designed by Fresh Lemon
Picture research Jacqui Black

ISBN: 978.1.84938.870.2
Order No: OP53977

**Exclusive Distributors**
Music Sales Limited,
14/15 Berners Street,
London, W1T 3LJ.

Music Sales Corporation,
257 Park Avenue South,
New York, NY 10010, USA.

Macmillan Distribution Services,
56 Parkwest Drive
Derrimut, Vic 3030,
Australia.

Typeset by Phoenix Photosetting, Chatham, Kent
Printed in the EU

A catalogue record for this book is available from the British Library.

Visit Omnibus Press on the web at www.omnibuspress.com

# Contents

For my beautiful Flora. Thank you for lending me your BEP player. It made all the difference.

For my darling Jules. Who would have thought, 25 years ago?

# Introduction

# Fill Up My Cup

*"This band is like musical hip-hop, like theatre, in a sense. We are not your typical hip-hop band. The people that come to our shows and buy our records don't seem to mind."*

Stacy Ferguson, 2005

*"You'd find it hard to make up our group. We are more like a mad, worldwide science project than a band. No record label could have invented us. I'm a black guy who grew up in a Mexican neighbourhood. Then we have a white girl, a guy from the Philippines and a Mexican rapper who was raised in a Chinese part of town."*

will.i.am, 2009

Every generation gets the music it deserves. When the Black Eyed Peas – the strangely monikered, multi-racial rappers, dancers and vocalists, will.i.am, apl.de.ap, Taboo and Fergie – started making computerized, beat-laden, simplistic post-hop with 'I Gotta Feeling' in 2009, the group who'd been together since the mid-nineties, became something else entirely. For many, it was the final detachment from their East LA hip-hop roots, and the ultimate adoption into the widest possible mainstream; they were no longer, as they had been so extensively on their earliest recordings, quoting their references. They had now created, with French DJ David Guetta, a potent brand of mainstream party house. As they occupied the top two positions in the US *Billboard* Hot 100 with this and their preceding single, the extraordinarily minimalist 'Boom Boom Pow', 'I Gotta Feeling' became the first digital download to sell a million copies in the UK, and demonstrated that the group had gained a whole new generation of fans who had no idea that the Black Eyed Peas had been recording for over a decade.

Their image was now what really struck a chord – the four group members had become strange cartoon images of themselves, with outlandishly futuristic clothes and matching headgear. And 'I Gotta Feeling', a call-to-action celebration anthem, seemed to top all of its predecessors in that well-trodden genre. Over an insistent computerized riff, will.i.am encourages people to party, with a simple hunch that the evening ahead will be an absolute stormer. And then it builds, and builds and builds, until the song explodes in a jump-inducing frenzy. All it asks its audience to do is to go out and have a good time, which in 2009 was a much-needed diversionary tactic, as the world teetered into a new recession and the first signs appeared that the amazing new dawn offered by the Barack Obama presidency wasn't going to be as great as all that. By March 2011, the song had become the first record in digital history to sell over seven million downloads. The group had truly created an anthem for the digital age.

This is the story of a group who enjoyed not one, but two rebirths. As *Entertainment Weekly* wrote in 2009, "Ever since the group's three core members transformed themselves from a middling conscious-rap outfit into the platinum hip-pop juggernaut of 2003's breakout *Elephunk*, featuring lithesome onetime child star Stacy 'Fergie' Ferguson, their energy has appeared to be virtually unsinkable." And it was true. When will.i.am, apl.de.ap and Taboo were joined by Ferguson in 2003, the Black Eyed Peas went from experimental to exponential. In Ferguson, the group – who at best resembled a raggle-taggle band of highly individual rappers – found a pretty, unique, public face, ready to dance, ready to sing, ready to do most anything. The selection of 'Where Is The Love?' from *Elephunk* as the first single with this new line-up was appropriate.

As the tragic events of 9/11 had become another excuse for nations to go to war with other nations, the seemingly simplistic rallying call for peace and harmony struck a chord. And it remained high in the US and the UK charts for most of the later summer of 2003. However, its sweet groove and marriage of the personal and the global masked its bitter attacks on the CIA and the inner turmoil in the US. Its use of the repeated refrain, 'Father, father, father' was a clear echo of Marvin Gaye's 1971 protest anthem, 'What's Going On', as 'Where Is The Love?' searches for the covert reasons behind conflict and looks for explanations of why hatred and war infect the minds of the young. Its pleas for overall unity at the end may be simplistic, but it put these messages on the radar for a generation.

One may wonder how the group's socio-political concerns of 2003 had become diluted to the point of releasing seemingly simple party anthems only six years later, but in a way, this says everything about the Black Eyed Peas. Often, their message requires a strangely apolitical social conscience, combined with an inclusive implication of unity, big, bold cartoon slapstick and a strong urge to dance, dance, dance.

The Black Eyed Peas have never been held in the greatest reverence by the hip-hop cognoscenti. Critics who see their cartoon-like rapping and reductive visuals as shallow and ephemeral view them perhaps as *arrivistes* but to do this is to miss the point entirely. The Black Eyed Peas have their roots firmly in the hip-hop scene, having been part of it for over 20 years from their outset. That they didn't take a conventional route to sucess is another matter.

In 1996, the Black Eyed Peas emerged at something of a crossroads for hip-hop. Its first wave of artists were now growing older, either going cabaret or caricature. Ice-T had lost his critical and commercial head of steam thanks to the controversy surrounding his track 'Cop Killer', recorded with his sideline thrash band, Body Count. Ice Cube was moving increasingly into film. Gansgta rap was the music of the day, and the outpouring of grief after the deaths of Notorious B.I.G. and Tupac Shakur fuelled enormous record sales and made them the most popular artists of the mid-nineties. A new breed of money-loving, business-minded rap mogul was emerging – Shawn Corey Carter, aka Jay-Z, and Sean Combs, the producer and rapper known as Puff Daddy. They would redefine the genre. On the other hand, there was the complex mysticism of Wu-Tang Clan.

If these were the major players, the Black Eyed Peas seemed like the bunch of geeks in the corner of the common room. They looked and sounded like none of their peers. If anything, they owed far more to the Daisy Age rappers of the late eighties/early nineties – De La Soul, A Tribe Called Quest and P.M Dawn – than the swaggering braggadocio or lofty ambitions of their peers. As with many things throughout his life to date, leader will.i.am was out of step with what was going on around him, looking constantly to reinvent what he saw as a tired genre. It would only be many years later that everyone else was banging his drum.

# Chapter 1

# The Birth Of The Visual Stereo Sound

*"If I was really worried about 'keeping it real' then I never would have put an album out – I would still be in my neighbourhood doing music for my homies. When we went to the next neighbourhood to do music for other people, my homies on the block said, 'Y'all sellouts, why the fuck y'all goin' to Hollywood?' If I really cared about that I would have stopped it back then, cuz in actuality those are the real cats – the people I grew up with that dug what I did."*

will.i.am, 2002

The story of the Black Eyed Peas is fundamentally the story of William Adams, who, under his *nom de rap*, will.i.am, provided the inspiration and drive for the group. As its producer, principal writer, lead male vocalist and rapper, he guided the group from their East LA beginnings to their stadium-filling everyman pop of the early 21st century.

Adams was born William James Adams on March 15, 1975 in Inglewood, California, and raised in the Estrada Courts projects in the Boyle Heights district of East Los Angeles. His father, William Adams

Sr was quickly off the scene. Little is known of Adams Sr aside from his Jamaican origins. His mother, Debra Cain, had three of her own children, Adams' sister Qiana and his brother Carl, and adopted four more. A strongly independent woman with an innate appreciation of art and music, she wholeheartedly encouraged Adams to stand apart from other children and develop his individuality. Adams was also raised by his uncles, Rendal Fay, Donnie, Roger and Lynn.

In 2011, Adams was asked by *Elle* magazine if he felt he had missed out on anything without a father around. "I asked my mother about it once," he replied." And she said, 'Willie, can I ask you a question? Are you happy with your perspective on the world? Are you proud that you're tenacious and driven? Are you happy how me and your uncles have raised you?' I was like, 'Yeah.' She said, 'Then you shouldn't feel like you're missing anything. I am your daddy. I protected you, and the proof is your happiness with who you are right now.'" Unlike many of the fathers of those who become famous, Adams Sr has not reappeared on the scene. "I've been truly protected by my uncles," Adams added. "All I know is that dude don't come around, and I'm happy it's that way."

Adams remains close to his mother, admiring her strength and positivity. He told *The Sun*: "My mom is the most awesome woman. She raised us all by herself... Mom adopted two other girls when they were infants. Then she just recently adopted two other boys." Adams knew that he would do right for his mother. He told her when he was 11 that he would buy her a house one day.

The Adamses were one of the few African-American families living in the largely Latino Estrada Courts. "We were the only black family in our neighbourhood, everyone else was Mexican," Adams said in 2007. "It was a great experience." His mother encouraged Adams to be his own man; not for him joining gangs and playing with others, rather he developed his own style and got others to join him. This was the birth of the restless individuality that has become the cornerstone of his work.

Adams excelled at sport and his first love was American football, which came in part from his uncle Lynn, who had been an NFL player since 1979, playing for the Atlanta Falcons between 1979 and 1984 and for the LA Rams in 1985. Adams also developed a youthful passion for rap. When he was four, rap moved from being a street corner phenomenon to gaining ground in the charts with the initial success of the Sugar Hill Gang's 'Rapper's Delight' and then Grandmaster Flash and the Furious Five's party tunes. By the middle of the eighties after 'The Message', rap had become something deeper, darker and more substantial. This combined with the global success of Michael Jackson's *Thriller*, which came out when he was seven, piqued Adams' interest and music was always playing in his house.

When he was 13 years old, Adams went from Paul Revere Junior High on 1450 Allenford Avenue to somewhere more up-market. "Mom sent me to school in Pacific Palisades, a wealthy neighbourhood. She wanted me to be challenged," he said. Pacific Palisades was an affluent, largely residential area, a world away from East LA and an hour's journey each way for Adams. Located between Brentwood to the east, Malibu to the west and Santa Monica to the south east, it is known as 'where the mountains meet the sea'; it also contains the western end of Sunset Boulevard. The area contains notable popular culture locations; the high school was the setting of Brian De Palma's 1976 chiller, *Carrie*, and the long-running James Garner TV detective vehicle, *The Rockford Files,* was filmed in the area. Pacific Palisades Charter School was a well-respected establishment situated on 15777 Bowdoin Street, and its alumni included actors Jeff Bridges and Forest Whitaker, and musicians such as Susannah Hoffs from the Bangles and musical mavericks Ron and Russell Mael, the duo behind art-rock group Sparks. Adams enjoyed school, although came away with no great love for literature. "I can read pretty well, but my attention span is really short," he told *Chicken Bones* journal. "When I read, the first paragraph is great, the second is great, but by about the third paragraph or so, I'm just reading the words and it's no longer sinking into my mind."

Pacific Palisades school, known as Palihigh, was largely white, but had a strong mix of ethnic minorities. In 2007, the student report noted that the ethnic mix was 49% White/Caucasian, 23% Hispanic, 18% African-American, 8% Asian, and 2% other. But in 1985, the mix was geared further towards whites. Adams told *Billboard*: "The black people hung out by the lunch tables, the Mexicans hung out by the bathroom, the white people hung out in their cars, the Asian people stood next to their lockers. I would always wander between the different sections. If I didn't go to that school, the Black Eyed Peas wouldn't be what it is. I don't think we would be able to relate to every country on the planet."

Adams went through a brief phase of rebellion, putting the graffiti tag 'Expo' – short for 'exposure' on walls. His Uncle Fay caught him and reported him to his mother, who for the first time in his life, if memory served him, administered a good beating. Adams thought twice about doing it again.

It was at school that he met his future partner in the Black Eyed Peas, Allan Pineda Lindo. Pineda was born on November 28, 1974 in the Sapang Bato district of Angeles City in Pampanga in the Philippines. He was the son of an American serviceman based at Clark Air Base on Luzon Island, just outside Angeles City. One of seven children, Pineda was raised by a single Filipina mother, Cristina Pineda, a domestic helper. The family lived in poverty and as a small child Pineda worked the local farms picking rice and corn after he had completed his hour each-way journey to school on a small bus-taxi that was known as a Jeepney. Born with a sight condition, Pineda had to wear thick glasses and was teased at school, which initially threatened to knock him off course for studying to become a nurse, his first ambition. When he was 14, Pineda was adopted by a Californian-based lawyer, Joe Ben Hudgens, who sponsored Pineda through the Pearl S. Buck Foundation.

The Pearl S. Buck Foundation was set up by author, missionary and humanitarian Buck in 1964. She had won the Nobel Prize for literature in 1938 for her "rich and truly epic descriptions of peasant life in China and for her biographical masterpieces". Her most famous book, the Pulitzer-prize winning *The Good Earth,* which focused on family life in a Chinese farming village, was published in 1931. Following on from the Welcome House programme she had introduced in 1949, which was the first international inter-racial adoption agency in the US, the Foundation was established to address issues of discrimination and poverty faced by children in Asian countries. Buck, who had been raised as the daughter of American missionaries in China, had a vision to create a bridge between east and west, a desire to create a better life for the underprivileged. Pineda first travelled to America when he was 11 for treatment of his eye condition, nystagmus, a series of involuntary eye movements that can come on from birth, and ultimately lead to only partial vision or even blindness.

Pineda was sponsored by Hudgens after the lawyer had seen an advert on American TV and a call-to-action for the Pearl S. Buck Foundation, initially on a dollar-a-day assistance programme. Within two years, Pineda had been formally adopted by Hudgens, and in 1988 Pineda moved to the US. Pineda was a deep, thoughtful child, who had enormous inner strength – particularly needed as he was to travel across the Pacific Ocean to grow up apart from his mother.

Future Black Eyed Peas member Taboo wrote later of Pineda, "He was born with an astigmatism in each eye. When I first met him, he had what appeared to be some kind of nervous tic. He'd shake his head and blink repeatedly. Turns out he was shaking his head to establish focus. He sees outlines, not detail, more shapes than vivid colour, but then you see how he dances, how he writes and how he thinks and it is mind blowing." Pineda's condition was further complicated by the fact that he also suffers from short-sightedness and colour blindness. When he was older, he really wanted to drive, and, with some foolhardiness, actually did so for a while. "One wrong turn and I'd be lost for hours," he later told *People* magazine.

Pineda was a student of John Marshall High School in the Los Feliz district of LA (and for a short while also lived in Chicago). Hudgens knew Fay, one of Adams' uncles, as they had roomed together. He was aware of Adams and thought that he would be a perfect friend for his newly adopted son. Adams saw beyond Pineda's sight problems, and began to instil his new young friend with confidence. Still at school, they hit it off immediately and, realising their shared love for music and dancing, soon began working on raps together. "He paid attention to my ability to do things: my break-dancing, my lyrics, my freestyling," Pineda said. Pineda and Adams were attentive pupils, attending raves in their spare time, which were later to have an enormous influence on the output of the Black Eyed Peas. A fellow Palihigh pupil of Adams was Pasquale Rotella, who would later be the organizer of LA's Electric Daisy Festival, and he would join them at early raves and club nights at Club What?

"We'd be going to Club What?," Adams told the *LA Times* in 2010. "We were like in 10th grade whispering, 'Yo man, you go to that rave last night?' 'Yeah man, it was crazy.' Our friend would be like, 'Dude, I'm still rolling.' People were on drugs – I'm talking about 11th graders, 15-year-olds in high school. Where I was going to high school people were rolling, and coming down from the drug. I didn't do that stuff, and Pasquale didn't do that stuff. But we went, and we liked the vibe and the scene." Another school friend of Adams was the son of Motown founder Berry Gordy, Stefan, who many years later would find fame as DJ Redfoo from partyrock ensemble, LMFAO.

At weekends Adams and Pineda would hang out at Glendale Galleria, the upmarket shopping mall on Glenwood's West Broadway. Although Pineda could speak little English at this point, he had a voracious appetite to learn, and soon was poring over dictionaries, working on his pronunciation. At this juncture, he and Adams would both adopt rap handles – Adams became Will-1-X (sometimes spelled Willonex) and Pineda took apl. de. ap – Allan Pineda Lindo from Angeles, Pampagna.

What they had in common was music, and Adams and Pineda formed a dance crew, Tribal Nation, adding third member, mutual friend, Dante Santiago, and another, rapper Mooky Mook. While dancing, they met producer Monroe Walker, who was performing as a DJ on the west coast. Walker, who was known by his stage name DJ Motiv8, was impressed by Adams' youth and passion for music, and set about teaching him studio techniques.

Tribal Nation performed at LA's first dedicated hip-hop club, Balistyx, held at the Whisky at 8901 Sunset Strip. The club was run by Nic Adler, son of record producer, Lou, Robert Gavin, Dan Eisenstein and teenage actor David Faustino, who was known for playing Bud Bundy in the Fox TV smash hit comedy, *Married… With Children*. The club became something of a phenomenon and represented, on the smallest scale, the impact hip-hop was having at the heart of mainstream America, crossing over from the African-American districts into the heart of middle- and upper-class white America, hungry for more hip-hop after the storming emergence of the Beastie Boys. Soon there were kids queuing round the block, thrilled by seeing these teenagers dancing while members of NWA DJ'ed. It was here that Adams met rap businessman Eazy-E.

Eazy-E had been tipped off by his friend, industry veteran Jerry Heller, who in turn had been given the word about Tribal Nation by Bret Mazur. Mazur was the 'Epic' part of the production duo Wolf and Epic, and was the son of Irwin Mazur, who had been one of Billy Joel's production team in the artist's early days. "I hosted a freestyle battle every week and it became really famous," Faustino told 215hiphop. com. "That's how Will got his record deal. He won battles and held the top spot for like, it was ridiculous, for like three, four, five months in a row. No one could beat him. And that's when Eazy-E came, and he signed him to Ruthless."

# Chapter 2

# Ruthless Times

*"We really were a garage band."*

will.i.am, 2005

*"We as a group wanted our music to be multicultural and mirror our own life experiences: will as the black dude, accepted within a Latino community; me, the Mexican accepted in a black community; apl, the Filipino embraced by America. Crossing divides. Building bridges. Finding acceptance among other races."*

Taboo, 2011

For such a peace-loving group, it might seem strange that Black Eyed Peas were born in Los Angeles during 1992, a period that saw the city become a seething hotbed of racial tension. The leaked video footage of the LAPD beating Rodney King the previous year had been beamed around the world. When the five police officers accused were cleared of charges in April 1992, the fermenting frustrations of a disenfranchised section of African–American youth went overground and six days of rioting ensued. It was during this period that Will-1-X and apl.de.ap signed to Eazy-E's Ruthless Records.

Always a controversial figure, Eazy-E actually sided with the LA

Police Department when questioned on the matter of King, something that did his business no end of good among the wider music industry. It was ironic, when one of his best-known songs was entitled 'Fuck Tha Police'. Born Eric Lynn Wright, Eazy-E was instrumental in the formation of Niggaz With Attitude (aka NWA) alongside Andre Young (Dr. Dre), O'Shea Jackson (Ice Cube), Lorenzo Patterson (MC Ren), Antoine Carraby (DJ Yella) and Mik Lezan (Arabian Prince). Wright was a true maverick, living the life of a well-heeled playa, courting controversy and goading public opinion.

Wright was immediately impressed with Will-1-X. Many commented that Will-1-X's peace-loving, hippie-inspired music was somewhat out of step with Eazy-E's previous outfit's work, but Eazy-E was an astute businessman, and he felt that these wild dancers with Will-1-X's freestying hip-hop sound would make good commercial sense. Jerry Heller wrote that Will-1-X "grew up in South Central and shared a lot of the same turf as Eazy – but their philosophies couldn't have been more different. Will connected to the peace and love tradition of the sixties. He was an incredible dancer, singer, musician. I always thought of him as the Paul Hornung of rap, after the triple-threat Green Bay Packer football great." Heller was apposite in this comparison – Hornung became idolised by America, and was renowned for being able to play with equal ability in a variety of positions. Although any wider recognition for Will-1-X was still a long way off.

School friends LMFAO would play a footnote during the early part of this period: "I used to record on my little sister's Teddy Ruxpin tapes to make Teddy Ruxpin rap. So I used to put my little demo inside his belly and press play and he used to kick my lyrics in homeroom show-and-tell," will.i.am said in 2011. "So after homeroom show-and-tell, I gave the tape to Stefan [Gordy]: 'Give this to your pops.' And he didn't give it to his dad, so he gave it to his brother, Kerry, and then Kerry says, 'You're really talented, this is cool.' To make a long story short, in the 10th grade I tell Stefan, 'Tell your daddy to get you some music equipment so we can record after school. In 11th grade, Stefan goes, 'Yo, my dad got me an Ensoniq and ADATs!' At the time, those were like the newest stuff. If you got ADATs, it's on."

It was these tapes that helped Will-1-X secure his deal. "I come to school with a record deal, like 'Yo, I got a record deal, 10 G's!' To a 17-year-old, ten thousand dollars – granted, it was, like, for life. Eazy-E had me signed like forever. I ghost wrote for Eazy-E. I know how to write those type of rhymes. I just don't want to rap them."

Will-1-X clearly couldn't believe his luck to be running with one of the most notorious figures in hip-hop. "I was in high school, so it was a dream come true," he said in 2007. "To be in 11th grade, 12th grade, and you're running with Eazy... That was unbelievable... You can't compare it to 50 Cent or Jay-Z, because Eazy-E was the first nigga." A few A&R decisions were made; the group changed their name from Tribal Nation to the far more in-keeping-with-the-times Atban Klann. Sounding like A Tribe Called Quest or the B.O.O Y.A.A. Tribe, Atban stood for 'A Tribe Beyond A Nation'. Atban Klann seemed very much of their time – post-Daisy Age rapping with a modicum of social commentary added into the grooves. Will-1-X and apl.de.ap had assembled their wayward crew that included friends and future Black Eyed Peas cohorts: Mooky Mook, Monroe Walker (aka DJ Motiv8) and Dante Santiago.

With Motiv8 and Will-1-X producing, Atban Klann made their debut recording on Eazy-E's EP *5150: Home 4 tha Sick* on the track 'Merry Muthaphuckkin' Xmas'. Released on December 28, 1992, it was Eazy-E's first release after his departure from NWA. It was a skittish piece of gangsta rap with festive songs and lewd versions of Christmas carols thrown in. It was a slightly inappropriate and certainly inauspicious start to Atban Klann's recording career, but then they had moved from hanging out in malls to being in the studio with one of NWA, arguably the most influential outfit of their era, in less than two years and Will-1-X was still at High School. After he left school, although he enrolled at the Fashion Institute of Design and Merchandising in LA, his mind was firmly on the possibilities for Atban Klann now they were signed to Ruthless.

The Klann began work on their debut recording, *Grass Roots*. Originally scheduled for release in the latter half of 1993, the album was to feature 16 tracks, and was to prove a very credible debut.

Steeped in old school influence, it showed how accomplished Will-1-X and Motiv8 were at piecing an album together. Will-1-X and apl.de.ap flow together very well, and the album teems with youthful exuberance. 'Adidas' really highlights the influences of A Tribe Called Quest following a 'Bonita Applebum' style rap, and references the Sugar Hill Gang and Run DMC. 'Lord Of The Flies' offers an insistent jazzy groove with the repeated buzzing fly sound effect. Although the music is frequently naïve, it still sounds like that which was to lay ahead of Will-1-X and apl.de.ap. "The music hasn't really changed since then," will.i.am said in 2007. "Not a lot of people have really heard our album on Ruthless. I was 17 years old. The only difference I can say is that I'm an adult now. I know the business, I understand the marketplace." The other thing about the album was that it seemed to remain a work in progress. "The album was fantastic, but it never seemed to get finished," Heller wrote. "It entered that black hole that a lot of recording projects fall into."

*Billboard* magazine was later to report that "many in the Ruthless camp were puzzled by the group and the enthusiasm of Eazy, who had no problem reconciling his own gangsta style with the peace-minded, break-dancing of Atban." And that was true. Nobody really knew what to do with the album, or which market to place it in – its sporadic bursts of hardness and cussing would sit uneasily with the Daisy Age crew; yet it was far too tree-hugging for the hardcore rappers; on top of that, it didn't have any out-and-out sex and violence that so titillated and captivated the burgeoning white marketplace. As a result the ever-shifting release date reserved for the album in Ruthless' catalogue was replaced by Eazy-E's latest signing, the Cleveland-based Bone Thugs-N-Harmony. E paired them up with DJ U-Neek and they released *Creepin On Ah Come Up* in June 1994. Their brand of something a little more hardcore was much easier to market and by the time of their next record, Bone Thugs, led by Anthony Henderson, known as Krayzie Bone, were scoring huge international hits with 'Tha Crossroads' and '1st Of Tha Month.'

All that did appear for Atban Klann was 'Puddles Of H20', released as a CD single and promotional 12" in 1994. It had an accompanying video showing four of them (Will-1-X, apl.de.ap, Santiago and DJ Motiv8) throwing jazzy, hip-hop shapes, wearing hats and dancing very much in the style of the moment, owing a little to the Pharcyde, a little to the UK Sumthin' Else signed jazz-rappers Galliano. Produced by Danish hip-hop production team Madness 4 Real (Lasse Bavngaard, Nicholas Kvaran and Rasmus Berg) it sounded loose and fluid. The B-side of the single was the Motiv8 and Will-1-X produced final track from the proposed album, 'Let Me Get Down'. What was interesting on this track was their production credit – whereas the A-side was 'Produced for Solid Gold Productions', the flip was 'Produced for Black Eye Peas'.

Atban Klann remained on Ruthless' books, playing live and developing their stage show, resolutely wishing to play with real musicians rather than backing tapes and beats, but 1995 would prove a turning point for the group. Two events would shape their future. Key member, rapper Mooky Mook, was jailed on an assault charge. It was only for six weeks, but when he emerged from prison, the experience had affected him deeply. Quick to argue, he quit Atban Klann in a heated moment. He was, however, later to rejoin the family and be one of the group's close ongoing associates.

However, the second event had far deeper significance. In early February, Will-1-X got a call from Eazy-E saying that MTV had heard the group's song 'Puddles Of H20' and were excited about it. The group were understandably delighted, as they now had a perfect opportunity to finally show what they were capable of, and its success could indeed lead to the final release of their long-delayed album.

Within a week of this call, Eazy-E was taken to hospital on February 24, with suspected pneumonia, but by the first day of March, it was discovered that E was suffering from AIDS. That week he issued a public statement which said that he had lived a "fast life, filled with fancy cars, gorgeous women and good living" and blamed no-one but himself. "I feel that I've got thousands and thousands of young fans that have to learn about what's real when it comes to AIDS. I would like to turn my own problem into something good that will reach out to all my homeboys and their kin."

He made peace with former colleagues and recent adversaries Dr Dre and Snoop Dogg. On March 14 on his sickbed, he married his current girlfriend, former Tabu and Motown employee Tomica Woods, the mother of his most recent son. On the following day, he went onto a life support machine. On March 26, 1995, Eazy-E was pronounced dead at the Cedars-Sinai Medical Center. One of the great tragedies of hip-hop was the speed of his passing and the irony, of course, was that he died of complications arising from AIDS, thus becoming one of the first high-profile heterosexual artists to die from the disease. He had said in interviews in the past that he preferred not to use a condom during intercourse, as the women that he associated with were 'clean'. But he had a voracious sexual appetite and fathered seven children with six different women. His funeral, held on April 7, was an enormous, star-studded affair. Eazy-E was buried in a 24-carat gold-plated coffin, wearing the traditional NWA outfit of Compton baseball hat, wraparound shades and chains. The grief was all too real.

Atban Klann were, like the rest of the rap community, absolutely stunned by the news. Due to Eazy-E's passing, Ruthless went into a quick freefall, and within a day of its owner's death there were legal wrangles over who owned the company. There was a quick cull of artists, and Atban Klann, whose work had hardly set the world aflame, were dropped. On top of that, Ruthless owned the copyright of the name. Will-1-X sensed it was time for a swift change. He knew that the group's recent past stood them in fair stead, certainly inasmuch as if Eazy-E had signed them, they were at a certain level, but it was time to move on. Dante Santiago left the group. However, Santiago, like most of the people who would work with Will-1-X, would remain part of the larger team, and as recently as 2011 is credited with 'Creative A&R' on the sleeve of the Black Eyed Peas' sixth album, *The Beginning*.

And so, in 1995, the group changed its name to the Black Eyed Peas, a name they had already used informally, and that had been used for the production team of Will-1-X and Motiv8. They toyed with other titles such as Blue Unit and Turquoise Vines. The name was taken from the cowpea bean prevalent in cooking in the West Indies and the US

Deep South, colloquially and commonly known as soul food. Its white appearance with a black speck in the middle seemed to symbolise the sort of music that the group was intending to make: soulful, multi-racial, unifying, warming. It also had a ring to it of the multi-platinum selling Red Hot Chili Peppers. Will-1-X also decided that his name would change accordingly, to will.i.am. "I liked playing with words," he told the *New York Times* in 2011. "I noticed that my name was a sentence, meaning one with will, who is strong-willed. And so I called my mom and said, 'Hey, mom, do you mind if I call myself will.i.am?' She was like: 'Whaaa? You're crazy.' She was cool with it." With this cartoon-like name, itself part-homage to Dr Seuss' character Sam-I-Am from his 1960 book, *Green Eggs And Ham*, will.i.am had his name in place, ready for the group to change its direction.

It was during this period of flux that the group added another member, Jaime Gomez, or as he became known, Taboo. Gomez was born on July 14, 1975 in Boyle Heights in Downtown Los Angeles to Mexican Jimmy Gomez and his wife, Aurora Sifuentes, known as Laura, an American with Native American ancestry, whom he had met at a Mexican market in East LA.

Although like Adams his father was quickly off the scene, Jaime was raised in Dogtown in an apartment full of love, by his mother, grandmother and uncles. When he was six, his mother married Julio Arevalo, and Jaime moved in with his grandmother 'Nanny Aurora' in South Central LA, going from a Mexican-American district to an African-American area. Taboo talked about the impact and influence of his grandmother in 2001: "My grandmother was one of a kind... she was the most influential person in my life. She was the motivating force for me to become the performer that I am today. She really lit the fire inside me which inspired the desire to become who I am. The beauty of it is that she believed in me even when other people didn't. The fact that my grandmother always had my back was pivotal because she also taught me a lot about values and about life in the process."

And it became the first place he heard hip-hop. By the age of 12, Gomez had settled in the LA suburb of Rosemead, living in a house bought by his stepfather Arevalo. According to his autobiography, *Fallin'*

*Up*, it was while at Rosemead High he aquired the nickname Taboo, from defacing school books, initially with the word 'tab' liking the shape of the 'b' and the 't', and then developing it to 'taboo', revelling in the forbidden. Realising he had a talent for rhyming and dancing, he would dance in the playground to the encouragement of fellow students, as well as making a few enemies with the older boys. As he got older, Gomez too would frequent Balistyx on Sunset Strip, and assemble his own dance outfit called Divine Tribal Brothers. Gomez and his friend Joey Jordan, aka Phoenix, got an opportunity to audition to dance for the Pasadena-based rapper Ron Johnson. They danced for his manager, Polo Molina. Although the gig they were hoping for with Johnson fell through, Molina was impressed with Gomez, and kept him in mind. Adding singer David Lara, the Divine Tribal Brothers morphed into rapping, singing and dancing outfit United Soul Children.

Gomez and the Atban Klann's paths had crossed sporadically over the past few years, and through a meeting at a club, Molina got to know will.i.am, who, in turn, got to know Gomez more through Molina. Because of friendships between Atban Klann and United Soul Children, the members formed an informal, flexible crew called Grass Roots, a title shared with the unreleased Atban Klann album. Gomez formed a duo with rapper Eclipse called Rising Suns, which became Pablo. An attempt to record Pablo with DJ Motiv8 producing ended badly. Soon, Gomez was working as a Disney employee – but will.i.am had kept Gomez's dancing and rapping in mind.

With his light-skinned Mexican/Native American appearance, Taboo looked the part of an LA *Cholo* rapper, adding to the overall eccentricity of will.i.am and apl.de.ap. According to Gomez, his invitation to join the group was straightforward. "So you wanna come and perform with us?" will.i.am asked. Taboo did not hesitate. "Life is a chessboard and someone is always moving things around and removing pieces from play. One man's prison sentence and one man's death had changed the entire board and would change the trajectory of my life." Taboo's first gig with the group was at Prince's Glam Slam West as part of a Ruthless Records showcase, which they were still contracted to do. Taboo recalled at length in his autobiography, *Fallin' Up*, the night when the three of them ("Two black cats with thick, long, Bob Marley-style dreads, wearing beatnik style, old-man vintage clothing, accompanied by one theatrical, scary-looking Latino dressed all ninja-style") slowly won over the audience of hard-as-nails, dyed-in-the-wool hip-hop brethren. will.i.am's freestyling was tailored to fit the moment, even when an ice cube was hurled at him from out of the crowd. Although an inauspicious beginning, this new line-up gelled, looking at once intriguing and eccentric, and offering something new. The crowd was won over if not by their beats and rhymes, by their spontaneity and warmth.

The Black Eyed Peas set about working out their masterplan. Taking the hip-hop that all three loved, they added a mixture of other influences – some soul, jazz and Latin, even a touch of rock and pop. Although they had been performing to DAT, they wanted to get the live ambience of a proper band behind them; Carlos Galvan joined on keyboards, 'JC' on guitar, Terry Graves as drummer and Mike Fratantuno on bass.

The trio, with their new band, would rehearse at apl.de.ap's house in Pasadena; recording and cataloguing the words to the freestyle raps they improvised. The first Black Eyed Peas gig in their new rappers'n'band line-up was at LA's Peace and Justice Center. It was not a great success but it showed them where they needed to tighten up and develop. They wrote and sculpted rhymes, looking at the best way for the words to integrate with the music.

A series of poorly attended shows ensued but soon they started to draw small crowds of 'pea-bodies', fans there to see them. Their mixture of live band and rap won over tranches of female fans. They acquired a manager, Yon Styles, who ran a company entitled Black Coffee Management along with Eddie Bowles and numbers man Johnny Johnson. Working with Styles and Polo Molina, the Black Eyed Peas began to build their reputation. Their use of mailing lists and flyers pointed the way to their full-scale adoption of social networks a decade later. will.i.am and Molina were also concerned that the group give something back, and around this time, the fledgling Peapod Foundation was set up, providing charity toy drives for LA-based children and local orphanages.

A further development came when the band met Kim Hill at a BMI showcase in 1995 where she was performing as were they. She knew Styles, and had been dating Eddie Bowles. There was a mutual appreciation between the two acts. "We met and we really clicked, will and I immediately had a connection as musicians," Hill told portalblackeyedpeas.com. "And he felt like a little brother to me, and we immediately started writing together... it was very organic, and at the time, their manager lived on my street, and he would talk about this group 'the Black Eyed Peas', and it just happened at that showcase, both the Black Eyed Peas and myself were performing and then we got to meet, and that's how it started, it was very random. But it was an immediate creative connection."

will.i.am asked if Hill would be interested in singing with the group; thus began a five-year association with the band. Taboo recalled the first time he laid eyes on her, as she played in the club Mogul on Fairfax Avenue in Hollywood. "She was sitting on a stool, with her tumbledown curly black hair, playing her guitar and singing true soul. Her voice wasn't extraordinary, but she had a soulful sound that was both edgy and ethereal. Unique."

Hill was born in Syracuse in upstate New York. She relocated to Philadelphia, where she had studied violin and piano, and had lived in LA since 1993. The addition of female vocals sweetened up the group's frantic freestyling. The blend clicked. Although Hill was not a full-time member of the band, and didn't attend every gig, maintaining her own solo career, she signed to will.i.am's newly formed label, I Am Music, and played with the group at all their significant concerts of this period.

The group put together a demo tape, consisting of two tracks, 'To The Beat Y'All' and 'That's Right'. The tracks were old school in their approach and didn't quite work. Faced with rejection, the group created their first major track – 'Joints And Jam'. They played campuses, rock clubs and hip-hop joints. Although perplexed by the lack of record company interest, they ploughed on, refining their stage act, and writing more material. The group continued to attract a large female following. Actress Gabrielle Union (then TV star of *Family Matters* and *Saved By The Bell*) came down to one of their shows, and returned with a group of friends. "She comes with all these girls, and, ever since then, we've always had girls at our shows," Taboo recalled. "She started off our girl fan base."

"When we got off Ruthless Records in 1995 we started Black Eyed Peas," will.i.am said in 2000. "But nobody wanted to sign us, they just didn't see it. We did a demo in '96 and '97 but they all said 'naw'. Interscope was one of the people who said 'naw'. So we were like, 'Fuck this shit'. We started playin' at colleges and at clubs in Hollywood, just doin' our own thang. Playin' at these colleges we met the people who make our videos today. Some people worked next to college as interns at record companies. That's how the record companies got interested. We always wanted to go to Interscope." EMI had told will.i.am that although they liked their music, it simply wasn't tangible enough. The word verily bent will.i.am's brain. He had to go home and look it up in a dictionary. He explored the deeper meaning of material that couldn't be defined.

As word of mouth had been growing, Black Coffee Management thought it a good idea to arrange a showcase gig for the group at the Dragonfly Club on Sunset Boulevard. This event changed Interscope's mind. Its boss, Jimmy Iovine, had been passed a Black Eyed Peas demo by his nephew, DJ and LA scenster James Mormile, and was keen to see them live. After the Dragonfly showcase, there was also interest in the group from major labels Warners and Sony. Although the band visited all the companies, it was Interscope's acceptance of will.i.am's request for tour support that sealed the deal.

Interscope was delighted with Black Eyed Peas, and it was clear that under the guidance of label head Iovine, they could develop. Iovine was something of an industry legend. He had worked as an engineer in the seventies on records by John Lennon and Bruce Springsteen before becoming a producer in the eighties working with Dire Straits, U2 and Simple Minds among others. But it was his foundation of the Interscope label with his business partner Ted Field in 1991 that made him an industry mogul. Interscope quickly established a reputation for high-quality, often but not always highly commercial, idiosyncrasy.

Set up with 50% backing from Warners, Iovine and Interscope

provided financial backing for the controversial Death Row Records, releasing albums by 2Pac and Snoop Dogg, and enjoying enormous sales. When Warners pulled out of Interscope in 1995, Iovine purchased the stake before selling the share to Universal. When Black Eyed Peas joined the roster they were labelmates with BlackStreet, Marilyn Manson and No Doubt. Also, unusual for a group so unproven, Interscope agreed to oversee will.i.am's own label, I Am Music, as part of the deal. With the label, he could nurture and develop talent, and offer Interscope the first option on release. The label's mark would be on all Black Eyed Peas releases from the off, yet it would not really expand until Venus Brown became the President and General Manager.

Black Eyed Peas signed to Interscope, according to Gomez, for $500,000 for a three-album deal. This was a generous deal and showed Iovine's faith in will.i.am and his crew. Working with A&R man Scott Igoe, they developed their demos, and a single release was slated for December 1997. The band took a variety of support slots with a whole host of groups, honing their live performance skills.

# Chapter 3

# Ice Cream Truck Music:
## *Behind The Front*

*'I just started making ice cream truck music. You know what I'm saying?*
*Slangin' muthafuckin lollipops.'*

will.i.am., 2007

Although they had created a video for the track 'Head Bobs', 'Fallin' Up' was the first time the wider world heard or saw the Black Eyed Peas. Released in December 1997 and backed with '¿Que Dices?,' they filmed a video with Brian Beletic, who had directed their 'Head Bobs' promo. It marked out their territory and displayed their difference. Shot in sepia to give the impression of old film stock and dressed as prospectors, the three of them, will.i.am, apl de. Ap and Taboo, were filmed in the San Juan Mountains in Telluride, California. The video opened with a slide declaring, "Keeping time is in a daily man's function..." before another slide said, "But frontiersmen move to a different beat." The band emerge over a hill with a pony, explorers on a mission to achieve new heights in hip-hop, with the words 'advancing the unknown' superimposed on the picture.

They travel through undergrowth, reaching summits, crossing streams.

The three are introduced by their names in captions on the screen as they break-dance, looking like a late 20th Century update of Laurel & Hardy's 1937 film, *Way Out West*. With its organic, back-to-nature feel, the overall effect is one of purity, cleansing the path from a rap scene that was dominated by fast cars, expensive jewellery and boasts of sexual, lyrical and gangsterish prowess. It is a first, early sign of the Black Eyed Peas' big, reductive simplicity. When they reach a hand-painted signpost marked 'west' and 'east', they ignore it and throw a hook into space, climbing a mountain to transcend the Westside/Eastside feuding that had begun to dominate rap music. A map showing them heading into uncharted territory demonstrates that they have loftier ideals. The lyrics make explicit that they are still very much relevant to rap, even though they refuse to wear the standard uniform of the day, Tommy Hilfiger outfits and baseball caps. Showing them in leather waistcoats and granddad shirts made explicit their absorption of the history, not only of American music, but also of America itself. At the end of the video, after conquering one summit, they look to higher mountains spread out in the distance. There were many peaks to climb, and they had only just begun their journey.

Recording sessions for their debut album spread out across the remainder of 1997 and into early 1998. will.i.am was impressed with a vocalist he had seen in Los Angeles, a statuesque woman with a striking clump of Afro hair and a strange, otherworldly presence. Macy Gray was a 27-year-old Ohio-born mother-of-three who had been recording demo material but had yet to release a record. Born Natalie McIntyre, her strange rich voice would be perfect in the Black Eyed Peas mix, and she was invited to sing on 'Love Won't Wait'. It marked her debut commercial recording.

*Behind The Front* was finally released on June 30, 1998. It was based on the material from demos that Atban Klann had made, supplemented with additional raps by Taboo. Recorded at Paramount and Benyads studios, it was largely produced by will.i.am, with contributions from DJ Paul Poli, C-Los and Brian Lapin. It bore several things in common with rap albums of its era, namely its length – filling up 74 minutes of CD and peppering the musical flow with 'skits'. But that was where most similarities ended. This was a positive album full of love, hope and passion. Taboo was later to write that the group didn't say that they made music between 1996 and 1998, rather that their music came from "the time we started dreaming and working as kids because it was a collection of inspirations and influences from childhood and adolescence. Music that effectively said, 'this is our life... this is our inspiration... this is the first album that reflects it all.'"

Black Eyed Peas' *Behind The Front* began with their debut single, 'Fallin' Up', which had already acted as a sophisticated, jazzy introduction to the group. 'Joints And Jam' was the core track, and the album's second single, getting somewhat overlooked on its initial US release in December 1997. It was released as a single in the UK in September 1998 when it reached number 53 in the charts and made the band the darlings of the then-fervent dance music press, such as *DJ*, *Muzik* and *Mixmag*. With support vocals from Ingrid Dupree, it borrowed the vocal riff from the theme from *Grease*, by Frankie Valli, and felt like a jazzy departure from hip-hop. The song was used to great effect in Warren Beatty's curious 1998 film, *Bulworth*, about a failing politician who wishes to get down with hip-hop culture. Although the film was another of Beatty's high-budget box-office letdown curios, it showed the Peas that synchronization deals – getting your music into films and adverts – was a lucrative way of propelling your group out into the wider world. The video to support the single, again directed by Brian Beletic, featured the group being sucked into a force field while on a street corner in LA. Kim Hill appears singing the infectious refrain. There was a special version of the song recorded for the promo video, which featured their live band performing a piano-based rendition. Halfway through, will.i.am, apl.de.ap and Taboo begin to break-dance.

*Behind The Front*'s pleas for peace and unity between the warring Eastside/Westside hip-hop rivals set against jazzy warm grooves was instantly appealing. As Peter Shapiro wrote in *The Rough Guide To Hip Hop*, "While their level-headed lyrics attracted pacifists, hippies and people that didn't understand metaphor, it was their warm, mellow production that really got heads turning." 'Clap Your Hands' is a stand-out example of what the Black Eyed Peas were attempting early on.

Sampling legendary New Orleans funk band The Meters, it utilises their 1970 track 'Hand Clapping Song' and adds an adaptation of the vocal from Jacob Miller's 'Tenement Yard' and a nod to Michael Jackson's 'Wanna Be Startin' Somethin''. With will.i.am increasing the bass and rounding the track out, it revels in its own exuberance.

The album had skits that cut through the tracks, in the form of a game show, with the group playing a variety of hosts, such as will.i.am welcoming the listener to 'The Rap Gamer,' where 'the business is music, but music isn't the business'. Although these are not overly successful, they demonstrate that the group were keen to bring more to the experience, to add variety and present some kind of show. 'Karma' the album's third single, had a beautiful, Latin-infused vibe, using the lazy bossa nova to emphasize the message that it was impossible to shy away from destiny. It spotlights their musical magpie-ism perfectly, as three-quarters of the way through the group begin to sing 'One Way Or Another', the Blondie standard from their 1978 *Parallel Lines* album.

'Be Free', one of the three songs to which Kim Hill contributed, was in some respects probably the most interesting track on the album, using as its sample the great lost eighties electro-dance classic 'White Horse' by Laid Back. The electro-bubble of the backing with heavily featured female vocals, pointed most presciently to the future. It seemed to offer a new take on the universal popular music placebo phrase, 'everything will be all right'. Of their newer tracks, 'Say Goodbye' incorporated a JBs style groove with an infectious sample from the obscure UK-based 20th Century Steel Band's 'Heaven And Hell Is On Earth', which had become something of a rare groove anthem. It highlighted the fastidious nature of will.i.am and Motiv8's sampling. 'Positivity' was another new number, another opportunity to offer optimism to the feuding rap scene.

'What It Is' is another outstanding track. Taking a sample from Tom Browne's gold-standard jazz-funk 1980 hit, 'Funkin' For Jamaica (NY)', it creates its own lazy, loping universe, with will.i.am sampling drum loops, keyboards and flutes on the Akai MPC-3000, underpinned by Mike Fratantuno's rubbery bass. It is again Hill's strident and assured vocal that makes the track stand out.

The sleeve of *Behind The Front* made it look like it was something that had been found at the back of an old record crate. Designed by band associate Mark Leroy, with photography by Storm Hale and illustrations by Suren Galadjian, it owed something to Blue Note, Prestige and Impulse in its house style. The words, 'recorded in visual stereo sound' across the top made it feel, too, like a jazz album. The inner booklet art was particularly clever. The cover depicts a fully clothed picture on the right hand page of Taboo, will.i.am and apl.de.ap. The next picture overleaf finds them naked and unadorned – will.i.am's glasses are off, as is Taboo's bandana. On the next page, we have an illustration of the three without skin, showing their muscles; and, of course, as the layers are dispensed with, they begin to all look the same – there is no longer a Mexican-Native American, African-American and Filipino standing before your eyes. This is taken to its furthest degree on the next illustration when the three are skeletons. By the final page all that remain are Taboo's heart, will.i.am's mind and the faint outline of apl.de.ap's silhouette.

As with many debut albums, the credits page was fulsome and the individual and group thanks went out of their way fully to acknowledge all who had helped them on their way. The final credit, aside from 'the whole world for her and his inspiration', was to the Grass Roots collective (Mr Shaha, Eclipse, Shaggie, Roycel, Phoenix, Scoober, Mooky Mook, Darkter Dre); all of the crews that had supported or played with them. The Black Eyed Peas were not going to leave their past behind.

Interscope was pleased with the release and threw a launch party at the legendary El Rey Theater on Wilshire Boulevard in Los Angeles. The famous art deco building had been opened as cinema in 1936, and its old school opulence seemed completely in keeping with the quality and difference of *Behind The Front*. To further justify the faith that Interscope had in the group, the album received largely positive reviews. *Rolling Stone* said that they had "an organic mixture of sampled melodies and live instruments... *Behind The Front* really takes off when the Peas challenge the status quo or indulge their braggadocios taste buds." *The Source* magazine said that their musical outlook was one that would "undoubtedly draw comparisons to the mostly sample-free sound of the Roots and the vibey, mellow bounce of Tribe."

*Behind The Front*, its title a dig at all the rappers who 'fronted' their machismo, showed that in Black Eyed Peas there was another route for rap to take. It was a credible debut that won a great deal of appreciation and found an audience: thoughtful, left-field serious-minded types who talked about rap as the science of sound. The album was a moderate but encouraging success; it reached number 37 in the *Billboard* R&B chart and number 129 in the *Billboard* Top 200, selling around 300,000 copies.

To support the album, Interscope put the band on the eight-week, 20-date *Smokin' Grooves* tour across summer 1998. Sponsored by the US-based restaurant and venue chain House Of Blues, it was a sort of rap version of Lollapalooza and featured an all-star line-up: Cypress Hill, Busta Rhymes, Gang Starr, Canibus, Wyclef Jean & the Refugee All-Stars and Public Enemy. It was a veritable who's who of the past decade of rap. Although its headliners were somewhat past their sell-by date in terms of relevance, it was the sort of bill that delighted white middle-class middle-American audiences, especially as it was the first time Public Enemy had played together since the early nineties. Playing in stadiums and arenas, it was, for all intents and purposes, a festival on the road. When the tour started Black Eyed Peas were very much the newcomers, opening the bill with a 20-minute set, often at around 6pm to a half-empty arena. That, of course, mattered little to the group, obsessed with honing their craft, and especially pleased at getting the opportunity to fill bigger stages.

VH-1 caught the show at the 12,500 seater Concord Pavilion in California on August 18. Obviously dwelling on the headliners, the channel gave the Peas a small but significant mention. "Those who showed up early on Sunday to catch the bohemian rap of Black Eyed Peas... showed their appreciation loud and proud – when they weren't bobbing their heads to the beat." The group's professionalism and energy struck a chord with the other acts on the bill, and gained them respect from all their fellow travellers. They also, through Polo Molina, looked at the opportunity to sell merchandise to their growing fan base – and nothing is more potent than the T-shirt purchasing opportunity after a fabulous live show. Their friend and associate Paul Chan had come up with a recognisable logo for the group, a merged B, E and P, almost like a hip-hop version of Roger Dean's 'Yes' logo for the famous progressive rock band.

*Smokin' Grooves* ended on August 29, 1998 at the Nissan Pavilion in Washington DC. The shows had sharpened the group's approach and had also shown them the joy and pitfalls of living on a tour bus. They were most smitten. The memories of that tour have never left them. "It was beautiful, man," will.i.am recounted in 2011. "This was our first tour. The first time we ever stepped out on the road was on a tour bus, not a van. There was no, 'Oh, I'm calling shotgun.' We were on the road with Wyclef, Cypress Hill, Public Enemy, M.O.P. and Gang Starr... this was dope"

Within weeks the group were off to Europe, visiting the UK in September 1998 to a muted response. Taboo wrote of the group's awe at their first transatlantic visit in his autobiography, *Fallin' Up*; "We fell in love with London the moment those jet wheels touched down at Heathrow Airport... If there is something perpetually showbiz about LA, there is something dreamy about being in London, especially for a southern Californian."

They played the Jazz Café in Camden, an intimate, specialist venue, as part of the run-up to the MOBO Awards at the Royal Albert Hall in October. The venue was showcasing artists who had been nominated. Both nights were a sell-out, as Black Eyed Peas seemed a glamorous, LA extension of the then-flowering trip-hop movement. *NME* was on hand to record the moment. "Funny. No-one onstage throws gang signs. Nobody yells 'Weeesssstside' or talks about their hellish life with a liberal use of swearwords and racial epithets. Is this a rap show? Do Black Eyed Peas represent Los Angeles to the fullest? will.i.am, apl de ap and Taboo certainly show a knowledge and love of hip-hop, it's just that their Los Angeles is a different one: a multicultural place populated by those with a positive outlook on life. And as for their approach, well it's just another way to see hip-hop." And it *was* another way to see hip-hop. The band had far more in common with the Daisy Age rappers than the gangsta rap that had become so adored and prevalent. Britons loved their alternative approach and the way their songs fitted in with the downtempo scene that had been around in the UK for several years, spearheaded by acts such as Bristol's Massive Attack and Austrian DJs Peter Kruder and Richard Dorfmeister.

Black Eyed Peas loved the experience. Despite the stage being minuscule and the band having to negotiate each other's space, the audience response was incredible. "We were so close to the audience," Taboo said, "that we could reach out with our arms and touch the shoulders of the dudes bouncing in the front row. It was sweaty and slick, and we brought that place alive." According to Taboo, apl.de.ap came off stage and said to them both, "Did you see how they were receiving us? I felt like one of the fucking Beatles out there!" Thus began the close relationship that the Black Eyed Peas would have with the UK, which culminated in them recording many of their later albums in London, in order to soak up the increasingly global vibe of the city. By the end of their European excursion, taking in shows in cities such as Paris and Amsterdam, word of mouth about Black Eyed Peas was spreading. The idea of marketing the group not only to the hip-hop but to the left-field audience was paying off.

# Chapter 4

# Uptempo, Energetic, Good-Time Songs:
## *Bridging The Gap*

*"We were not saying the n-word, and we didn't have our pants sagging and... I wasn't naked."*

Kim Hill, 2011

After their sojourn in England and Europe, the group began to write new material, while taking support opportunities with OutKast but not before another genre-warping tour that opened them up to new audiences. The Vans Warped tour was another US-crossing enterprise that had grown up in the shadow of Perry Farrell's Lollapalooza; a multi-band enterprise taking an all-in-one evening festival to provincial, moneyed audiences. And again, it was a marvellous line-up to be part of: Suicidal Tendencies, Agnostic Front, Sevendust, Pennywise, Blink-182, Ice-T and the new rap phenomenon, Eminem. The Black Eyed Peas had to work harder than ever on this tour, which attempted to show just how broadminded the Vans brand was, when in reality the tour was playing to fairly closed-minded punk and metal audiences. For the shows, the band had gained two newcomers in their live band who were to become mainstays for the rest of the Black Eyed Peas' career – guitarist George Pajon Jr. and keyboard player Priese Prince LaMont Board, known as Printz Board. The pair would soon prove invaluable to the group's writing and recording process. Although audience responses may have been mixed, the backstage camaraderie was second to none, and the band played basketball and forged a close bond with Blink-182.

The group returned to Paramount studios in September 1999 to commence work on what was to become *Bridging The Gap*. In the period between the first and second albums, Interscope, which had been part of the Universal Music Group, was merged with the A&M and Geffen labels as a result of Universal's purchase by global drinks company Seagram. Iovine retained control of Interscope, and his love for the Black Eyed Peas, plus an eye for their potential, ensured there was still a place on the roster for them.

Ahead of *Bridging The Gap*, the group was interviewed by hip-hop site urbansmarts.com, and apl.de.ap explained what they were up to in the near future. Aside from working on Kim Hill's album (which was ultimately rejected by Interscope as it allegedly wasn't "black enough"), and finishing their own album, he said: "After that we're gonna do some collaborations with the Propellerheads, Portishead, Beck and Stereolab." The interviewer was shocked, as these were hardly conventional hip-hop acts. will.i.am replied, "Well it's music, you know what I mean? Of course we wanna do shit with De La Soul, Lauryn Hill, A Tribe Called Quest, Busta Rhymes and shit like that. Hell yeah. We just wanna bring a different thing to hip-hop." The group was the squarest peg in the roundest hole.

Selecting material from an initial pool of over 50 tracks, *Bridging The Gap* was released on September 26, 2000. It was unmistakably the same group that had released *Behind The Front*. It marked a development from their debut but it was probably not the stellar leap that the group would have really wished for. Taboo made clear the group's intentions with their second album: "We wanted to deliver an international flavour and take this album to the wider world, beyond America, beyond Europe. This album was designed to be the bridge that connected us with all continents, and we eyed Australia and New Zealand for the first time." will.i.am told MTV, "The album's title means we're bridging the gap between rock-hop and hip-hop. There are a lot of cats that don't like rock, and a lot of rock cats that don't like hip-hop. So we're bridging that gap." He continued, "This one is basically our experience from dropping the first album until now. It's been a lot of touring and a lot of performing so a lot of songs on this album are very uptempo, energetic, good-time songs." And it *was* packed with energetic, uptempo songs, while lacking some of the depth of *Behind The Front*.

It found them again working with Macy Gray, who in the interim had become something of a megastar in Europe with her millennial soul anthem, 'I Try', which was a fabulous update of torch singer material; Gray's album *On How Life Is* had been Grammy-nominated, as well. "She was on our last album," will.i.am told MTV. "She didn't even have a record deal when she did our first joint, and she's a good friend. All the collaborations are with friends. Even if Macy Gray wasn't blowing up, she would still be on the album." His pride in Gray went on, as he said in 2005: "Macy Gray's been part of our family since before she put out her first record. She was on our first record that came out in 1998, and I remember hanging out at the studio watching, being inspired like, 'Wow... I try to say goodbye and I choke.' I was there while she recorded that and I remember what it felt like."

*Bridging The Gap* also drew on the respect that they had gained by playing on so many support bills across the years. will.i.am's hard work and devotion to his material had earned him a great deal of respect. The album, which also featured a wealth of guest artists such as Wyclef Jean, Mos Def and Les Nubians, was cram-packed with ideas and grooves. 'Weekends' took a short sample from Sly & the Family Stone's quintessential 1971 US number one, 'Family Affair', with a fine wah-wah guitar breakdown, before moving into something reassuringly jazz-tinged at is close, sounding not unlike German label Kompost's roster of jazzy downtempo. It featured the vocals of Canadian chanteuse Esthero. Born Jenny-Bea Englishman, her woozy, off-kilter vocals seemed to fit the track's unusual ambience. She sang the refrain from the underground hip-hop smash 'Look Out Weekend' by Debbie Deb from 1986. To add to this already potent brew, its trio of samples was completed by the introduction to 'Lord Of The Golden Baboon' from Brooklyn funk group Mandrill's 1972 album, *Mandrill Is*. In a way, there was simply too much going on.

The opening track, 'BEP Empire', was also the album's first single. Mixed by DJ Premier, it was a lurching, loping groove, not a million miles removed from their touring partner Eminen's debut hit 'My Name Is', with a deeply funky Blaxploitation flavour and laying out the group's manifesto – looking at 'bridging the gap from rap to calypso'. The accompanying promo, directed again by Brian Beletic, showed just how amusing and sophisticated the group could be. Filmed in the style of an infomercial, it offered Middle America an opportunity to buy a 'Discover Hip-Hop' kit. will.i.am appears as a salesman with the content of the kit laid out in front of him. Included are a series of VHS tapes – 'Hip-Hop Tricks', 'Hip-Hop Scratching', 'Hip-Hop Is Fun' and 'How To Hip-Hop'. There are language tapes in order to acquire a hip-hop vocabulary, a set of sunglasses, 'freestyle flashcards', a T-shirt and visor. It then shows many happy people around the country, on their lawns, by fire engines, washing their cars and in their swimming pools holding one of the kits. Easy to use, easy to store, it acts as a witty metaphor for how rap had infiltrated all areas of US society. A tickertape comes across the screen exalting the benefits of the language cassettes "Listen to a motivational experience of hip-hop vocabulary" and continues to list a series of key phrases that America can familarise itself with: 'buggin', 'iced out', 'I keep my gear tight', 'laid up with my shorty' and 'blazing'. There was also a set of gold front teeth in the set so everyone could look the part of a hardcore MC. The video ends with the classic infomercial 'call to action' – a static screen with everything you need to purchase your discover hip-hop set, including its own URL – www.discoverhiphop.com. The whole enterprise will take a week to arrive and is sponsored by 'Shady Credit'. There was also a supplementary short film called *Discover Hip-Hop*, with 'BEP Empire' being played discreetly in the background. It was a full ten-minute infomercial for this imaginary set. The parody of commercialisation was, of course, doubly ironic for the group, as Polo

Molina's T-shirt and merchandise operation was proving extremely lucrative.

'Get Original' has the phrase 'in the mix' from the Indeep record 'Last Night A DJ Saved My Life' and a rap from the then-ubiquitous Chali 2Na from fellow LA rap travellers Jurassic 5. It is also underpinned by a fabulous, nagging guitar figure. The track was later featured on the flipside of the 'BEP Empire' single. The album's title track encapsulates the modus operandi of the original incarnation of the Black Eyed Peas; languidly relaxed, unhurried grooves with Kim Hill's vocal floating over will.i.am's rap. 'Go Go' however, typifies the issues confronted by this early line-up; the music is too meandering and the rap unfocussed. Over a skittering beat with elements from Afrika Bambaataa and Soul Sonic Force's 'Planet Rock', it spends a long time getting nowhere in particular.

'Cali To New York', too, is leisurely, and featured some of the group's heroes, De La Soul. The three-piece hip-hop group – Kelvin Mercer (Posdnuos), David Jolicoeur (Trugoy The Dove) and Vincent Mason (Pacemaster Mace) – had travelled a long way since their groundbreaking 1989 debut, *3 Feet High And Rising*, which had heralded a new era in rap, introducing the so-called and fondly remembered Daisy Age. The debt owed by Black Eyed Peas to De La Soul is clear and this recording began a long-term friendship and recording association between the groups.

'Rap Song' acts as something of a baton pass between the Fugees and the Black Eyed Peas; featuring Wyclef Jean, it showcased the nursery rhyme quality that was soon to be so prevalent in the Black Eyed Peas' work. It is hard to overestimate the importance of the Fugees to the future success of the Black Eyed Peas. The Haitian-American hip-hop group fused R&B, soul, Caribbean grooves and funk. Although they released only two albums before effectively splitting in 1997, 1995's *The Score* was one of the biggest selling rap albums of all time. The combination of two Haitians – Wyclef Jean and Pras Michel – with American singer Lauryn Hill proved irresistible and their ability to adapt well-known standards and add samples to make them their own was a huge hit with the buying public. Their version of Lori Lieberman's

'Killing Me Softly With His Song', 'Killing Me Softly' was a number two US hit and topped the charts in the UK. The combination of a sweet female soul vocal with rap interjections and freestyles by the other two performers had a great impact on will.i.am. Wyclef had met the group on the *Smokin' Grooves* tour and was thoroughly impressed by their influences, their stagecraft and their professionalism.

'Rap Song' also showed that they were steeped in old school funk, by taking its spine from James Brown lieutenant Bobby Byrd's seminal track from 1971, 'I Know You Got Soul', best known to the hip-hop community through Eric B & Rakim's legendary 1987 update. 'Rap Song' was almost perfect for Black Eyed Peas, and it referenced the jagged edges of 'Clap Your Hands' from the first album. Its refrain of 'she like a rap song', demonstrated again how the group were playing to their burgeoning female audience. It also writ large the group's love of A Tribe Called Quest, making sure that their hit 'Bonita Applebum' was well referenced in the chorus.

'Bringing It Back', with DJ Motiv8 on turntables, is a direct plea to all the group's b-girls and b-boys. It is another dig at other rappers, suggesting that Black Eyed Peas were the only crew who were keeping it real. Of course, suggestions of superiority are a standard theme within rap – and very much a recurring theme within the Black Eyed Peas' work; however deriding those who aimed only at the charts, and the group's aim of taking hip-hop back to the days of Mantronix and Soulsonic seems a tad ironic in the light of what was soon to happen musically to Black Eyed Peas. Also, its case is somewhat weakened by some of the least original beats a listener could imagine. 'Tell Your Mama Come' is much better, taking a vibrant salsa groove with acoustic guitars and understated horns. Kim Hill adds a fine chorus vocal on yet another call to one large unified party.

The best is left right until the end: 'Request + Line' is very special and has the hallmarks of what was to be. With Macy Gray's sing-song delivery over the acoustic samples, it namechecks the favourite artists of the band – De La Soul, Les Nubians – and features a sample of the sitar from Traffic's 1967 hit, 'Paper Sun' (with a strong nod to John Martyn's 1977 album track 'Big Muff' in its guitar sound). It was a simple, potent patchwork. This became the final single from the album, and, in turn, the album's biggest hit, reaching number 63 on the *Billboard* Hot 100. The video, directed by Joseph Kahn, was perfect and showed how the group was coming together so well visually. Highly stylised and less down-home than Brian Beletic's efforts, it showed them in dayglo colours in a stylised radio station/nightclub set and heavily featured Gray, by now an enormous selling point. Gray dominates the promo with her mixing and scratching, wearing enormous sunglasses behind a pair of Technics turntables.

The UK version of *Bridging The Gap* ends with 'Magic', a join-the-dots of the Police's 1981 chart-topper, 'Every Little Thing She Does Is Magic'. Recorded for the film *Legally Blonde*, this song was a small, but extremely significant track for the Peas. It brought them into contact with writer/producer Ron Fair.

By the end of the album, the listener feels as if they have been bombarded by a collage of other people's material; indeed, one can argue, that is the fabric of hip-hop itself, but there seemed something ultimately unappealing about the blend.

*Bridging The Gap* received mixed reviews: those who loved it seemed to be very happy with the group's ongoing musical stew. *Hip Hop DX* suggested, "For the most part listening pleasure is guaranteed. The musical interludes are so good that in some cases you will wish that they were complete tracks." Q magazine said in November 2000, "Although less retro than chums Jurassic 5, their Hispanic-flavoured style constantly edges between sounding cool and simply withdrawn." Rapreviews.com said, "This is not a revolutionary album; but then again, neither was their debut. Both albums have one thing in common – they are a good listen from start to finish." *Rolling Stone* argued that "uncluttered but muscular production, deft samples and smart rhymes all ensure that the album's power increases with repeated listening", while noting that "garbed in boho gear, comprised of various races and stressing positivity, the trio is a pointed anecdote to gangsta and ghetto fabulousness." *Spin* magazine in November 2000 got closest to the bone: "While *Gap* is tougher and more fun than 1998's bland debut, *Behind The Front*, the Peas just aren't that good."

*The Village Voice*, the perennial hipster magazine that emanated from Greenwich Village was scathing. Under the heading 'DUD OF THE MONTH', it said: "Refusing to preach about politics, guns and bitches, as one admirer puts it ('Thankfully there's no inkling of misogyny or homophobia – how refreshing!'), these well-meaners are the Jurassic Five's answer to Arrested Development. Proficient, bland, and dauntingly dull, their only threat is a promise to 'take it back to the days of Mantronix' (no, please, anything but that). I can only guess why they clock corporate cash while accessible and manifestly civilized West Coast alt-rap mega-talents like Lyrics Born, Del, and Aceyalone explore bootstrap entrepreneurship. Maybe they lucked into connected management. Maybe they take good meeting. Or maybe their very lack of content has the advantage of cosseting the commercial preconceptions that count for so much more with sellers than buyers."

*The Rough Guide To Hip Hop* was similarly dismissive, suggesting that it followed *Behind The Front's* blueprint but without "any passion or inspiration, the title of *Bridging The Gap* seemed to indicate the only places that would play such insipid hip-hop". The review was a reference to the bland, safe San Francisco clothing chain store that had taken the world by storm at the turn of the 21st century.

*Bridging The Gap* was launched at the Grand Avenue Club in downtown LA in September 2000. There was a simple feeling among the hip-hop hardcore that, no matter how hard they tried, Black Eyed Peas just were not authentic. But already, this didn't necessarily matter, as the group had growing grass-roots student support.

# Chapter 5

# Lost? Change!

*"Nobody really knew who we were. It was more like, 'Oh, yeah, those are the hip-hop kids from LA.' It was proving ourselves. There was no success. There was no fame. There was no fortune, none of that."*

Taboo, 2011

*B*ridging The Gap suffered from a new 21st century phenomena – Internet piracy. Of course, bootlegging had been a music industry problem for years, but then you had needed to know the right people in the shady underworld of pop's twilight regions. Now, you could simply sit by your computer and have access to a never-ending supply of new music. For free.

"The record leaked. The Internet came into existence, and we suffered from it big time," will.i.am told iTunes. The band realised this when they were invited to a party after one of their shows, and heard their new soon-to-be-released album playing there. After eliminating any of the band members from bringing a pre-release copy along, will.i.am realised that they had fallen foul of the new craze of file-sharing as the Internet took control. If their audience had been more traditionally hip-hop, it may not have affected the group so much. But their core fan base was students, the most tech-savvy of the lot. "We got signed because our whole theory was we go to colleges, so when they graduate they take us with them," will.i.am said. "Our whole fan base was college kids, so they downloaded our stuff off the Internet. The download thing messed up *Bridging The Gap*. The bridge never truly got built, because there was a gap in it." Taboo recalls hearing 'Weekends' ahead of the release in clothes stores in LA. He later wrote, "Aside from the kick-to-the stomach feeling of being cheated, the main emotion was confusion. We felt violated that our piece of art – months in the making – was stolen and now hanging in someone else's gallery before we had even the chance to display it, showcase it and sell it." The recriminations and fall-out from this episode were an early wake-up call for the group. Recognising how technically literate the group's audience was, the group immediately established www.blackeyedpeas.com and began to communicate with their fans. By the time Napster had been shut down, the group had ensured it would be on the cutting edge of developments and would support iTunes wholeheartedly from its inception in 2003.

As a result of the Internet leak of the album, the anticipated leap in their fortunes did not happen, and *Bridging The Gap* sold only around 250,000 units. Steady, but hardly stellar sales. The group was downhearted, especially as Macy Gray, to whom they had given such an opportunity, was now a recognisable headliner in Europe. That said, Napster's black economy had also done the group a world of good. Now known as 'going viral', the message of Black Eyed Peas penetrated far further than it would normally have done. An inquisitive new audience heard the group and it did their reputation little harm.

A further merger of Interscope meant that *Bridging The Gap* languished somewhat because of record company politics. However, senior company executive Ron Fair could see the potential in the group and felt that they should move to the A&M wing of the Interscope-Geffen-A&M family. "I said, 'Look, you're on Interscope, I'm president of A&M and we could switch you over to A&M,'" Fair told MTV. "It's really the same company. The only difference is you get me. So let's put our heads together and try to make this thing work." The group moved across to A&M for their final album of their deal, with Jimmy Iovine's blessing and ongoing involvement.

The band toured again to support *Bridging The Gap*, and played the Mean Fiddler in April 2001 at the heart of London's West End to their small but fervently devoted followers. *NME* captured the moment again. Writer Dele Fadele was absolutely right when he noted that the group's version of their hometown was "emphatically not one of drive-by shootings, police corruption, ghetto runnings and huge bottles of malt liquor. It's more akin to an endless party in the sunshine, programmed by eclectic music fans, who might be conscious of society's rifts and shifting political faults but are determined to celebrate people's diversity and differences." Their eclecticism was now their strongest selling point. But eclecticism was not going to bring in the sort of money needed to keep them financially afloat.

In the period following *Bridging The Gap*, Black Eyed Peas felt strongly that they needed to get their house in order, so throughout 2001, there were several wholesale changes to their operation. They were buoyed by Jimmy Iovine and Ron Fair's faith in them. Iovine instructed them to go and create a fabulous third album. David Sonenberg replaced Yon Styles and Black Coffee as the Black Eyed Peas' management. will.i.am was most impressed with Sonenberg's track record. A straight-talking, no-nonsense industry professional, he was everything that Styles, who had grown with them, was not. Sonenberg was a Harvard-educated entertainment industry lawyer when, at 24, he began managing Meat Loaf, who was then looking for a deal for his album *Bat Out Of Hell*.

By carefully selecting the artists that he took on his roster, Sonenberg built a small, successful client base for his company, DAS Communications. "I've managed very few people," Sonenberg said in 2004, "and years may go by when I don't sign anybody, unless they're unbelievably gifted and unique." One of the groups that impressed him the most was the Fugees.

"When I met the Fugees, for example, I was blown away," he said in the same interview. "Lauryn Hill was magnificent-looking, incredibly smart, and had an unbelievable voice. Wyclef Jean was talented and charismatic. They were playing real instruments and writing real songs – something that wasn't happening in hip-hop. I thought they could make a difference, and they became major successes." The Fugees' stellar career in the late nineties proved that he understood how a multi-faceted rap group could become international superstars, and the Black Eyed Peas too maintained their live band and wrote real songs. Sonenberg employee Seth Friedman was put in charge of day-to-day management and Polo Molina, who'd been there since before day one and proved so successful with his merchandising operation, became their on-the-ground tour manager.

Also in this time of some tumult, Kim Hill left the group to pursue her own solo career. According to Taboo, it had been on the cards for some time. The band did not enjoy her wordy monologues on stage, and her dynamic was different from the rest of the group's. Hill commenced a solo career, releasing, to date, three critically acclaimed albums, *Surrender To Her Sunflower*, *Suga Hill*, *Okada Taxi* and *Pharoah's Daughter*.

Hill gave her reasons for her departure to portalblackeyedpeas.com in 2010: "It was less about the Black Eyed Peas, it was more about myself and will.i.am... Will was the closest thing to a little brother... Things just started kinda to go a little bit downhill... So when things started to get a little tricky with Will and I, it was very difficult for me to stand on stage and perform, because I felt like the chemistry had been tainted, and once your audience doesn't believe that what you projecting is organic, it's just not gonna work. So I had to make a decision." Hill also felt that change was on the cards and she wanted no part of it: "[I] really knew that the band was about to take a turn, because there was a lot of pressure on me for the label, to sex it up. They were like: 'You are size 4, you are attractive; wear some roller stakes and some panties and call it a day'. And there's a difference between over sexualizing the band that feels like your brothers, 'cause those guys were like my family. So it didn't feel comfortable to take on a sexual role in that band... I knew that a song like 'My Humps' was on the horizon and this is not an insult to Fergie or the Black Eyed Peas, that's just not a record that I wanna make. Cause I wanna make a record that when I'm 90, I still feel comfortable singing them."

Black Eyed Peas were in a state of flux. That said, the group always looked back on these years with a great deal of fondness: "The innocence of us being new to the industry and travelling for the very first time and performing, opening up for a lot of people," Taboo told *Miami New Times* in 2011. "Nobody really knew who we were. It was more like, 'Oh, yeah, those are the hip-hop kids from LA.' It was proving ourselves. There was no success. There was no fame. There was no fortune, none of that. It was just raw energy. Passing out flyers for our concerts and us going into the audience after our show and mingling with people. We wanted to get our name out there. It was like the new freshmen in college." But it was time to move on.

On May 28, 2001, Minneapolis Radio station KDWB held a concert with Black Eyed Peas playing with California-based girl band Wild Orchid. Their singer Stacy Ferguson, who was on the verge of leaving the soft-rock trio, approached will.i.am, whose work she admired, about producing something for her upcoming solo album. It wasn't the first time that Black Eyed Peas and Ferguson had been in the same room.

"I first went to see the Black Eyed Peas in 1998 at a place called the El Ray Theatre in LA," Ferguson told *Blues And Soul* magazine. "Because they were hip hop–yet-abstract and their style was eclectic and theatrical, there was something about them I knew I could gel with. So years later, when Wild Orchid and the Peas happened to be on a radio show at the same time, I went up to will.i.am, got on my hustle, and told him I'd been wanting to work with him for ever!" will.i.am took her number and was impressed with her confidence and front.

The changes gave Black Eyed Peas an opportunity to start again from scratch in many ways. Adams had also invested in his own studio-cum-HQ, where the Peas could base themselves for all future recordings. Situated between Glendale and Los Feliz in Los Angeles, the building became known as the 'Stewchia'. will.i.am also decided that he could attempt to sing the female vocal parts himself and that the group should continue as their core trio. After all, Hill had not been the only voice in the Black Eyed Peas – Esthero, Macy Gray and others had all sung vocal parts. They could surely import female vocalists as and when the occasion called for them.

Throughout, the group continued touring and recording. They

joined ex-Fugee Wyclef and De La Soul on the *MTV College Campus Invasion Tour* throughout October 2000 and supported both No Doubt and Macy Gray on her US and British tours, getting their first UK taste of playing big halls, opening for her at the famed 12,000 capacity Wembley Arena. Although it was just as a support act, it was a noticeable step up from their previous UK gig at the Jazz Café.

While sessions were taking place for what was to become the next album, Black Eyed Peas had an offer to record music for a new Dr Pepper commercial. They were excited, yet some people felt the group was selling out. "I remember thinking, this is important to the band, but it's taking up a lot of time," original band bassist Mike Fratantuno told the *Wall Street Journal*. "Ultimately the goal was to be a world-famous band." will.i.am saw it as a massive opportunity to spread the band's name further. The band got a $100,000 advance, and it sent a very clear message to corporate America that here was a band, which was in many ways a marketing executive's dream of mixed races, singing non-threatening rap music. The track, which would eventually become known as 'Be You', went out with the Dr Pepper TV campaign in 2002.

The advert – which took seven days to film – was a blatant attempt for Dr Pepper to reach out to the important African-American and Latino communities of America, with a stylised ad that reached back into the Harlem Renaissance. A curtain reveals huge cut-out heads of jazz legends Louis Armstrong and Ella Fitzgerald, and there is a flurry of jazz dancing and strategic product placement. The group appears, introducing the moves they had been making in Los Angeles for at least half a decade with will.i.am singing, "Here's to individuals, like Dr Pepper, the original." Its cry for individuality chimed with the group's ethos, and it was a shrewd move as it placed the extremely photogenic group into millions of American homes.

It was also a clear message that David Sonenberg had enough clout and forward thought to utilise these wider platforms for his charges, and this would therefore be a notable way to break the band across America. Taboo said, "The music industry was about getting visibility and getting our music into as many ears as possible – and one hundred Gs helped at a time when we needed money. It made no sense to turn it down." This would be the beginning of many product tie-ins that would become a key feature of the group's next decade.

will.i.am had no qualms about accepting the corporate dollar, and understood that this was the way to go: "Hip-hop was never supposed to stay in the South Bronx – it's whole purpose was to be the biggest form of music in the world...," he said in 2002. "Run DMC would never have made a song called 'My Adidas' – muthafuckas didn't get a dime for it. They were selling Adidas and Adidas didn't even have to do a marketing campaign. They didn't have the little marketing meeting – 'let's get these black guys to sell our shoes... and have all these urban kids buy our gear'. These corporations – Nike, Sprite, Coke, Panasonic, Motorola – they're gonna utilise urban music anyway to sell their product because most urban people buy these products. Every rapper talks about Motorola in their video for fuckin' free. So why not get paid for a commercial when people are doing it for free anyway?... Why not the Black Eyed Peas to do Dr. Pepper? We're the only muthafuckas that like that soda. I don't see nobody drinkin' no Dr. Pepper in no video. We're an odd ass group – why not us? I don't understand why people hate."

will.i.am reflected on the repeated question of sponsorship several years later in 2010 to *Newsweek*: "I did a Nivea hair-product commercial – that's how I paid my mom's mortgage. Then I did a Dr. Pepper commercial, and I bought my mom a new house. I got paid more for 30 seconds of music than I did making 72 minutes of music, and it allowed me to move my family out of the projects. From Otis Redding to Miles Davis to every single major artist I think about, all their record deals sucked. Ads paid. I knew at least that much."

The band toured Australia and New Zealand, playing the Big Day Out Festival, a moving festival that took in Sydney, Melbourne, Perth, Gold Coast and Auckland. The bill would be largely rock/dance based, playing alongside artists such as Placebo, Coldplay, Queens Of The Stone Age, PJ Harvey, Rammstein and DJs Carl Cox and Darren Emerson. The tour was soured by the death at the Sydney concert of 16-year-old Jessica Michalik, who passed away five days after being asphyxiated in the mosh pit at the front of the stage.

Continually coming up with new tunes and ideas, it was during this period that will.i.am released his first solo album, *Lost Change*, for Barely Breaking Even (BBE), Peter Adarkwah and Ben Jolly's UK based left-field label with impeccable US west coast connections, and distributed through Atlantic. It was part of a series of releases for the label that included Pete Rock's *PeteStrumentals*, DJ Jazzy Jeff's *The Magnificent* and J Dilla's *Welcome To Detroit*. Based in the decidedly unromantic Cricklewood, north-west London, Adarkwah and Jolly had a strong feeling of what was right about old school hip-hop, and gained the respect and the ear of many left-field beat merchants. They also supplemented their new albums with impeccable, often vinyl-only compilations of rare grooves and classic soul, *Strange Games And Funky Things*.

Working with a select team including long-time BEP collaborator Printz Board, guitarist J. Curtis, LA underground rappers Mykill Myers and Jason Green, known as Planet Asia, *Lost Change* was a freewheeling development for will.i.am. It was intended as, and remains, a low-key release and offers proof positive that he was sincere and innovative as a producer and performer. The sleeve of *Lost Change* featured a high gloss and high production values photograph by Scottish art and fashion photographer Albert Watson. It shows will.i.am crossing a busy LA street, with his hand resolutely and somewhat conspiratorially over his mouth suggesting that his raps were to be used sparingly across the album's 14 tracks. The key track is 'I Am', which acted as something of a theme song in the intervening years. The album has a sharpness and clarity that was missing from *Bridging The Gap*.

"The mood of *Lost Change* ranges from fuzzy funk to jazzy downright jiggy. will.i.am utilises some creative production tricks... BBE might want to change its name to BBA – with tracks this good, you can Barely Break Away," *Atlanta Vibes* said at the time. It's probably the great hidden treasure out of the whole Black Eyed Peas' canon. Its blend of beats, instrumentals and raps emphasizes just how difficult will.i.am was to pigeonhole whether as a solo artist or within his group. The idea of creating the title tracks as the theme to an obscure, Internet-only movie allowed will.i.am and his players to stretch out – 'Lost Change' is a spy pastiche, while 'Lost Change In E Minor' is Spaghetti Western-hued, and then 'Lost Change In D Minor' is all incidental detective movie music. 'I Am', an underrated theme song if there ever was one, was a rather splendid piece of incessant chanting, enlivened by will.i.am's freestyling.

Allmusic.com said: "*Lost Change* is a sophisticated, musically enthralling endeavor, which still manages to be accessible." It is a joy from start to finish and takes today's listener back to a time when blunted beats and loping funk seemed such an exciting future for the dance movement. It sold next to nothing, but that was hardly the point. "It wasn't really supposed to," will.i.am said in 2002. "The only people I really cared about listening to it and liking it was the Okayplayer community and the Breakestra community. That's not really a lotta people — it's just tastemakers, people that care about music integrity. That's pretty much all I cared about. I got the video played on MTV — shot the video, paid for it myself, and I took it to MTV's offices and they added it. That was kinda surprising cuz it wasn't like it was [selling] mad units, and there were a whole bunch of other groups that they weren't playing."

Black Eyed Peas had begun their third album, working in a rented house in Bodega Bay, Sonoma County, in northern California between June and September 2001. The whole band decamped there along with their musicians, and Polo Molina, DJ Motiv8 and Dante Santiago. Vocalist Terry Dexter came along too, as Adams was experimenting with female vocalists in place of Kim Hill.

Ron Fair had approached Adams with a proposition: "I asked them, 'How would you feel about taking a leap and going more into the pop world?' They replied, 'We don't want to lose our credibility or our fan base.' I said, 'Well, if you don't take a shot at it, it's gonna get worse, because the backpack crowd are the people who will download the records for free." It was a prescient statement: for the group to survive, they had to go overground. It was clear from the strength of the new material that they may be aiming for a wider market than simply their old student crowd. However the material they were attempting just didn't somehow feel right. They had the house booked until September, before they were to return to LA to take part in the Coca-Cola sponsored *If You Don't Know You Don't Go* (IYDKYDG) tour.

It was towards the end of their stay at Bodega Bay that the group watched, with the profound shock, fear and sorrow of the whole world, the events of 9/11 unfold on the television. Being on the west coast of America, it was 6.30 am, and they knew immediately that they did not want to continue work on a day of such tumult and confusion. After trying to book a flight home then realising that this was not an option, the band rented cars in which to rush back to Los Angeles to be with their families. In the days of rage and bewilderment that followed, they considered cancelling their place on their upcoming tour but after sage advice from will.i.am's grandmother, the band went ahead and played. They felt, after much soul searching, that to cancel the tour would simply mean that the terrorists had won.

The IYDKYDG tour was based on competition winners who sent in their special ringpulls from Coca-Cola cans. The varying success of the promotion led to some wild discrepancies in attendances for the shows. Sharing the bill with Black Starr and Bismarck, the group used it as another opportunity to hone their live act. They incorporated a minute's silence into their set, and called for mass lighter waving during their closer, 'Positivity' from *Behind The Front*.

In December 2001, Adams and Printz Board began working on a song that would have an enormous impact on Black Eyed Peas' career. Originating from some experimentation with music they were to provide for ringtones, they pieced it together in the Stewcha, and Adams came up with a guitar riff and a beat. With the events of 9/11 still on his mind, he began to craft raps that reflected his feelings about the state of the world. When the band reconvened the following year at Glenwood Studios in Burbank, Taboo and apl.de.ap added their own verses. Taking different approaches to the problem of terrorism and living through the 'war on terror' era, which brought suspicion and questioning into the heart of the community, the three rappers sang verses examining the state of the world and the ameliorating need for universal love. It was good, but needed something extra. All three felt that it needed a well-known male vocalist to sing the chorus to spread the message as far and as wide as possible.

There is some dispute about whose idea it was to bring in Justin Timberlake to record with the group. Ron Fair heard the song and recognised its enormous potential. He has said that he came up with an idea – to team them with the current hottest phenomenon on popular music, former *NSYNC dancer and vocalist Timberlake, who was then on the verge of a solo career. Fair has said that he told will.i.am to get in touch with Timberlake under the radar – the last thing he wanted it to look like was that a record company mogul had instructed a group, for a cynical marketing ploy, to get the hottest thing on the block to join them. will.i.am and Timberlake knew each other, and Taboo had recently danced with him in a club in Hollywood. will.i.am played the track down the telephone to Timberlake and the words 'where is the love' inspired Timberlake to write. Within 15 minutes, he had come up with a chorus melody and sung it back to will.i.am on his voicemail. However, Taboo eloquently states in *Fallin' Up* that it was his idea after speaking with Ron Fair to get Timberlake. He called Timberlake about the song, played what they had, and soon the *NSYNC star came back with the new chorus. Taboo then played it to will.i.am, who was initially skeptical.

Whichever way it actually was, everybody liked what Timberlake had done, bringing a sweet and soulful – and highly commercial – touch to the record. Within a matter of days, Timberlake had come to Los Angeles to record the vocals at Glenwood Studios in March 2002. He had just split up with his paramour of three years, Britney Spears, and felt the need to open his heart to his new allies. "He went into the vocal booth and poured all of his heartbreak into that hook," Taboo wrote. "He shit on that song, and the studio was blown away by his harmonies, the way he hit his falsettos, and the whole way he was trained."

With this momentous track in the bag, the band set about recording the rest of the album, utilizing some of the characters they had met on the *Warped* tour, namely drummer Travis Barker from Blink-182 and Papa Roach, alongside their studio regulars George Pajon Jr., Printz Board, Mike Fratantuno, and J Curtis. The album became a lengthy work in progress, and its title and outlook were already in place when Adams talked to MTV in June 2002.

He reflected on Hill's departure ("We had a falling out") and those original fans who believed the Peas were selling out due to the relative success of 'Request + Line' and the Dr Pepper ad. "A lot of fans are like, 'I love the Black Eyed Peas. Y'all so positive,'" he said. "Then as soon as you're on 'TRL' [*Total Request Live*, MTV's heavy rotation video section] they're like, 'I hate y'all. Y'all sold out.' I don't understand what selling out means. If I changed what I was talking about, now I treat women like bitches or now I hate white people or now I hate black people, that's a sell-out. But if you just get recognised for the things you do or the song the record label chooses as a single, which you have no choice over, is not your hard, aggressive one, I don't see how that's selling out." If people thought that they had sold out thus far, what was about to happen would only reinforce all of their concerns and prejudices. The group was about to get a permanent female vocalist. A white chick from a soft rock band.

# Chapter 6

# Make Way For The Dutchess: Enter Fergie

*"We exchanged numbers and it was when they needed a singer for their song 'Shut Up' that we actually started working together."*

Fergie, 2006

During the sessions for the group's next album, Taboo and will.i.am developed an idea that originated from an argument Taboo was having with his then girlfriend over the telephone at the mixing desk in the studio. Adams got the idea to turn the phrase 'shut up' into a chorus, a call-and-response between man and woman. But who could do it? Terry Dexter had sung some back-ups for Black Eyed Peas, most convincingly on 'Magic', the track recorded post-*Bridging The Gap* that was included on the European edition of the album and later on the *Legally Blonde* soundtrack. She was good but not right. Costa Rican vocalist Debi Nova, and Eden Crush vocalist and dancer Nicole Scherzinger were discussed as possible alternatives. Band associate Dante Santiago suggested that they should hook up with Stacy Ferguson, the singer from Wild Orchid, who had introduced herself to will.i.am over a year ago at the radio broadcast in Minneapolis.

Stacy Ann Ferguson was born on March 27, 1975 in Hacienda Heights in the Puente Hills of the San Gabriel Valley in Los Angeles County in California, the daughter of teachers Theresa 'Terri' Ann Gore and Jon Patrick Ferguson. Of Scottish, Mexican, Native American and Irish descent, the young Ferguson went to Mesa Robles Middle School, and then on to the Glen A. Wilson High School in Wedgeworth Drive, also in Hacienda Heights.

Ferguson was encouraged wholeheartedly in the arts by her parents: "My mom would have to quiet me down in church," she told *Billboard* in 2010. "They're big music lovers, and they exposed me to things at a very young age. My mom would take me to musicals on our mother-daughter dates. She also took me to the Madonna *Like A Virgin* tour." Ferguson also attended a Tina Turner concert with her father around the same age. "I saw Tina Turner, second row, with my dad," she later told *Rolling Stone*. "She pointed at me. I love how she was energetic and raw. Those early impressions tell you how things are supposed to be." Seeing that the young Ferguson was clearly bitten by the bug, her mother spotted an advert for a theatre group, Karen's Kids, that performed and sang in shopping malls.

The children's performing group was established in 1978 by Karen Blackburn, who used her music education degree to put together a team of 12 children between the ages of five and 14 who could sing, dance and act. The group would perform at malls, predominately in southern California, but also as far afield as Las Vegas and Hawaii. Ferguson was a natural for the group and was encouraged by her mother to participate, singing 'On The Good Ship Lollipop' and songs from *Annie* and *Cabaret* at the age of six.

Ferguson's mother also bought a season ticket to their local venue, the La Habra Community Theatre, and together they went to see every suitable show that came along like *West Side Story* and *Peter Pan*. Ferguson's love of theatre and early potential meant that she – and often her younger sister Dana – would appear in television work, mainly adverts. When Ferguson was promoting *The Dutchess* album in 2006, her mother gave the Tyra Banks show permission to show some home videos of Ferguson when she was five years old. She is standing with her sister in her kitchen making up adverts about items from the family refrigerator. A natural performer, she was also a diligent, straight 'A' student, performing especially well in the Spelling Bee competitions, as well as being a Girl Scout and a cheerleader.

A big break came for Ferguson at the age of seven, when she became a voice actor, working with Bill Melendez and the Charles M. Schulz Creative Team and CBS on the animated *Peanuts* cartoon specials. *Peanuts*, the cartoon strip created by Schulz in 1950, was a venerated American institution syndicated across the globe in newspapers that introduced the world to Charlie Brown and his beagle, Snoopy. Snoopy was a dog whose fantasy life marked him out over the years as anything from a writer to a World War One flying ace. After it made the transition into animation in 1965 with the Emmy-winning *It's A Charlie Brown Christmas*, a further 24 half-hour specials had been made. Ferguson joined the series for two specials, *It's The Flashbeagle, Charlie Brown* in 1984 and *Snoopy's Getting Married, Charlie Brown* in 1985. Ferguson voiced Charlie Brown's smart young sister, Sally, who had a crush on the strip's spiritual core, the blanket-holding Linus Van Pelt.

It was clear that Ferguson was destined for great things; between 1984 and 1989 she starred in the Disney Channel's *Kids Incorporated*. *Kids Inc.* as it was often known, featured the ups and downs of a group of teenagers who performed together as a rock band. Ferguson played 'Stacy', and was one of the original cast. Each show would feature the band singing a selection of songs, a mixture of originals and cover versions of the day, against a storyline of their lives. In a particularly poignant episode in season three, an 11-year-old Ferguson sings Lionel Richie's 'Say You Say Me' to a heavily made up clown, who twirls a broomstick and then fails to make a yo-yo return. It was a showboating performance, and encapsulated perfectly the show's potent ratings-grabbing use of popular pathos.

"In *Kids Incorporated*, I'm in the studio at eight years old, behind a microphone, learning the techniques," Ferguson told *Rolling Stone* in October 2006. "I was a little adult. I had to be professional on the set – you can't break into a tantrum, so [I] learned. I always wanted to appease and put on a strong face and not let anyone know if there was something bothering me." It was also during her stint at *Kids Incorporated* that she broadened her musical horizons. "Part of my affinity with urban music comes from being on *Kids Incorporated*, 'cos we used to sit around and listen to Chaka Khan and Prince, and I got influenced by all that," she told *The Guardian* in 2006. "Then gangsta rap got started, and I was infatuated with that."

*Kids Incorporated* became a fertile breeding ground for future talent; of its alumni, Eric Balfour went on to star in *Six Feet Under*. Martika, known as Marta on the show, became a successful recording artist. Mario Lopez – who was Ferguson's 'boyfriend' at the age of 10 – ended up a dancer and presenter, and Jennifer Love Hewitt became a Hollywood star. After leaving *Kids Incorporated* in 1989, Ferguson got occasional TV work, most notably – and showing, in reality, how small the Los Angeles scene is – playing Bud Bundy's girlfriend, Ann, in an episode of *Married With Children* in 1994. Bundy, of course, was played by David Faustino, the promoter of the Balistyx nights on Sunset Strip which led to Atban Klann being signed to Ruthless.

When it became clear that Ferguson would soon be outgrowing *Kids Incorporated* (which was to run for nine seasons until 1993), at the age of 15 she joined a new group that was being put together by producer-writer Ron Fair. Fair was an industry veteran by this point, having worked his first hit in 1976 when as an engineer he worked on the *Rocky* soundtrack and the number one single by the Bill Conti orchestra, 'Gonna Fly Now'. At the turn of the nineties, he was working both in A&R and had gained a reputation as motion picture soundtrack coordinator and producer, working on such enormous-selling titles as *Pretty Woman* and *White Men Can't Jump*.

Ferguson's new group was to be known as Wild Orchid. The trio was Renée Sandstrom – who had played Ferguson's sister on *Kids Incorporated* – and Stefanie Ridel. Ferguson was full of admiration for Fair. "He signed us to RCA. We took nine months to make our first album. He let us nurture our voices and learn how to record in the studio, harmonise, techniques of the mic. He actually let us splice an actual tape reel. We were old school. I would do 50 tracks of the same song and we'd go through each one and talk about them. Ron was an amazing guide."

However, try as they might, Wild Orchid – described by *Billboard* as a 'disco Wilson Phillips' – simply didn't fully connect with the record-buying public. They released two albums – *Wild Orchid* and *Oxygen* – and supported Cher on her *Believe* tour. "The record company put a lot of money into us, Ferguson continued. "We released a ballad called 'At Night I Pray'. We thought, 'We're gonna go tour the world now,' but it never did connect to people... It was very frustrating. We worked really hard and had a lot of letdowns, a lot of rejection. Those girls are still my sisters, but my career didn't take the path that I thought it would. I'm a better artist for it, though."

What it did leave Ferguson with was an addiction to crystal meth. She had wanted to leave the group in 2000, but her desire to please others and keep the show on the road, a hangover from the *Kids Incorporated* days, meant she carried on, propping herself up initially with Ecstasy and then with increasing use of crystal meth. Methamphetamine, known by its street name, 'crystal meth', is a seductive and assiduous drug. Its positive benefits include increased alertness, concentration and energy; it also increases libido and self esteem. It is also extremely addictive.

Ferguson lost at least two years to her crystal meth addiction. Disguising her weight loss to her friends and band members by saying she was suffering from the eating disorder bulimia nervosa, her worst moment came when she took herself, riddled with paranoia and an obsession that the FBI were after her, into a Korean church on Wilshire Boulevard. In her dialogue with God, she said that if there were no FBI agents outside the church when she left, she would begin to rid herself of her addiction. There were, of course, no Feds. Her rehabilitation began.

And so, Dante Santiago brought Ferguson along to Glenwood Studios for her to sing the female vocal part to 'Shut Up' for Black Eyed Peas. will.i.am was at once impressed with her vocal style but also the way she performed the record in the booth; and then the way that she could add her own harmonies. "Like a seasoned pro, she knew about thirds, and layering, and stacking, and she brought that song to life," Taboo said. "But it wasn't just the voice that impressed, it was the performance she gave. The majority of people walk into a booth to lay down vocals and concentrate on the delivery, keeping the mouth close to the mic, not wanting movement to affect the projection of her voice. But Stacy started rocking out like she was on stage, in her zone – and kept her vocals pitch perfect. It was incredible to watch. She was a fireball."

Ferguson remembered, "I basically became a studio rat! I'd go to the studio, put a background part here or there – and ended up becoming the record's background singer." The group started developing a relationship with Ferguson in a way they had never done with Hill. They began hanging out and going to clubs with each other. When Jimmy Iovine heard 'Shut Up' he suggested that Ferguson become a full-time member. The group was initially skeptical, especially as they had recently bonded back well into three-man mode.

Given Iovine's suggestion, will.i.am was impressed enough with her to invite her to sing some spots on their already-booked Australian festival tour, to see how she fitted into the group dynamic. They played The Falls Music And Arts Festival at the seaside resort of Lorne, south west of Melbourne. For their first performance on New Year's Eve 2002, an incident happened that was to go down in folklore. Ferguson had needed to go to the toilet, but, in the excitement before beginning their performance had forgotten to – and on stage she wet herself. "That's when she became a Black Eyed Pea," apl. de.ap was later to say.

"It's like there's one or two things the public knows about every famous person," Ferguson later told *Blender*. "With me, everyone knows I wet my pants on stage and had a crystal-meth addiction. That sucks. You have to laugh." Fortunately, as 2003 was rung in, she saturated her pants in champagne to cover her misdemeanour. Ferguson commanded the stage in a way that the group's other vocalists never had. She immediately created a contrast to the rest of the band, a sort of white rock chick-hip-hop hybrid.

Soon afterwards the other three decided Ferguson should become a full-time member. "Though I was working on my solo stuff at the time – I made the decision to become a full-time member of the Black Eyed Peas. And I'm obviously very glad I did! It finally gave me the rock'n'roll lifestyle I'd craved, but never had, with Wild Orchid – where the most we'd got to do was open for Cher!" When Ferguson joined the group, their fortunes changed. Here was a street-smart vocalist with the looks and sass; her striking appearance and mixed–race descent gave the group yet another colour to add to their image.

Just why the group had brought Ferguson – who they renamed 'Fergie-Ferg', or 'Fergie' for short – became an ongoing question. It seemed like a purely commercial move when they had been left-field darlings. "We put Fergie in because of her amazing voice, her edge and her rawness," will.i.am said in 2009. "When you follow your heart, you're never supposed to do things because of what you think people might say. You do it for the opposite reasons... We did it because she was a true talent." There was always an understanding that Fergie would, at some point, have her solo career and that it would run alongside the group's work but now, they had an album to finish.

Sessions for *Elephunk* continued into the start of 2003, now with vocals by Fergie being added to key tracks, and the track 'Fly Away' was included as a showcase for her. By the time of the album's release in June of that year, Fergie was on the cover with the other three. Ron Fair kept his eye on the proceedings, knowing that something special had to be delivered, and importantly, the message song that will.i.am had started recording in 2001, 'Where Is The Love', needed to be the strong lead track. In Fair's opinion, the song still needed work doing to it.

"Will tends to make records very quickly, on the fly, with a lot of heart. He cops a vibe and then moves on," Fair told MTV in early 2004. He asked will.i.am if he could go into the studio and 'fool around with it', on the proviso that if Adams didn't like what he did, he could veto it. Fair went in with musicians, an orchestra and a production team and reworked the original that will.i.am and the Peas had put down. He re-edited Timberlake's vocal parts and added Ferguson's voice to it. Most notably he added the string part and trimmed down will.i.am's original. "We basically buffed it and made it a lot more powerful and concise."

will.i.am heard the new version. Liking some of it, but not all, he then added his own touches to curb some of the potential schmaltz in Fair's arrangement. By the end, they had one *enormous* pop song. There was talk that the infectious, Fergie-driven 'Shut Up' should lead the album, but it soon became clear that no-one could ignore the, um, *Elephunk* in the room, and that 'Where Is The Love' should be the album's lead single, a clear marker, if it were needed, that Black Eyed Peas were about to move on. As if to mark a clear distinction between the old group and the new group, a decision was taken to add the definite article to the group's name. Black Eyed Peas became the Black Eyed Peas.

# Chapter 7

# The Shiniest Pop Product
# Imaginable: *Elephunk*

*"We were behind the front, so we built a bridge and bridged the gaps... so now we need to travel across that bridge on an elephant's back and bring you Elephunk."*

will.i.am, 2003

*"It was a long 2 ½ years, but those 2 ½ changed me tremendously forever."*

will.i.am, 2003

In 2003, there were but two pop records to stand out – Beyoncé's coming-of-age track, 'Crazy In Love', and the Black Eyed Peas' 'Where Is The Love'. While Beyoncé was all going-out sass and strut, 'Where Is The Love' was a pensive, introspective call to arms. Released as a single in the US on June 16, 2003 'Where Is The Love' was the first taste of the new Black Eyed Peas. It became a breakout success and its video, directed by will.i.am himself, introduced this new configuration to the wider world. It marked a departure from the slick promos that accompanied *Bridging The Gap* and returned to the style of their earliest Brian Beletic-helmed clips. Filmed around the Estrada Courts and Royal

Heights areas of LA, it had a guerrilla feel, with the group and friends posting question mark stickers on various items of street furniture and walls, while will.i.am, apl.de.ap and Taboo travel the streets in a van, broadcasting their song, looking not dissimilar to the Lone Gunmen, the trio of conspiracy theorists from Chris Carter's *X-Files* series.

A question mark is put into the torch of the Statue of Liberty. As the band head to the streets, Fergie makes her first appearance as a member of the group. To circumvent Jive Records' embargo on Justin Timberlake's appearance in the video, the chorus is mimed by a variety of children. Ironically, with his shorter dreads, sideways baseball cap and tracksuit top, will.i.am looks more like a conventional rapper than he had ever done before in Black Eyed Peas videos. However, he appeared almost cartoon-like as an MC and gave the world's viewers something easily understandable to watch and immediately identify with. will.i.am said during the making of the video that it was "about four people that influence four billion people; it's our own propaganda campaign where we are trying to educate people to ask where is the love within themselves."

Communities were involved and, importantly, children are seen playing war-enactment computer games which are interrupted with the question mark. The marks are seen as tattoos, on road signs, on liquor bottles and as crop circles. As Taboo delivers his rap furiously into the tannoy in the van, a street preacher is seen waving his bible with a question mark on it. It is as if all conventional and traditional places to look for love are under question – a neat video précis of the confusion and introspection America had been going through for the past 18 months. apl.de.ap's dark, searing rap is played out with him running from, and being captured by, aggressive police, portraying another strong stereotype for discussion. The video, which also features Fergie heavily, ends with the refrain of 'one world', as all races and genders come out of their houses and look to the skies. It was the first of the Black Eyed Peas' simplistic, easily accessible videos that could play out across the globe and, alongside the record, it proved an immediate talking point. As a result, 'Where Is The Love' went into heavy rotation on MTV and began to assail the world's charts.

Taboo told the *Daily Mirror*: "It was a success because it was letting people ask the question of themselves, not just the government. A lot of people have been feeling the message that we send out in the song but were too scared or couldn't find a way to say it. Whether it was being asked about terrorism, or racism or gang violence or politicians didn't matter. Take mentioning the CIA for example – that isn't something that is often spoken about in pop music. It's not just blatantly saying that George Bush is a terrorist, but it is making people think, 'Perhaps there is something more to what is going on than what we are being told.' I'm so proud that one of our songs can have that kind of effect."

will.i.am said: "The song relates to the tension of the world today with the personal struggles the members of the different groups have gone through. The last couple of years haven't been easy. Is it guilt or is it stress? But there is uncertainty over what's gonna happen in the next five years." He told MTV: "It's like if Marvin Gaye was alive today. It's classic soul, some thinking shit... The world needs this song right now. There's no song like that in urban music, pop music. We're saying some pretty deep stuff, some conscious stuff." Ron Fair was delighted with the outcome, saying that the finished result was a "mixture of a lot of things. It's a hip-hop record, a pop record, a sing-song kind of nursery-rhyme record and a soulful record. And it's certainly a message record."

The increasingly stellar profile of Justin Timberlake did much to help the success of the record. Since recording the track with them in March 2002, his debut solo album, *Justified,* was released in November of that year and had reached number two in the US and topped the charts in the UK. A string of singles made him ubiquitous. Working with the Neptunes, Pharrell Williams and Chad Hugo, his distinctive falsetto had been framed by their brand of futuristic hip-hop-tinged neo-soul.

Certainly, Timberlake's international profile and the continued interest in his high-profile split-up with his childhood sweetheart Britney Spears made 'Where Is The Love' exceptionally newsworthy. It tapped into the conflation of the personal and the global that had occurred in the months and now years since 9/11. The fact that Timberlake was uncredited made the record all the sweeter. It seemed as if people had stumbled across this connection rather than it being some superstar confection.

The track's parent album, *Elephunk*, gleaned its title from a time when the group visited a club while staying at Bodega Bay and saw a woman playing a tuba which sounded like an elephant. It was released on June 24, 2003 three years after *Bridging The Gap.* "An elephant ain't the fastest, swiftest animal, but it walks smoothly," will.i.am told MTV. "It's fat. It's heavy. Thump, thump. You can just picture an elephant's movement. That's the sound of the album. We have a lot of trombones, fat bass lines, fat grooves, and nice, thick horn layers and arrangements. Just fat funk."

*Elephunk* certainly was a different listen from its predecessors; commerciality was emphasised, and the production sheen given to key tracks by Fair made it far more radio-friendly than their previous releases. It sleeve marked out the difference between this album and their earlier work; where *Behind The Front* and *Bridging The Gap* had fairly interchangeable portraits of the three group members; here, an illustration of an elephant occupied sleeve middle. With an illustration of a vinyl record to its side, the elephant could possibly represent Ganesh, the Hindu 'remover of obstacles', 'lord of beginnings' and patron of arts and sciences. The four Peas are in the four corners of the sleeve with Ferguson bottom right perfecting a street sneer. The A&M logo is prominent on the middle of the rear sleeve, alongside will.i.am's 'I Am Music' imprint on the rear. It was all a clear indication that this was very much a new outfit. The first photograph of this new line-up together was Markus Klinko and Indrani's heavily stylized portrait on the final page of the album's inner booklet. Fergie's hand is resting on a legs-apart Adams' shoulder. Taboo is in a suitably ninja-esque pose. apl.de.ap looks on from behind. The group, instead of striking their previous benign, bookish poses, look ready for battle.

The album is crammed with ideas – as allmusic.com suggests, "It does possess some of the most boundary-pushing productions in contemporary (mostly) uncommercial hip-hop, right up at the level occupied by Common and OutKast." Album opener 'Hands Up' is a perfect example of this new direction. It isn't that stylistically removed from what has gone before, but is just so much more developed – its mariachi trumpet refrain, its sample from the Billy May-written, Yma Sumac performed 'Yo Mambo' at once unites the group with the past and the present. Its loping groove with the feel of a forties-style orchestra demonstrates the new ambitions of the group – but they are still very much here to rap.

'Labor Day (It's A Holiday)' continues in the same vein. Not overly commercial but featuring Fergie's vocal prominently in the mix, it feels as if Madonna has been visited by the JBs (their 1970 anthem 'The Grunt' is used as the main sample). will.i.am delivers a high-speed rap before it swings into the 'holiday' chorus. There is already a lot more grit in their mix than had been heard previously; the 'holiday' refrain takes something from Madonna's signature 1983 hit but it is insistent, incessant, apparently endless. Fergie's sweet interjections lighten the frenetic mood of the track, celebrating the September 5 US holiday that commemorates the economic and social conditions of workers. There is a suggestion to get 'buddy buddy with our friend Mary Jane', but unlike on *Behind The Front* and *Bridging The Gap* the group have made their good-time stoner-influenced rap harder, faster and stronger.

Without drawing a breath, the group launch into 'Let's Get Retarded', one of the earliest tracks they had worked on for *Elephunk*. Recorded between January and September 2002, the idea for the track, with its fairly questionable title, grew out of a sample from Busta Rhymes' old group Leaders Of The New School 1991 track 'Bass Is Loaded' from their album *T.I.M.E (The Inner Mind's Eye)*. It starts with a vocal homage to Alicia Keys' 'Fallin''. The breadth of the group's influences underlined their ambitions. The title derived from the dance term to lose control on the floor, in the same vein as going dumb or crazy, though in the wider context, it could easily be construed as having negative implications for those who are cognitively impaired.

The track went through a variety of changes before it was finally released as a single. "The first 'Retarded' was nothing like the 'Retarded' we have now," will.i.am told emusician. "We were married to the first one because of the magic when we recorded it. That was retarded." The second version added its walking bass line. "We were in rehearsal with our bassist and guitarist. We were trying to figure out these chords. And [Mike Fratantuno] was trying to find the right note. So he was just going down his frets, and we're like, 'Loop that!' So he does, and then we say, 'Can you resolve that?' And then we're like, 'Hey, George, write some chords to that.' We were just listening to the old version in the car, and we were excited. But then I sang the hook and verse to the fuck up that happened in rehearsal, and that's how the 'Retarded' that we have now happened."

By the time it became *Elephunk*'s fourth single in June 2004, it had become the much more radio-friendly titled 'Let's Get It Started', which reached number 21 in the US charts and number 11 in the UK in that summer, almost a full year after *Elephunk* was released. Its video, directed by Francis Lawrence, complemented the upbeat party action of the song. It opens with Fergie getting instructions for a party from a then state-of-the-art mobile phone. Behind her, an office block starts throbbing with all its lights flashing on and off as will.i.am rises towards the camera from the road on which he has been lying. As the camera pans around we see the other three Peas in various stages of their live routines. apl.de.ap looks as cool as a cucumber, while Fergie and Taboo both show off their latest moves. Using camera panning and CGI effects, the group are seen at various angles, dancing and in close headshots. As the song progresses, various items, from an egg to a house, fall out of the sky, narrowly missing the band. The action is then intercut with in-concert photography of the band playing live in front of an audience that predominately appears to be rock fans. The tension builds toward the end with members of their crowd now out on the road junction where the group have been performing, stretching on into oblivion, with various members elevating from out of the throng.

The song, another party-call-to-arms, was selected for use as the play-off music for the NBA. It became ubiquitous on the ABC network, which led to it becoming adopted as a Democratic party theme tune. The group aligned themselves with Senator John Kerry and were asked to play the Democratic National Convention in Boston in 2004. Although none of them had been particularly politically motivated in the past, they knew simply that they no longer wanted George Bush in the White House. 'Let's Get It Started' also became the fastest download success of its day, working hand-in-hand with the newly expanded iTunes, selling 500,000 downloads in the US alone.

iTunes had been launched in September 2001 as a legitimate follow-up to the Napster phenomenon. Developed by Apple, it began to alter the way Americans (initially) purchased their music. By 2003 the iPod, the portable device that enabled listeners to carry their record collections in their pocket, had launched its third generation player. The next track on the album, 'Hey Mama', was used in the initial television advertising campaign for the must-have device. Against a vibrant changing backdrop of pinks, greens, yellows and purples, in darkened silhouette various people dance with abandon to the track. The only other thing visible is the pure brilliant white of the new device and its trademark white earphones, plugged into the dancers' ears. It screamed modernity, freedom, happiness. Now you could hear your favourite music anywhere with the minimum of fuss or complication. 'Hey Mama' with its fusion of Latin, jazz and reggae seemed perfect for this new method of carriage. Suddenly, it seemed that the Black Eyed Peas were everywhere.

Released in January 2004, 'Hey Mama' became the third single to be taken from *Elephunk*, and reached the Top 10 in the UK and the *Billboard* Top 30. It acted as the perfect platform to keep its parent album alive and the group's name current. Aside from its advertising prowess, it was incorporated into *Garfield: The Movie* as well as a variety of computer games. The song, unlike many others on *Elephunk,* was put together very quickly. "That was one of those days," will.i.am said in 2005. "I was showing somebody something in the studio. They were like, 'Hey, why don't you do a reggae song,' and I was like, 'Eh, if I'm going to do a reggae song, I want to fuse bossa nova with the kind of bone structure of dancehall but using bossa nova rhythms.' And he was like, 'What do you mean? Bossa nova and reggae don't go together!' And I said, 'Actually, they kind of do. It's all Afro rhythms, just a different emphasis on the kick or snare, but they're influenced by the same thing.' So I was showing him, 'Look, you can do it just like this.' And the song came out like that."

The video for 'Hey Mama' gave a generous nod to the iPod commercial – with the group initially dancing in silhouette before moving to what appears to be a Jamaican club underlining the song's infectious dancehall rhythms. It was perfect subliminal cross-promotion. It also featured British reggae star Tippa Irie. Born Anthony Henry, Irie's fast-talking reggae style had given him chart success in the eighties, and something of a cult status in the US. will.i.am became aware of him when Irie worked with Jurassic 5's Chali2Na on the Long Beach Dub All Stars project in 2001. Irie's authentic dancehall vocal added spice to 'Hey Mama' and he too features heavily in the highly stylized video.

*Elephunk* continued apace with 'Shut Up', the track which made it clear that this was very much an update of the old group. The first voice the listener hears is that of Fergie. 'Shut Up' was a perfect introduction to the new Peas. An infectious pop song about relationship strife, it portrayed a melodrama and captured will.i.am and Fergie as a couple. The track was released as a single in November 2003 and became a huge international success, topping the charts in many countries and reaching number two in the UK.

will.i.am described the lengthy gestation period of the next track, 'Smells Like Funk', in 2005: "I was listening to some Disney thing, and I liked the baritone men in it, so I was like, 'Oh, trombones! I want to use trombones! Nobody uses trombones and tubas.' So we came in and put the trombones and tubas on 'Smells Like Funk.'" It was one of the first tracks recorded for the album, and featured Terry Dexter and Dante Santiago on backing vocals. The track was problematic as it gave the group's critics ample ammunition with which to question their new direction. Conflating the dictionary definition of 'funk' as a pungent smell with the musical form, its lyrics feel as if a sledgehammer is being used to crack a nut. We learn that the group like to "keep it stinky" and then that "We drop enough shit to keep the toilets clogged." It may not be high art but there is something endearing in this cartoon music, the vocal refrain of which owes a debt to Irving Berlin's 1929 standard, 'Puttin' On The Ritz'.

'Latin Girls', complete with Mike Fratantuno on guitarrón, created a lovely, sensuous stew praising all forms of Latin women. Featuring Debi

Nova on vocals, it would not sound out of place on any package holiday soundtrack. It tapped into the concurrent craze for Cuban music, made popular by the Buena Vista Social Club, a group of immensely skilled elderly Cuban musicians who were recorded on a 1997 album by guitarist Ry Cooder. The Latino interlude continued with 'Sexy', a slinky slice of lounge music based on Joao Gilberto's 'Insensatez' ('How Insenstive'), written by Antonio Carlos Jobim and Vinicius de Moraes. The bossa nova rhythm gives will.i.am the opportunity to perform a sultry duet with Fergie – it's refrain of 'yes to sex' and 'no to war' continues the album's pacifist theme. It is a millennial interpretation of the hippie ethos of making love, not war, and is largely successful in updating that flower-drenched tenet. This being will.i.am, there had to be yet another idea at play: the chorus also manages to weave in a generous homage to The Kinks' 1965 hit 'All Day And All Of The Night'. It demonstrated again will.i.am's fearlessness in mixing up his references.

None other than bossa nova legend Sergio Mendes played on the track and performed its languid piano solo. It was another of Ron Fair's astute suggestions. Fair knew of will.i.am's admiration for the Brazilian superstar, and thought he would be perfect for the session. "I received a phone call from the president of A&M Records," Mendes told *Blues And Soul* in 2006. "He told me that he had a band I hadn't heard of called the Black Eyed Peas, and the leader would like to come to my house and talk to me. I agreed, and the next day I opened my front door to find will standing there with a bunch of old vinyl records of mine – including some really old instrumental piano things I'd done for Atlantic Records! As I was kinda surprised, he explained how – as a 16-year-old – he'd gone to a record store, discovered my records, and been my biggest fan ever since! And, because he really did seem very sincere in his passion for the music, when he then asked if I'd come and play on one song for his group's new album, I agreed."

The pair hit it off so well that, within a couple of years, Adams would be producing *Timeless*, Mendes' first new album since 1992. The song was also featured (along with the group and Mendes himself) in *Be Cool*, the 2005 sequel to the 1995 blockbuster *Get Shorty*. Adapted from the novel by hipper-than-thou author Elmore Leonard, it followed the career of gangster Chili Palmer (John Travolta) as he left the film industry and crossed over into the music industry. The Black Eyed Peas play the scene in a club where Palmer and Edie Athens (played by Uma Thurman), move out to dance. It is a fulsome and knowing pastiche of the scene from Quentin Tarantino's 1994 masterpiece *Pulp Fiction* where Travolta as Vincent Vega danced with Thurman as Mia Wallace. Although *Be Cool* enjoyed mixed success, the group's performance was posted on a global card around the world, prolonging the success of *Elephunk*.

The album's mood is suddenly broken for 'Fly Away', a showcase for Fergie, with rock guitar provided by occasional Peas guitarist and Fergie's then-paramour, Ray Brady ("My love, my inspiration and my friend through these tough times," as she wrote on the sleeve). It is big, bouncy and strident, with its Jamaican-influenced shout of 'live it up'. There is also a brief reprise of 'Fallin' Up' in 'Fly Away', the first track from the first Black Eyed Peas album to suggest continuity between the new Peas and the old Peas. The song dissolves to the sirens that usher in the urban funk of 'The Boogie That Be', a celebration of all things Saturday night with co-writer John Legend (billed by his birth name John Stephens) assisting on vocals. There is a fabulous funk-phased guitar solo by George Pajon Jr, complete with increased synthesizer sirens. It is a beautiful, accomplished song that shows that the group had many strings to their bow.

'The apl Song' is a showcase for apl.de.ap, outlining his childhood in the Philippines, showing just how different his upbringing was from the rest of the group. Influenced by the folk songs he heard during his early life, he sang the chorus in his native Tagalog; it was partially a musical letter to apl.de.ap's uncle Marlon, a Filipino war veteran. It featured a sample from the song 'Balita', written by Cesar Bonares for the Filipino group Asin. The idea came when apl.de.ap had been listening to the song, and feeling homesick. "One day I was just sitting around, maybe I should sample this and make a Tagalog song," he said in 2005. "It just went perfect with what's going on in my life. I was adopted and I haven't been able to go back home for 13 years, and my brother committed suicide. That was like a release song for me – I got to, like, showcase where I'm from, where I was born, my roots and share a little bit of my culture." Alongside the sweet chorus, apl.de.ap adds a commentary as if he is some village elder. He talks about being reunited with his mother, and reflects with great sadness on the suicide of his younger brother, Arnel, who had taken his life in the Philippines the previous year.

The video that accompanied the release featured Filipino stars Chad Hugo from the Neptunes and actor Dante Basco. Shot by Patricio Ginelsa, it has apl.de.ap showing movie footage of his home country, while Fergie wheels apl.de.ap's uncle Marlon around the nursing home in LA into his flat in his retirement home. As apl.de.ap emotes, the other three Peas stand silently behind him. It was a sensitive and unusual subject for a pop video, especially when the elderly protagonist of the video stares into his mirror and sees the young soldier version of him staring back. A shot shows the protest marches that called for Filipino war veterans to be afforded the same status as their US counterparts. The song, which incorporated a tribute to all of the Filipinos who died for the US in the Second World War, was deeply moving and added a degree of gravity to *Elephunk*. will.i.am was forever proud of his best friend's work, and marvelled at his story to MTV: "I don't think that's ever happened to anyone, to be adopted from a Third World country as a sponsored child and be a global international artist. That's an accomplishment... Seriously, man, the ghettos we know ain't ghettos. This dude was pumping water out of the ground, killin' chickens, washing his clothes on rocks."

The sombre mood was immediately lifted by yet another glimpse into the Peas' relentless adaptation of styles. 'Anxiety' demonstrates how far the group was prepared to travel from their original formula. It is also clear how the influence of the other bands they had toured with had seeped into the Black Eyed Peas' consciousness. It was recorded with one of America's most popular alternative rock bands, Papa Roach, and features their leader Jacoby Shaddix on vocals and rap. "I was like, 'Damn, man, I saw you on the *Warped* tour, and you guys fucking rocked,'" Shaddix told MTV in 2002. "They play with a live band, and I'm totally a fan of hip-hop groups that play with live bands. And they were like, 'Yeah? We're putting out another record and we're looking for people to work with.' And I said, 'Dude, what's up? Let's do something.'" The swoop from Filipino hymn to a dose of abrupt nu-metal may have alienated old fans and hip-hop purists, but it certainly advertised the Black Eyed Peas' diversity to a whole new audience.

After the late flourish of 'Where Is The Love' sequenced perfectly to display the album's commercial embarrassment of riches before its killer single, the reggae influenced, low-key 'Third Eye' closed the album. A subtle duet between will.i.am and Fergie, its eastern feel locates the track in the material of the first two albums, suggesting that even after all of these changes, it is still fundamentally the same group offering the same message of hope and criticism of the system. Its lyrics are explicit in their desire to remove the current political system of the United States, suggesting that George Bush is Pinocchio, but wondering who is Gepetto, his puppet master. The final words from Fergie are as much about the state of America as a manifesto for the group, asking whether they should "Leave the past behind or shall we look into the future?" Before she reassuringly adds, "Look ahead, that's right" as the sampled trumpet, synthesizer and bongos peter out into the ether.

*Elephunk* became an undoubted sleeper hit; propelled by 'Where Is The Love', it continued to sell well for over a year. It reached number 14 in the *Billboard* charts, and number three in the UK, while topping the charts in Switzerland and Australia, going on to sell over eight million copies worldwide. There was, of course, a feeling that the group had sold out for *Elephunk* – no longer were they running with Ozomatli and Jurassic 5, they were firmly tilting their cap towards the charts populated by Timberlake and Timberland. The *Village Voice* retrospectively suggested that they "skitched onto the pop bandwagon by inducting melanin-challenged siren Fergie as a permanent member, enlisting cameos from similarly melanin-challenged celebs like Justin Timberlake, and serving up an all-you-can-eat stylistic buffet: a safe-for-Wal-Mart alternative to gangsta theatrics."

However, at the time of release, the paper wrote it was the album where "the unbelievably dull El Lay alt-rappers fabricate the brightest actual pop album of 2003. They remain unbelievable, but in pop that's just one more aesthetic nuance. Titles like 'Let's Get Retarded', 'Shut Up' and the guitar-driven 'Anxiety' are what you'd hope except cleaner – tremendous ups every one."

*Entertainment Weekly* noted that the "problem is, that kind of constant high gets as dull as life on Prozac." Yet *Elephunk*'s safety was its strongest suit – this was family-friendly rap with intelligent lyrics and instrumentation and a complete lack of fear about taking an overly commercial, straight-ahead route.

*Drowned In Sound*, on the other hand, was very positive: "Everyone will know the hits, the slightly saccharine hippy anti-gulf war anthem, 'Where Is The Love' and the pin sharp R&B/rap of 'Shut Up' and 'Hey Mama', and perhaps a few folk might be a little tired of the way they've carpet-bombed the airwaves in the last year. Cool your boots, stand back for a moment and when you've calmed down, come back and give the album an objective listen. I'm not going to pick out other tracks because I tend to listen to this record beginning to end, but the listening experience feels like putting on a great P-funk/70s disco/Daisy Era hip-hop album".

*Alternative Press* said, "Better partiers than preachers, these Peas have found their pod." Influential UK website *popmatters* commented that, "The organising principle of this band seems to be that you have a good time and that no one gets hurt in the process. If *Elephunk* doesn't move you, if you don't end up with a massive grin slapped across your face, if you don't heed the built-in dance demands, then check your pockets; there should be a receipt for your soul in there somewhere." Even august journal *Rolling Stone* was amused: "Freeing themselves from the shackles of playing underground for cred, the Black Eyed Peas made the shiniest pop product imaginable." *Spin* noted that the group was able to "pick up where the Fugees left off." Tom Reiter at Music Critic said, "While *Elephunk* offers something different for Black Eyed Peas fans, it's also a fun album that is irresistible from start to finish for newcomers." The album was simply a quantum commercial leap forward from their first two albums.

Although there was a general unease from their original fan base about the blatantly pop direction they had taken, to will.i.am it was simply the next step. "All that 'sell-out' stuff comes from the same people who held us close to their hearts for our first two records," he told *Faze* magazine in 2004. "And they call it 'sell-out' for what reason? Because we have a white girl in our group now? I don't think that just because one day you do a jazzy record and then you do a funk record means you sold out. It just means you like music and you're trying to dabble in every ray of colour in the music world."

Fergie was well aware that people held her responsible for the shift in direction that the group were already making before she came on board. Understanding that they had lost some of their original fan base, she told papermag.com that, "This band is like musical hip-hop, like theatre, in a sense. We are not your typical hip-hop band. The people that come to our shows and buy our records don't seem to mind." And it was the live shows where it was really happening; for those who had just tuned in, here was an outfit, playing with a live band that had honed their skills. Fergie was typically forthright on the album credits, thanking god for "lifting me out of the dark and leading me back 2 the path I'm supposed 2 be in" and thanking "will, Tab and apl 4 welcoming me into your crazy, wonderful world. It's only the beginning of this adventure…"

There were also changes to the Peas' long-serving backing band. Beat Pharmacy had been in place more or less since *Bridging The Gap*. Drummer Terry Graves became disgruntled over pay and, deciding to leave, took longstanding bass player and songwriter Mike Fratantuno with him. As a result, the Peas' band regrouped: Keith Harris joined them on drums and multi-instrumentalist Timothy 'Izo' Orindgreff joined, primarily on bass. With Printz Board and George Pajon Jr., the players changed their name from Beat Pharmacy to Bucky Jonson.

Coinciding with the album's release, the Peas signed a lucrative publishing arrangement with Cherry Lane Music, which aided the group's profitable sideline of product endorsement deals. Founded in 1960 by composer and arranger Milton Okun, the company oversaw the catalogues of some of the biggest artists in history such as Quincy Jones and Elvis Presley. Acquiring the rights for *Elephunk* and everything forward, Cherry Lane President Aida Gurwicz said, "This year, we've been aggressively diversifying our client roster and signing the Black Eyed Peas fits perfectly into our business model. We're looking forward to exploiting the many opportunities for the band's increased exposure that this record promises." Working in conjunction with managers David Sonenberg and Seth Friedman and will.i.am, they ensured that the Black Eyed Peas would not miss an opportunity to extend their influence. Sonenberg said, "The Peas have worked very hard over the years to get where they are today and we're optimistic about the future with Cherry Lane as their publisher." With this established and a powerful team behind them, it seemed that little could halt the Black Eyed Peas' inexorable move forward.

# Chapter 8

# The Four Headed-Dragon

*"I want us to be like the Grateful Dead of hip-hop. I want to be touring forever."*

will.i.am, 2004

Remarkably, in the middle of the Black Eyed Peas career take-off, will.i.am found time to release another low-key solo album. Again working with ultra-cool, left-field BBE, he released *Must B 21* in September 2003, just three months after the release of *Elephunk*. Subtitled 'Soundtrack To Get Things Started', so discreet were the markets he was aiming at few knew that *Must B 21* had been released. Many of its cult purchasers clung to the totem of will.i.am as an underground hip-hop producer, few realising it was the same man blazing up the world's charts in the new, improved Black Eyed Peas.

The album, released initially as double-pack vinyl only, was the ninth release in BBE's *The Beat Generation* series (*Lost Change* was the third). Since the 2001 release of *Lost Change*, Marley Marl, Jazzy Jeff, King Britt and DJ Spinna had all contributed to the series. Though it received scant media attention, *Must B 21* featured the full back-up Black Eyed Peas crew and marked Adams out as something of a hip-hop auteur, working with talents such as KRS-One, Phife Dawg and John Legend.

Moving away from the genre homages/pastiches of *Lost Change*, it was an old-school jam, a full-on rap album. 'Swing My Way' was a superior groove with John Legend laying down a sumptuous, languid vocal. The track was later featured on Adams' clothing line website.

Mainly recorded and assembled at the Stewchia, will.i.am arranged the beats and some of the rhymes, while giving his guests full reign; Fergie drops in on 'Mash Out' on which she duels with MC Lyte. It is interesting to hear this out-and-out example of Fergie rapping. Dante Santiago sings with Taboo and Niu on 'Somethin' Special'. The *Rap Reviews* site was one of the few voices that commentated on the album and was very impressed: "At a little over 48 minutes long, *Must B 21* is an exercise in hip-hop in its purest most unadulterated form, packed into a highly concentrated dose. From the opener until you rock 'We Got Chu' featuring FL II and Planet Asia, it's a non-stop roller coaster ride of jazzy, funky, ill and uniquely original beats and rhymes. The only downside of reaching the will.i.am solo finale 'Go!' is that it makes you wish he had dropped more rhymes on his own album... If you're looking for something refreshing and new, pick up this album to help will and his label do better than Barely Breaking Even or going triple wood. It deserves to go gold, because it's that damn good." The 'triple wood' in the reference alludes to a line in the track 'B-Boyz', featuring a full-bodied rap from MC Supernatural. 'Ride Ride' shows how happy will.i.am was in sharing the limelight. He doesn't actually appear on this Printz Board solo enterprise, again featuring John Legend. It slips effortlessly into the album's mix.

As with *Lost Change*, no tracks were taken for singles, although closing track, 'Go!', one of the few tracks on which will.i.am took a solo lead vocal, was later used as the theme for *NBA Live 2005* and *Madden NFL 2005* seasons. 'Go!' was the great hit that never was. After the languid beats and old-school approach of the rest of the album, the track arrives following a short instrumental interlude, and then we're off on a high-powered romp with will.i.am in full freestyling effect. Built around a sample of James Brown's super-rare 1963 B-side 'I've Got Money', he shouts out to the rest of the Peas, who join him on the track, and states his plea that he doesn't want to leave the party while it's in full swing. It is reminiscent of House Of Pain's 'Jump Around', but that is not even the half of it — it is frenetic, full of Printz Board's trumpet and will.i.am's beats. Also, furthering will.i.am's policy of letting few things go to waste, elements of the thumping 'I'm Ready' went into the 2004 reworking of 'Let's Get Retarded', the radio-friendly 'Let's Get It Started'.

"The whole mindset was if it takes longer than a week, don't put it out," will.i.am said in 2005. "If it's not done that day, throw it away and that was just it. It's not for radio, it's not for video, it's just for us to go out and make music that says, 'Oh wow, rewind that part, you wanna hear that!' That kind of stuff."

One of the most fascinating aspects of the release was its cover, an illustration of will.i.am, line drawn in shades of blue, next to a huge red exclamation mark. Nodding to classic Impulse or Blue Note sleeves, it was designed by 32-year-old South Carolina-born artist Shepard Fairey, who had made his name with his art sticker campaign, *Andre The Giant Has A Posse*. It would mark the beginning of an association between will.i.am and the artist, who would later design the sleeve for the Black Eyed Peas' fourth album, *Monkey Business*. Fairey would achieve world-wide fame in 2008 with his poster for Barack Obama's presidential campaign; a stylized interpretation of Obama's profile with the single word 'Hope' beneath. With its striking cover and interesting hip-hop collaborations, *Must B 21* remains one of the most interesting left-field items in will.i.am's catalogue.

To support the album, Justin Timberlake invited the Black Eyed Peas to be the opening act on his US *Justified & Stripped* tour, a co-headline enterprise between himself and Christina Aguilera, at that point two of the hottest pop stars on the planet, promoting their huge-selling albums of the same names. The tour started on June 4, 2003 at the America West Arena in Phoenix, before ending in September at the 20,000 seater Xcel Energy Center in St Paul, Minneapolis. During the tour, the group's popularity escalated. Fergie fitted effortlessly into the group's dynamic, bringing sass and glamour as well as well-honed experience. "Our sound was different, and better, because of her," Taboo was to write in *Fallin'*

*Up.* "She was as powerful and hard as she was sensual and soulful, and her inclusion provided that cross-over into pop-rock that we never had before. As she carved out her role, she became the siren of what she refers to as 'the four headed-dragon', and, throughout 2003-2004, she started to unveil, bit by bit, the marketable sex appeal that also brought the 'wow' factor to the Peas."

As a result of all this legwork, by the start of 2004 the Black Eyed Peas were enormous, and 'Where Is The Love' was nominated for the Record Of The Year Grammy at the 46th Grammy Awards on February 8 at the Staples Center, Los Angeles. Coldplay won the award for their piano-driven rock anthem 'Clocks', and among the other nominees were Beyoncé and Jay-Z's 'Crazy In Love', Eminem's 'Lose Yourself' and OutKast's 'Hey Ya', three of the most powerful records of the first decade of the 21st century. The rise in the Black Eyed Peas' profile was astonishing. Ron Fair was delighted and could see how important the record would become to the group and to will.i.am in particular. "It's actually one of the biggest records of all time in terms of its radio spins. Will's fears about losing credibility and his audience base worked in reverse. He actually gained credibility, and people realized what a talented heavyweight he is. He's on his way to becoming the next Pharrell or OutKast. The whole thing is just a giant miracle."

In early 2004, the Black Eyed Peas recorded an appearance on the NBC drama series *Las Vegas*, set in a fictional resort hotel on the fabled desert city's Strip. It was during the recording of the show that Fergie met actor Josh Duhamel, who played the show's heart-throb head of security, Danny McCoy. The couple began dating. At this period, however, there was little time for romance. In March 2004, the group undertook a US tour supporting N★E★R★D. By the time the show hit the Wiltern Theater in LA, the Peas were clearly displaying the upper hand. MTV reported, "The crowd at the sold-out Wiltern LG Theater went into an uproar midway through the Peas' encore of 'Where Is The Love' when Timberlake casually strolled onstage to sing the song's classic 'People killing, people dying' hook. At that point, the promoters might as well have added Justin's name to the marquee... at the top. After 'Where Is the Love' Timberlake busted into some beat-boxing, which gave will.i.am a great excuse to show off his freestyling talents, even as a stagehand (probably with N.E.R.D.) standing nearby yelled at them to clear the stage." The gigs continued to confirm the Black Eyed Peas as a must-see live act.

To underline how far the group had travelled in such a short space of time and just how the UK had taken to the Black Eyed Peas, they were invited to play Glastonbury, the prestigious event that opens the UK's burgeoning festival season. On June 26, 2004 they found themselves as the penultimate band on the Pyramid Stage on the festival's Saturday night. Topping the bill that year was none other than Paul McCartney, making his long-awaited Glastonbury debut, and performing a set that relied heavily on Beatles songs. The group were personal guests of ex-Police superstar Sting, staying at his nearby Jacobean castle Lake House. They had met when Adams was asked to remix two tracks from Sting's 2003 album, *Sacred Love*: 'Whenever I Say Your Name' and 'Stolen Car (Take Me Dancing)'. The Black Eyed Peas had arrived.

Another Beatle connection came about when the group's manager David Sonenberg offered them the opportunity to become associated with the John Lennon Educational Tour Bus, a non-profit state-of-the-art mobile music studio, while on tour with N★E★R★D. Founded in 1998 by former Iam Siam keyboard player Brian Rothschild and Sonenberg, the vehicle is a fully equipped studio. They asked Yoko Ono for permission to use Lennon's name on the enterprise. At first she was sceptical. "I'm so used to saying no," she said in 2008. "So many people come to me to use John's name, mostly to do with making money, and I always feel that if I'm going to say yes to using John's name and likeness, it has to do... something with spiritual awareness, changing the world for the better. This one was right on because it was about children, and I really thought it was a great idea."

The bus provides an opportunity to learn about the recording process and travels to various schools, festivals and venues around the US, often where the state-funded schools' programme meant that there simply are no facilities in their place of learning. It reaches around a quarter of a million children a year. While assisting with its educational programme, the group took the opportunity to outline demos on the bus. It would mark the start of a long association with the JLET Bus, and the Black Eyed Peas would become judges of the John Lennon Songwriting Contest, a competition that was set up in 1997. They remain on the executive committee to this day.

The group had considered taking a break in 2004 in order for Fergie and will.i.am to release solo projects. However, it was patently apparent that *Elephunk* had an afterlife all of its own, and if there was a time to continue as a unit, this was probably the most important period for their long-term career. It was time to think about a follow-up. "We felt it was important to install the next Black Eyed Peas record this year with the momentum that we've had," Adams told MTV in June 2004. "Which will only allow our solo adventures to be successful and continue to keep our franchise going." By the end of the year, their franchise was going very well indeed, buoyed up by their performances and the slow-drip of releases ensuring the ubiquity of *Elephunk*, now 18 months old, with some songs on it written three years before.

On February 6, 2005, the group was invited to play with Earth, Wind & Fire at the Super Bowl XXXIX pre-game show in Jacksonville, Florida. will.i.am had been working with the group on a track on their forthcoming album, so it seemed wholly appropriate that the two should play together. The performance consisted of 'Where Is The Love' and the EWF classic 'Shining Star'.

A week later, the tireless work the Peas had put in over the past 18 months was validated on February 13, when the group won Best Rap Performance by a Duo or Group at the 47th Grammy Awards at the Staples Center, Los Angeles for 'Let's Get It Started', as well as being nominated for Record Of The Year and Best Rap Song. The group opened the show in an extraordinary 12-minute set piece in which they interspersed verses of 'Let's Get It Started' with performances from Gwen Stefani and Eve, Maroon 5, the Lonely Boys and Scottish art-rockers Franz Ferdinand. At the end, every group played their song together – what should have sounded like a caterwauling cacophony actually worked. The award itself was not televised. Taboo recounts in *Fallin' Up* that they were simply informed that they had won by a member of the Grammy staff, who popped her head round the dressing room door. The group received their actual trophy some months later through the post.

The Black Eyed Peas seemed to be on a permanent tour. The group returned to the Big Day Out festivals in Australia and New Zealand in early 2004, their first time at the festival since 2001. This time, far from being the left-field act they had been, they played with 'Shut Up' at the top of the chart, and more than held their own on a bill which included Metallica, the Flaming Lips, Massive Attack, Kings Of Leon and Muse. The group played at dusk and were a huge success.

The group received a hero's welcome when they played the Philippines. "When we get down, every news crew possible is there documenting the landing," an incredulous will.i.am said in 2005. "We get off the airplane and the news crews come and rush us. We get to the hotel and turn on the TV. There is a four-hour special on apl's life, and it ends with the crew's documenting of our landing. They were shooting till the moment we landed, and then went in and edited that footage in. The next day, we did a show in front of 30,000 people, and they have the army in front holding the people back with the President in the middle! Every time apl goes back to the Philippines, there's a news crew. He's bigger than any government official in the Philippines. That's nutty."

The band came to London in February 2005 and played the Hammersmith Apollo in west London. Formerly known as Hammersmith Odeon, the venue was dripping in history. It was the venue for the Beatles' 1964/5 Christmas shows, David Bowie's final show as Ziggy Stardust in July 1973 and Bruce Springsteen's UK debut in 1975. The first time the Peas had played London it was at Camden's homely, passionately run 400-capacity Jazz Café in September 1998. Now they were on the same stage as the greats. The erudite David Sinclair of *The Times* saw the show. "Rapper William 'will.i.am' Adams was keen to emphasise that the group had not forgotten the Jazz Café days," he wrote. "Indeed, by about the sixth time he came to mention that venue during the course of their Monday night show at the Apollo he was beginning to sound decidedly wistful." Although the review was not wholly positive, Sinclair singled out Fergie for her command of the stage. "While the bustling performance was very much a group effort," he continued, "it was the singer and rapper Stacey 'Fergie' Ferguson who most often caught the attention and tended to hold on to it. A vision of designer street cool in her pink hoodie and plaits, she added sparkle and fizz to an already colourful show, especially when playing the nagging girlfriend to will.i.am's feckless boyfriend during 'Shut Up', a performance which evolved into an extended piece of acrobatic street theatre." The group felt the need to give something back to the London crowd.

Also in 2005, the Peapod Foundation (PPF), set up all the way back in the late nineties when the group were playing around Los Angeles by Adams and Polo Molina, became a donor-advised fund of the Entertainment Industry Foundation (EIF). A leading charitable organisation of the entertainment business, EIF oversees a range of charities, their principle function to raise awareness and gain funds for health, educational and social issues. The PPF had grown and was now run in association with marketeer and strategist Christine Hansen's Thirty-Three Productions. The PPF looked to support social issues involving children worldwide, looking at alleviating and assisting in shelter/housing, poverty, starvation, education and healthcare through music and fundraising. The group were tireless ambassadors of this work, and took many opportunities to visit children while on tour.

As the BEPs continued touring, will.i.am carried on piecing together the follow up to *Elephunk*, while also finding time to produce and co-write a track for one of his favourite groups of all time, Earth, Wind & Fire. 'Lovely People', which he wrote with long-time cohort Keith Harris, was chosen as the lead track for the seasoned funkers' 2005 album, *Imagination*. will.i.am was one of a series of artists chosen for their empathy with the era from which EWF initially sprang. Verdine White said at the time, "It sounds just like Earth Wind & Fire ought to sound, for a first time at attempting a project like this we were all really impressed with the way it turned out... a lot of their music reminds me of the early seventies soul movement. It's all really organic and it has a really good message behind the lyrics too. I think it's a very conscience movement at the moment but it's still very hip." will.i.am was energised working with his heroes, and also used the time to come up with some new ideas that again would be incorporated into the Peas' forthcoming album.

# Chapter 9

# Politics And Format:
## *Monkey Business*

*"Somebody asked me what's the difference between* Monkey Business *and* Elephunk. *It's that there was not a lot of fucking-around time."*

will.i.am, 2005

*"*Monkey Business *will be the first for the Quad Squad."*

will.i.am, 2004

Written over a period between January 2004 and early 2005 in hotel rooms around the world and captured on will.i.am's Macbook and Pro Tools, the fourth Black Eyed Peas album, *Monkey Business*, was largely recorded at Metropolis Studios, in Turnham Green, West London. Situated in an old power station next to Chiswick bus garage, Metropolis was a million light years removed from the sunshine of LA, but in a way it suited the sharpened purpose of Black Eyed Peas. For the first time in their career, a mass audience was hanging on their every word. "We wanted to zone out somewhere that inspired us," Taboo wrote in *Fallin' Up*. "Where better than the first place where our music was first and foremost appreciated. London had always had a special place in our heart so we headed there from July to October to build on our success and prove that *Elephunk* was no fluke."

The vibe of the big old West London building inspired the group; they enjoyed watching the red double-decker buses coming and going from the depot. They liked the long stretch of Acton Green behind the garage, their rented house in Chiswick and the fact that the studio, although just off the High Road in W4 was "close enough to feel the city's pulse". "The cultural aspects of London are really good," Fergie said in 2004. "We get a lot of love there. It'll be interesting to see how that influences the music."

Before arriving at Metropolis, the album had been simmering at a variety of locations: will.i.am told *allhiphop* in 2005, it was "made on my laptop on airplanes. At the time, we were travelling the world on *Elephunk*. 'Where Is The Love', 'Let's Get Retarded' and 'Hey Mama' was *huge* all over the planet. We were doing shows in Vietnam, Lithuania, Brazil, Japan, South Korea, and Philippines... I was thinkin' like 'When are we gonna make a record? 'Cause if we keep touring, we'll *never* make a record.' So I was doing it on the airplane, trying to feed the whole market at the same time. I wanna make an album that's gonna have songs that are relevant to every single country we are hitting at once."

This diversity is apparent for all to hear on *Monkey Business*. It sounds, however eclectic, like the work of a band. It is big. Glossy. A bit daft and resolutely commercial. And although not overdoing it, the album had the starry sheen of some superstar friends dropping by. In just over an hour, Justin Timberlake, James Brown, Q-Tip and Sting, among others, make an appearance. A rumoured update of Run DMC and Aerosmith's version of 'Walk This Way' with Justin Hawkins of briefly brightly shining UK faux-rock band the Darkness, whom they'd met in Australia on the Big Day Out events, thankfully failed to materialize.

Designed again by Shepard Fairey, complete with the first full-cover shot of the four-piece Black Eyed Peas on its front, and a small monkey logo in the style of the elephant on *Elephunk,* the CD booklet for *Monkey Business* was set out like a novel. It was full of information about the band, including rooming lists, tour riders and a BEP Q&A,

giving as much information as possible; will.i.am was ensuring that his fans could enjoy all the small print detail of album releases as he had as a kid. According to the group, the album was called *Monkey Business* for two reasons. The first was to do with their new success, as "people view you differently. They can go from viewing you like a person to viewing you like a product." The second definition was draped in classic BEP-speak – "Elephants have nothing to do with PHUNK and monkeys have nothing to do with BUSINESS... or do they? Our business is PHUNKIN' MUSIC."

Among the other standard Q&As on the sleeve, one stood out as somewhat contradictory. will.i.am had been keen to embrace whatever changes had come along within the music industry and commerce but in response to the question, "If you could change one thing about the music industry what would it be?" the group reply with the line, "To focus more on the music and less on politics and format." will.i.am's focus was undeniably on music, but his grasp of politics and formats was outstanding as well.

Also in the 32-page booklet (its increased size from previous releases a clear marker of their success) was the '*Monkey Business* Plan': travel itineraries, hotel and catering riders, stage plots and fan club details. Tellingly, there was also a mock (or indeed not-so-mock) profit statement for the band showing how their earnings had exploded in the mid-00s with the release of *Elephunk*.

In February 2005 will.i.am was candid with interviewer Kylee Swanson when talking about the phenomenal itinerary the group undertook after the release of *Elephunk*: "The idea with *Monkey Business* was like organ grinders. You're working out there, and you only get a peanut, and you give all the money made to the monkey owner. There is a good pay-off, but you work hard. Last week, we flew from South Africa to LA. It was a 20-some-hour flight. And before that, we flew from Pittsburgh to Rome to Johannesburg, like, in five days. In Rome, we sat in traffic for, like, four hours, got to the hotel, washed up, went shopping, sat in traffic for two hours, went back, left the hotel to go to the awards show. Four more hours of traffic, then went to an after-party for two hours and then left to get on a plane. I sound like a dick to say that it's hard, but it is hard on your body when you are on three hours of sleep." Taboo had his own theory about the album's title: "It represents the spirit of the Peas, because we were always dropping bombs on each other. It requires a thick skin and merciless humour to be on our tour bus, and no one is safe from the bagging, the sarcasm and the punking." The album was shaped very much by the touring experience, which had a deeply profound effect on will.i.am: "*Monkey Business* is very much about the types of songs we play live. It's about a party. It's layered differently and has energy to it that reflects how we tour – from the beats to the types of instruments we used to how we interact with the audience. It's very much about us and the crowd on this record."

The 15-track album, clocking in at just over an hour, was a breathless bump through the Black Eyed Peas' new world. It has a great deal in common with other albums that have been made in the first flush of success (De La Soul's *De La Soul Is Dead*, Terence Trent D'Arby's *Neither Fish Nor Flesh*, Oasis' *Be Here Now*) that survey the world from planes and hotel rooms as opposed to long-term crafting in a studio in relative obscurity. However, although will.i.am seems to have a moderate obsession with those who disrespect the group, *Monkey Business* is not a bitter work. It is the sound of newfound success and, for the first time in their career, recording with a cohesive unit. Although there is indeed a great section of guest artistes, it feels like the work of a four-piece vocal group with a four-piece band playing with them.

Again, Ron Fair kept his hand on the tiller with will.i.am to ensure a commercial cohesion. Acutely commercial, 'Pump It' showed that the Peas' eclecticism had not deserted them; a gritty, uptempo call-to-arms, using Dick Dale's surf-guitar classic 'Misirlou' as its sample. The idea for it came about when the group were on tour in Brazil in early 2005; will.i.am had bought a CD which had 'Misirlou' on it. The track had had a new lease of life after it was featured as the main theme for Quentin Tarantino's boutique gangster film, *Pulp Fiction*, in 1994. Within minutes he had started composing using his laptop. The dirty surf-garage guitar undoubtedly added something new to the Black Eyed Peas' mix. The group then moved onto Japan, where will.i.am developed

Munich, 1999, the three-man Peas touring Behind The Front. From the very start the group realised the value of world-wide promo. Note Taboo's Charlie Brown jumper. BOZI/CORBIS

Narrowing the gap: the early Peas play to the rock and punk crowds on the Vans Warped Tour at Randalls Island on July 16, 1999. SCOTT GRIES/GETTY IMAGES

Wild Orchid backstage at the Joint in the Hard Rock Hotel at Las Vegas, November 26, 1999. L to R: Stacy Ferguson, Renee Sandstrom, Stefanie Ridel. SCOTT HARRISON/RETNA LTD/CORBIS

Stacy on stage with Wild Orchid BARRY KING/WIREIMAGE

will.i.am at the Rock The Vote Party at House of Blues in West Hollywood in February 2001. S. GRANITZ/WIREIMAGE

apl.de.ap and Taboo at Rock The Vote. S. GRANITZ/WIREIMAGE

"The four headed dragon". will.i.am, Fergie, Taboo and apl.de.ap; promoting *Elephunk*, France, 2004.
JEROME DOMINE/GAMMA-RAPHO/GETTY IMAGES

Backstage with Justin Timberlake at the Vinyl Club in Hollywood, California, 2003. Timberlake's vocal on 'Where Is The Love' combined with an infectious tune helped take BEP into the world's hearts.

Before the bodysuits: a more informal approach to stage wear at one of Fergie's earliest shows with the band, at the Air Party at the Suede in Park City, Utah, 2003.

Fergie and apl at the Whiskey Beach in Henderson, Nevada, May 14, 2004. The show was the group's second of three planned concerts in three cities in 24 hours to showcase Elephunk. ETHAN MILLER/REUTERS/CORBIS

Only presenting this time: at The MTV Europe Music Awards in Edinburgh, November 2003. STEPHANE CARDINALE/
PEOPLE AVENUE/CORBIS

will.i.am and Taboo at Whiskey Beach, May 14, 2004.
ETHAN MILLER/REUTERS/CORBIS

Fergie celebrates after winning the Best Pop Act at the
MTV Europe Music Awards 2004. ALESSIA PIERDOMENICO/
REUTERS/CORBIS

will.i.am, Panama City, Nov 2005. His riddle-wrapped-in-an-enigma, non-stop butterfly mind, love of people, the cutting edge and musical history has ensured that the group have been at the forefront of contemporary pop for more than a decade. ALBERTO LOWE/REUTERS/CORBIS

the song. The credit actually states 'recorded at Bullet Train Japan', as will.i.am began the rap on the train after first hearing the music. Taboo recalled the moment when the inspiration hit will.i.am: "All we heard was him shouting out 'Louder!... LOUDER!... LOUDER!', which made him look like one of those crazy people who sit on trains alone and hear voices." will.i.am worked on the song and then recorded more vocals in a park in Tokyo. It was clear with the song's very difference and compelling rhythmic thrust that 'Pump It' could only ever be the album's opener.

'Pump It' became the album's fourth and final single, released in February 2006. Although it briefly made the Hot 100 in the US (due to digital downloads from the album when it featured in a Best Buy commercial), in the UK it reached number three. The song hit the top spot in Belgium, and, unsurprisingly, Greece (as 'Misirlou' is in fact an adaptation of an old Greek folk song). Its afterlife was huge for the Peas, with it appearing in the Pixar film *Cars*, *Big Momma's House 2*, Pepsi adverts and in the trailers for the two *Kung Fu Panda* films.

The video had a futuristic film noir vibe, set in an underground car park in two separate sequences, supposedly two weeks apart. Francis Lawrence – who had directed the 'Let's Get It Started' promo for the group, as well as a host of other millennial promo showstoppers – captured the foursome initially having a dance off with three opposing dancers. Arriving at breakneck, stunt-driving speed in perfectly placed customised Honda Civics (the sponsors of the *Monkey Business* tour), Adams slays his opponents with his rhymes and his moves. The rivals speed off. Two weeks later, we return to find the group encircled by at least 20 opponents in a similar parking lot. This time Adams juggles with a bowling ball, which breaks holes in walls, yet to him is as light as air. The best, most futuristic moment is when apl.de.ap raps, runs in circles, and, as he gains momentum, begins to run horizontally, bouncing off the chests of the men standing in the circle. It was a humorous take on standard fight scenes, possibly influenced by the fight sequences in David Fincher's 1999 masterpiece, *Fight Club*.

However, it was the album's second track, 'Don't Phunk With My Heart', that became its most successful single. Influenced by the group's visits to bhangra clubs in London, it represents a perfect slice of Bollywood style music; 'Ye Mera Dil Pyaar Ka Deewana' and 'Ae Naujawan Hai Sub Yahan', composed by Kalyanji Anandji and Indeewar, and originally sung by Indian singing legend Asha Bhosle. It had a marvellously dirty, grungy sixties guitar sound, which was achieved by will.i.am miking up a Mesa Boogie amp from a distance and playing a compressed Yamaha electric guitar through it. The noise was at once commercial with a somewhat otherworldly undertow. The track was topped off with comedy horse noises, raps and a complex rhythm arrangement.

'Don't Phunk With My Heart' also came as a happy boost for eighties rap and production outfit Full Force, as Ferguson's vocal was based on their 1985 hit for Lisa Lisa and Cult Jam, 'I Wonder If I Take You Home'. The song was instantly and remorselessly commercial, with the message of various lovers professing their love and admiration for her, while all the time she suspects that all they actually want is sex. Bolstered by a humorous date-show promo by directing brothers the Molloys, who had helmed the 'Shut Up' promo, the song became the Black Eyed Peas' biggest US hit to date. will.i.am saw the song as a follow-up to 'Shut Up' – "not sonically but in subject matter", he wrote in the publicity material for the album. "When you're on bad terms with a significant other, you don't want to break up. You tell her things and at the time you really mean them. But she's saying, stop fucking with me."

The video featured will.i.am as 'Voodoo Thursday', the host of the imaginary show that shared the same name as the single itself. Ushered on stage by two glamorous assistants, he says, 'We've got ourselves a real nice crowd here tonight' before staring at the ample bosom of one of his assistants and then mugging directly to camera, reiterating, 'real nice'. Fergie arrives carried aloft on a carpet, singing the opening bars of the song and 'Voodoo Thursday' is off, into a dancing frenzy. All three male members of the Black Eyed Peas attempt to win Fergie over for a date. will.i.am wins the opportunity to go horse riding with Ferguson and, after being teleported from the studio, a heavily stylized horse ride ensues. While it plays on a TV screen in the studio, Voodoo Thursday larks about with dolls of horses, ultimately performing voodoo on those who want Fergie's hand. Suddenly will.i.am is thrown from his horse, thwarting any chance of love. As the pair return, will.i.am holds his groin and back to emphasize the roughness of the ride he has just had. apl.de.ap is next in the frame, and he and Fergie win the opportunity to 'Boogie Down'. While will.i.am raps his tale of increasing bitterness on a split screen to the left, apl.de.ap takes Fergie onto the dance floor.

Every time she goes to kiss him, 'Voodoo Thursday' in the studio inserts a pin into a doll of apl.de.ap and he shakes away, leaving Fergie frustrated and annoyed. Finally, when it is Taboo's turn and they teleport to a restaurant, Voodoo Thursday is up to his tricks, making Taboo's arm touch the backside of a woman at the bar. Fergie is mightily disappointed but, by the time they get back to the studio, the video closes with her being scooped up into the plotting Voodoo Thursday's arms. All the while the house band – will.i.am on drums, apl.de.ap on bass and Taboo on keyboards, plays, their mannerisms a clear reference to the band played entirely by Andre 3000 in the 2003 video for 'Hey Ya' by OutKast. It is post-modernism running riot. It is little wonder, with such a compelling promo, that the single reached number three in both the UK and the US and topped the charts in Australia, New Zealand and Finland. The single also became a huge hit in Latin America.

As it became such a global hit, the group endured low-level questions such at the one posited by the UK's *Top Of The Pops* magazine, regarding how they were able to avoid swearing (a reference to the title's 'phunk'). will.i.am gamely replied: "We don't really cuss that much... I mean we cuss amongst each other but mine, like, turns off when I'm around my mom automatically, it turns off. My mom told me that your words make you what you are, they're the result of how you respond to things, emotionally and constructively, so you might as well have a whole bunch of good words in your head to describe how you feel in given situations." However the clear use of 'phunk' for 'fuck' meant that certain radio stations in the US were a little shaky about playing the track, so a re-edit was done substituting the word 'mess' for 'phunk'.

'My Style' maintained the relentless rush of the album's opening, featuring group friend Justin Timberlake returning the favour for

'Where Is The Love', which helped propel him as much as the Black Eyed Peas onto the world stage. will.i.am was now slated to produce tracks for Timberlake's follow-up to 2003's *Justified*, provisionally titled *FutureSex/LoveSounds*. A low-key blues, it also featured Timbaland, Justin Timberlake's long-term associate and one of the most influential artist/producers of the early 21st century. "I like experiencing things I've never experienced before," will.i.am said of working with Timbaland. "It brings you out of your comfort zone and that can be creatively inspiring. And Timbaland is an incredible talent." Ultimately, however, the total is not as great as the sum of its parts. It's good, but it's not as good as it could have been.

'Don't Lie' was the track that took the group outside their hip-hop roots. A straight radio-friendly slice of AOR, it was as if group friend Jack Johnson had suddenly added a hip-hop edge to his sound. Written by will.i.am from an experience with an ex-girlfriend, Fergie's chorus could have been delivered by Heart or Stevie Nicks. As the second single from the album, it marked a clear line between their previous work and the future. It had sampled beats and scratches, but the additional production by Ron Fair suggested that this was to be this album's 'Where Is The Love'. It was partially sampled from a demo made by Ferguson prior to her Black Eyed Peas career, and featured a sample of Slick Rick's 1991 track, 'The Ruler's Back'. George Pajon Jr. and Ray Brady laid down addictive acoustic guitars. "It's a song about owning up and apologising and realising your faults," will.i.am said. "It's about being a man or a woman – an adult – and confronting situations honestly."

The highly stylized video was directed by Justin Francis and the Saline Project, and portrayed the group in a kind of stop-motion scenario, towering initially above the skyline of Rio De Janeiro, before moving through rainforest, beaches and inner city areas. The men of the group all appear to be courting the same love interest. The video culminates in a group performance at the Parque Lage in Rio. After the frivolity of the 'Don't Phunk With My Heart' promo, here was something relatively downbeat. With its anthemic feel and mellow vibe, it became the group's biggest hit in Latin America to date. Released as the album's second single, it made number 14 in the US and number six in the UK.

One of the more controversial tracks on *Monkey Business* was the international hit single, 'My Humps'. Although the UK interpretation was that it was a song about breasts, it is actually about backsides. Either way, it came under a great deal of scrutiny and was quickly reviled, seen as the singular reason for the Black Eyed Peas' artistic decline. Over a skeletal beat, it uses an amalgam of several sources, the main one being the song 'I Need A Freak', an underground electro classic by the group Sexual Harassment that was originally released on the Great label in 1982. Written by Lynn Tolliver under the pseudonym of David Payton, its spindly proto-techno gave the track its propulsion. Although Tolliver was credited on the sleeve (as Payton), he sued the band for unpaid royalties on his sample, which made it through the courts finally in June 2011, earning him a $1.2 million settlement.

Beginning with mariachi trumpets, it falls into a lazy Tone Loc 'Wild Thing' type groove, with some clear references to 'Push It' by Salt'n'Pepa. It features Fergie more or less solo (a calling card for her long-planned solo album), telling of how men are bewitched by her 'humps', her 'lovely lady lumps', with the others performing cameos as her punch-drunk admirers. will.i.am asks what she is going to do with that 'junk in her trunk', and it is clear that Fergie will do all that she can to entice her men. Fergie was quick to dispel any controversy. "No, no, no, it's a character," she told the *Toronto Sun*. "It's a definite character. It's all tongue-in-cheek. It's just a fun song portraying that situation. It's going to be really fun to perform."

"It's funny, because that 'My Humps' thing was rare," will.i.am said in 2006, "once in a blue moon. It's a beat with a synthesizer. Here I am arranging horns for Earth, Wind & Fire and miking guitar cabinets for Carlos Santana, and here comes [the music for the song], and that one got people going, 'Hey, give me a beat!' Which is cool – I see the desire and the temptation to have those types of beats. Those are hard to come by. In the middle of the session, in 10 minutes, I just did that beat – *boom, boom, boom* – and I breathed on the mic. Played a little synth on it, and that's it. Now I can pay my kids' college tuition for life!" It wasn't actually going to be a single, but it was downloaded so much it began to race up the charts, giving Interscope little option other than to release it.

The song reached number three on both sides of the Atlantic. It is not high art, and virtually impossible to defend.

What is interesting are the Arabic influences over the minimalism and the piano outro with will.i.am chanting 'so real', which almost sounds like an enormous in-joke on the word 'surreal' and a raspberry to critics who are not in on the joke. Influential and somewhat superior site *Pitchfork* voted it one of the worst releases of the year: "Hearing this song for the first time was 2005's most sobering musical experience. Like 'Who Let The Dogs Out' before it, 'My Humps' is so monumentally vacuous, slapped together and tossed-off that it truly tests the definition of 'song'. It's actually more like listening to a five-minute commercial jingle – a point driven home by the miles upon miles of product placement that attempt to pass for its verses." *Slate* magazine suggested, "'My Humps' is a moment that reminds us that categories such as 'good' and 'bad' still matter. Relativism be damned! There are bad songs that offend our sensibilities but can still be enjoyed, and then there are the songs that are *just really bad* - transcendentally bad, objectively bad. As a piece of music, 'My Humps' is a stunning assemblage of awful ideas."

The video – which won Best Hip-Hop Video at the 2006 VMAs – added to the controversy, suggesting that a woman reaches a state of empowerment by men lavishing gifts on her because she has a shapely backside. Directed by Fatima Robinson and Malike Hassan Sayeed, it showed Fergie dancing with the men looking on. For all the group's considerable advances and innovation, this was practically stone age, with the male gaze firmly attached to Fergie's behind and bosom. Fergie making will.i.am work to get a glimpse of her 'breasts inside that shirt' sounds like something even James Brown would have rejected as an idea in the early sixties. Even Taboo wrote in his autobiography, *Fallin' Up*, "'My Humps' turned into a monster hit, but not in a socially conscious way."

It certainly became a target for parody; Canadian experimental electronic chanteuse Peaches sent it up with 'My Dumps', a song about female bowel movements; Afroman made 'My Chunk', taking the subject matter as his penis; cult TV show *Flight Of The Conchords* featured a version called 'Sugarlumps'. One of the more interesting aspects of the 'My Humps' release was a YouTube cover version of it by Alanis Morissette. Morissette, whose 1995 album *Jagged Little Pill* is still one of the biggest-selling albums of all time, dismantled the song and turned it into a plaintive ballad, sending up the video, showing her head-butting various suitors who tried to get too near. It also seemed to lampoon straight-facedly the increasing ostentation of hip-hop promos. "I was in the studio one day," Morissette told *Access Hollywood*. "I think at one point I said it would be fun to do a song that is really simple and I said, 'I'm gonna try to write it,' and [the guys in the studio] looked at me and laughed and said, 'It's not possible for you to do.' So I said, 'I'm going to write a song like 'My Humps.' So we just decided to cover it. Within a week I was recording the video for it in the garage at my house with my comedian friends. I just thought I would put it up on YouTube just for fun, a couple hundred people would get a kick out of it." It became a viral sensation, smashing records for most-watched clips.

Fergie was deeply amused and touched that Morissette, seen as a highbrow artist, would even be aware of her work. She sent her a cake made by Exotic Cakes of Los Angeles with the simple message, "Alanis, you're a genius, love Fergie". The cake was in the shape of flesh-coloured buttocks. 'My Humps' certainly made the group a cause célèbre and gave them pop notoriety for the first time. Denounced in the US media as setting the case of feminism back several decades, it was also lastingly successful, not least because a mobile ringtone taken from the original album master tapes became the first track to sell over two million mastertones. *The Seattle Times* took up the argument: "The song has been denounced for 'setting feminism back 40 years' – as if feminism has any meaning for today's young pop-music fans – and praised for coining a new hip-hop term for female erogenous zones. While few would deny that the repetitive lyrics are stupid, the subject matter is funny to some listeners and daring to others. What really sells the song is what the Peas are best at – creating music that is simple, fun and easy to dance to." It was clear that this one would simply run and run.

By 2011, even will.i.am had had enough of his premier novelty record: "It got to the point where we didn't want to play 'My Humps' no more," he told MTV. "You know, 'cause 'I met a girl down at the disco,' I just didn't want to say that no more, lyrically. It wasn't like my best lyrically, but it was fun. It wasn't lyrical miracles, but the beat was rocking, so we throw the beat in there and just let the beat linger." The storm over 'My Humps' continued. It isn't the best song ever by any means, and even if it is ironic, it sails a little close to the wind. In some respects, it marks Adams out as a latter-day Paul McCartney – in love with a tune and an idea so much that quality control can be impaired; for every undoubted classic that McCartney has penned, many will snipe that he also delivered songs of the novelty value and variable quality of 'Maxwell's Silver Hammer', 'Mary Had A Little Lamb' or 'We All Stand Together'. That said, all those songs have also been tremendously popular and introduced his work to different markets. At best, 'My Humps' can be categorised under that most debatable of genres, that of 'having a laugh'. What is remarkable, however, is the almost skeletal minimalism of the musical track.

By the time of the old-school apl.de.ap-led 'Like That', it's almost as if it is too late for the group, as discussion on the importance and supremacy of the Black Eyed Peas had been undermined by its preceding track. It is built over the infectious sample of Astrud Gilberto's version of 'Who Can I Turn To (When Nobody Needs Me)'. As if to reinforce the group's hip-hop credentials Q-Tip, Cee-Lo Green, Talib Kweli and John Legend perform guest raps, giving a message of positive vibes and consciousness, with the knowing, ironic message that Black Eyed Peas 'represent selling out' in the track.

'Dum Diddley' manages to take in Musical Youth's 1982 UK number one 'Pass The Dutchie' and a vocal line from the Bangles' 'Walk Like An Egyptian'. Again featuring *Elephunk* guest star Tippa Irie, this time on backing vocals, and a 'featuring' credit for long-term associate and 'fifth Pea' Dante Santiago – without actually stating what he does. It is an accomplished and exciting performance with all four members toasting and rapping over an infectious, growling, reggae-tinged beat. Although not released as a single, a promo was shot of the band playing it live in the studio. Bucky Jonson demonstrates in it how very capable and inventive they were as a live band, while the Peas display their showmanship and vocal ability.

Redemption arrives in the majestic old-school funk and soul of 'Feel It', a just beautiful jam that sounds like it drifted in from a 1981 New York dance album. Produced by apl.de.ap and Printz Board, it is an incredibly successful track, another call to the dance floor. Written by will.i.am, Fergie and apl.de.ap, it is one of those records that actually manages successfully to express the joy of music and dancing. With Santiago and Fergie providing chorus vocals, it makes marvellous use of old-school clavinet and layered strings. The track was used in the 2006 Antonio Banderas dance film, *Take The Lead,* and appeared on the soundtrack, among new hip-hop and some selected classics. Ironically, it followed the title track of the film, recorded by Bone Thugs-n-Harmony, the group who usurped Atban Klann's position at Ruthless Records just over a decade previously. The song dissolves into a jazz coda with Fergie vamping.

Recorded entirely at the Stewchia, 'Gone Going' actually offers an amusing sideways glance at the rags-to-riches tale of a pop star who becomes removed from his original fan base. Something of a hip-hop update of Bad Company's 'Shooting Star', it interpolates Jack Johnson's 'Gone' from his 2003 album, *On And On.* Son of surfer Jeff Johnson, Hawaiian-born Johnson had from the early 00s created a close-mic'd down-home acoustic music that very much set him apart from the excesses of the pop charts, selling millions of records in the process as a 'best-kept secret' artist. Johnson had met the Black Eyed Peas while on tour and struck up a friendship. He re-recorded his acoustic guitar part of 'Gone' with will.i.am, and created what was effectively a will solo track, with no other Black Eyed Peas present.

On top of all this, there was time for a real legend to drop into the *Monkey Business* mix. The track 'They Don't Want Music' effectively marked James Brown's only relevant recorded performance of the 21st century. The liaison came about as a result of the group meeting Brown at the inaugural *Mojo* Magazine Honours Awards at the Banqueting Hall in London's Whitehall on June 22, 2004, where Brown was awarded a Lifetime Achievement Award. It was in the days prior to the Peas' performance at Glastonbury and their host, Sting, was also a guest. will.i.am approached Brown and asked whether he would be interested in collaborating.

"I said, 'Thank you for all that you did for hip-hop. You may not know it or realise it, but hip-hop would not be what it is, without it,'" will.i.am said in 2005. "So, I asked him the most daring question 'You think we could do a song with you?' He said, 'Send me a reference for what you want me to do, and I'll do it.' So I go to the studio. James comes the next day with his whole crew. He pulls me aside and he says, 'Ya know, Mr. Will, I don't got to work with nobody. But something tells me to work with the Black Eyed Peas. But I like how y'all do what y'all do. Y'all got the band. In hip-hop music you don't see enough of that.' So, we started talking. I started talking to him about Malcolm X, Martin Luther King Jr. and Elijah Muhammad. He knew all of them personally. I mean there are not that many people that have seen as many things as he has seen back in the day that's still alive. I asked him what's the difference between black America today and black America back in the day. He said, 'Black America today is fighting a fight that we [the older generation] fought. Y'all ain't got nothin' to fight about, and it shows in y'all music.' That blew my mind. He said, 'I appreciate the fact that you took the time to write songs like, 'Where Is The Love'. That's brave. But I don't work with nobody because I don't got to.'"

Taboo recalled that Brown marched into Metropolis with his entourage and again stated: "I don't really do collaborations. I'm James Brown. But something told me that I needed to work with the Black Eyed Peas... and that's why I'm here! So let's work." Brown arrived with 10 people – three assistants, three of his band the Soul Generals and four female backing singers. His vocalists – Venus Brown, Cynthia Moore, Kelly Jarrell and Sheila Wheat – were joined by Dante Santiago to create the one-off group, the Bittersweets. Tim 'Izo' Orindgreff was joined by Brown's long-term sax player Jeff Watkins alongside Printz Board on trumpet. Recorded in two takes and based on Brown's 'Let's Make It Funky', although the song is nothing more than a mere sketch, it tapped into Brown's energy and created something special.

It is also clear that all concerned were having the time of their life while making it. Brown took control of the studio and put the young band members firmly in their place when they attempted to question any of his suggestions. For all involved, it was a memorable experience.

Taboo wrote in *Fallin' Up*: "I still look at that track's title on the album cover... and say a quiet 'wow' to myself. It remains one of the greatest memories of my life." Within 18 months of the recording, James Brown died, on Christmas Day, 2006 at the Emory Crawford Long Medical Center in Atlanta, Georgia, of congestive heart failure brought on by complications from pneumonia. He was 73.

After all the showbiz of the last few numbers, the album continues with 'Disco Club', a relatively straightforward paean to ladies and the dance floor. Co-written with long-term collaborators and Stewchia cohorts Jean-Baptiste Kouame, Melvin J Lewis, Michael Mathews, Anthony Tidd and D. 'Mazik' Saevitz, it references the opening note of the beat and later hip-hop classic 'Apache', and has an oriental influence. Although it initially appears to be in favour of women that attend discos, it then offers a word of caution suggesting that the ladies there may not be the kind that the men would wish to fraternize with. Fergie counters this: she suggests that women who go to discos are *not* of low morals. They are strong, too, and equally like to party just as much as the men. Allmusic.com described it as "one of the few serviceable tracks, an apt re-creation of Cassidy's 'Hotel'". It talks about having sex while still fully clothed, with a safe sex message. will.i.am carries a 'Trojan' (a US brand of condom), in case the action escalates.

Recorded entirely at the Stewchia, 'Bebot' was a classic apl.de.ap interlude, with him again singing in Tagalog, building on the success of 'The apl Song' from *Elephunk*. However, whereas that song was wistful and pensive, this is a full-on battle cry for the Philippines, with apl.de.ap in bold, aggressive form. With beats by will.i.am, instrumentation by Jimmy Limon and scratching by DJ Rocky Rock, the first verse details apl.de.ap's struggle, coming over like many Filipinos to Los Angeles to find work to support family back home. He catalogues how and what Filipinos eat; before moving on to eulogize both pretty women ('Bebot' literally means 'a hot chick') and his home country. It was released as a single in Australasia and, unsurprisingly, became number one in his home country.

Unusually there were two promotional videos shot for 'Bebot', both by Filipino American director Patricio Ginelsa. As the subject matter was so close to Pineda's heart, he actually funded the video out of his own pocket, with some assistance from the other Peas. "It's not just about doing a video," apl.de.ap told MTV in July 2006. "Filipino culture is like a community movement, and it feels good to represent my culture and to be embraced by my people." With both videos shot in a remarkably quick two days, the first promo shows how first-generation Filipinos dealt with living in America during the Great Depression. Set in Stockton, California, in 1936, it follows asparagus farmers, who work during the day and go out in the evening. apl.de.ap finishes on the asparagus fields and is picked up by will.i.am and Taboo in a smart car, taking him downtown to the Rizal Social Club. apl.de.ap sings on stage at the cub, before moving next door to a bar where girls are dancing. It is beautifully shot and shows the vibrancy and pride of the immigrant community. It also shows great detail; for instance, there is an amusing sight gag when DJ Rocky Rock scratches with a 78 on a horn gramophone. The closing shots show an old Filipino man in the present day looking at the disused site of the dancehall that had been re-created in the promo. Its aim was to increase visibility of the Little Manila Foundation, whose aim was to build a museum for Stockton.

However, the second-generation video for 'Bebot' caused controversy. It updates the life of a Filipino and is a full-on early 21st century extravaganza. Again, set in LA, it begins with Taboo and Fergie going to apl.de.ap's house, where they are greeted by his overenthusiastic mother, played by Filipino comic actress Louella Albornoz, a sketch of an overbearing matriarch, shouting for apl to come down from his room. In a scene that was entirely improvised, she only lets him go out to the park to hang with his friends if he takes with him his kid sister, Jasmine (played by *American Idol* finalist, Jasmine Trias). They go down to Kenneth Hahn Park, in the Baldwin Hills (also the location of Dr Dre's 'Nuthin' But A G-Thang' video), where they are joined by will.i.am, and all manner of youths standing and then dancing in front of low riders. All male members of the group gyrate with women and there is a vague side-plot of apl.de.ap keeping an eye on his sister to make sure the testosterone-packed young men do not become *too* interested in her.

In August 2006, a group of academics, led by writer Veronica Montes, wrote a letter to apl.de.ap, director Ginelsa and Xylophone Films, their production company, stating their dismay at the stereotypes portrayed in the video. The letter was simultaneously circulated around the online Filipino community.

"The video uses three very limited stereotypes of Filipina women: the virgin, the whore, and the shrill mother," they wrote. "We find a double standard in the depiction of the virgin and whore figures, both of which are highly sexualized. Amidst the crowd of midriff-baring, skinny, light-skinned, peroxided Pinays – some practically falling out of their halter tops – there is the little sister played by Jasmine Trias, from whom big brother apl is constantly fending off Pinoy 'playas.' The overprotectiveness is strange considering his idealization of the bebot or 'hot chick.'" The mother character was also particularly troublesome, but for very different reasons. "She seems to play a dehumanized figure, the perpetual foreigner with her exaggerated accent, but on top of that, she is robbed of her femininity in her embarrassingly indelicate treatment of her son and his friends. She is not like a tough or strong mother, but almost like a coarse asexual mother, and it is telling that she is the only female character in the video with a full figure."

There is a lot of truth in what they write. In the lengthy and fair letter, they praise apl.de.ap's wholehearted championing of his culture, a stance unlike many other expats. They applaud, with reservation, the first-generation video, but feel that the second promo does nothing to further the cause in a culture where most Filipina women are portrayed "as willing prostitutes, exotic dancers, or domestic servants who are available for sex with their employers", and that the "representation of Pinays in these particular videos can only feed into such stereotypes".

The claims were quickly countered by actors and director: "I'm so proud that they're representing the Philippines mainstream, 'cause we need that representation," Jasmine Trias told MTV. "More power and success to all of them, and just to be a part of it, it's definitely an honour." James 'Slim' Dang, a Vietnamese-American dancer and a participant in the video, said, "The open letter discusses the exaggerated [Filipino] accent of the mother. What if they replace it with a perfect English accent? I know some people are proud of their accents. By getting rid of your accent, you might be destroying part of your cultural identity."

Ginelsa was horrified by the debate, as he had spent so much time with apl.de.ap getting the video off the ground, and as he hadn't been approached before the letter was sent and published online. There was never any intention to portray women in a negative light, merely a capture of a multi-racial party led by Filipinos. "I'm just glad that 'Gen Two' turned out the way I wanted it to rather than what I know it could have been," Ginelsa said in 2006. "So people can misread it and say this and that and it was my intention to portray them as negative or as whores or whatever. I'm always aware of the responsibilities I have as a filmmaker."

The video received scant attention from VH-1 and MTV. Ginelsa added, "It is hard to say that four-minute videos will spark the entertainment industry's awareness of Filipinos but I can say that we should take it day by day, like taking baby steps." Like all Internet storms, it blew over relatively quickly, but both apl.de.ap and Ginelsa were saddened at the response it provoked. The video was included as bonus content on the group's 2006 DVD, *From Sydney To Vegas*.

Recorded entirely at Metropolis, 'Ba Bump' is a straight return to the floor. Featuring samples from Cameo's 1986 dance filler, 'Candy', this Printz Board-produced track is a dirty, crunk-influenced number. Crunk, a southern call-and-response-dominated hip-hop, had become popular through artists such as Lil Jon from 2003. Although it is relatively minor in comparison to other heights on the album, when it breaks into its rock-influenced middle eight, the song has all the trademark anthemic power of the Black Eyed Peas. Blackmon's vocal signature, 'Ow!' – as central to the eighties dance-floor as any of Michael Jackson's vocal tics – adds gravitas to this slight entry into their canon. will.i.am's impression of Blackmon is respectful and engaging.

'Audio Delite At Low Fidelity' was reminiscent of the Peas' early albums. A straight duel between will.i.am and apl.de.ap, it is based around a sample of the Rick James-produced and written Mary Jane Girls' 1983 hit, 'All Night Long'. It is a straight soulful celebration of the group's ability and prowess, reminiscing about how hip-hop has changed, casting back to the duos rapping and dancing at the mall, and how the group stand out like "chubby people in checkers". Over 16 verses, it has all the elements of will.i.am's slick and sophisticated rapping and would not have been out of place on either of the early albums. The track ends with a jazzy interlude and the repetition of the word 'change', with the message not to be afraid to move on; a thinly veiled note to those who wanted the group to remain in their back-packer hip-hop box. An amusing built-in CD glitch speedily concludes this free-forming and the final track on the album, 'Union', begins.

By now, the success and scale of the group meant that they could pull in almost any special guest they wanted. Sting, impressed by the work will.i.am had done with his remixes, was more than happy to assist when apl.de.ap had the idea to incorporate Sting's 1987 standard 'An Englishman In New York' into one of the tracks on the new album. The group's schedules meant they had to work on location, and they met when the Black Eyed Peas and Sting's respective *Elephunk* and *Sacred Love* touring schedules would allow. They ended up recording in Berlin, at the studio that had been used in the thirties for recording National Socialist propaganda records. "It's all the original equipment from when it was originally put in. So we recorded a song called 'Union'. It's weird because we're talking about the opposite of what Hitler was talking about – in the same studio. It was mad eerie. You don't understand how big this facility is. They gotta room as big as a basketball court that's just filled with organ pipes and one organ. It's bigger than any basketball gym... Fergie was singin' on the mic and I said, 'What kind of mic is that?' The guy's like 'This mic was made specifically for Hitler.'"

Recording with his musicians (Kenny Kirkland on keyboards, Manu Katché on drums, Branford Marsalis on sax and Mino Cinelu on percussion), Sting was the consummate professional throughout, and sounds as if he is greatly enjoying himself. He added bass and rewrote the song as if he'd been listening to 'Where Is The Love' for a year solid. "He came in, he wasn't even expecting to write and Will said, 'Why don't you flip something on the track?'" Fergie told *The Toronto Sun*. "So he came up with some of the most beautiful lyrics on the album, I think: 'I'd change the world if I could change my mind.' It just came spontaneously, which is how our records are made anyway. So it was perfect." The song ends the album on a hugely positive note, making a plea against war and calling for peace, one for all and all for one.

Given that the album had been largely written on the run all around the world, it had a unity in its diversity and *Monkey Business* was a huge, immediate success. Released on June 7, 2005 it was to become a fixture in charts worldwide as the group toured and pulled singles from it one by one. Nevertheless, it received decidedly mixed reviews. The *Los Angeles Times* said: "[It] hurries from one strangely unsatisfying sparkle to the next." *Rolling Stone* argued that, "Some cuts are dragged down by soul-pop clichés, but 'Don't Lie' is a breezy, grooving romantic apology... and 'My Humps' is an irresistible, butt-stupid ode to Fergie's ass. If anything, *Business* is too breezy – but from a group that once burdened us with rhymes about how its 'technicalities die hard like batteries', that's not such a bad thing." *Rap Reviews*, however, suggested that "While it's understandable that the Peas would want to follow up on the huge crossover success *Elephunk* had, they've only captured the pop aspects of that success and seemingly forgotten the hip-hop soul the album had when NOT being played on radio. While this album will be commercially successful for them, it feels to this reviewer like a seven-year regression backwards. The Peas forgot to stir the porridge in the pot, and now it tastes nine days old. No wonder they need so much sweetener."

The negativity seemed across the board: *Pop Matters* grumbled "two major problems that plague the Black Eyed Peas on this record: unimpressive rapping and, surprisingly for this erstwhile socially conscious hip-hop troupe, a distinct lack of substance... For a band that has made its mark by making positive music about important issues, the only issues being explored in any depth on *Monkey Business* are, as in 'Don't Phunk', a fairly sophomoric conception of love and desire, and just how awesome the Black Eyed Peas are. On track after track, the Black Eyed Peas boast about their prowess to get people dancing better than anyone else. In so doing, the Black Eyed Peas come over as so... unoriginal."

Even previous champion *The Guardian* offered the album just two stars in its review on May 27. Betty Clarke wrote: "The lyrical inspiration has evaporated. The dance-floor fillers are – in every sense – arse: the band's obsession with the female form, or 'lady lumps', takes precedence over their desire for world peace." The *New York Times* went even further: "Perhaps it was inevitable that a group like this would eventually emerge, peddling an energetic but inoffensive variant of hip-hop. But did we have any way of knowing that the results would be so unpleasant?"

However, the album was not about the critics, it was about taking the Peas' message to the widest platform possible. Not everyone was disparaging; Jason King wrote in *Village Voice* that, "Like pre-*Riot* Sly, the retro-integrationist Peas have been accused of selling out. White chick Fergie is usually the scapegoat, but with her mellifluous riffs, she's no hack. Besides, her residency transformed the Peas into the only multi-gender, multi-racial, multi-ethnic rap act in mainstream America. For my money, the Peas crossed over because they finally translated the kinetic exuberance of their live act on record, a trick that eluded them on their plodding first two albums." And it's absolutely true, that the album is pitched at full-speed as its starting gear. The album was the dawning realisation that the Peas had moved further away than ever from their roots. The preachy idealism was, of course, still there, as was a surfeit of guest stars, but here was something unashamedly commercial. "I think the fact that we just have fun with music is the reason why it works for us," will.i.am said on the album's release. "We love music and melodies and don't try to distinguish ourselves from regular music fans. It's really that simple."

It mattered not. The group was delighted with *Monkey Business*. It was a proper group album that symbolised the group as a unit, the four members working in unison with the band, crafting songs as a group. will.i.am said *"Behind The Front* was the idea, *Bridging the Gap* was the plan, *Elephunk* was the execution and *Monkey Business* is a documentary." The album went on to sell 4.6 million units in the US alone. It reached number two in the US album charts and number four in the UK, topping the chart in Argentina, Australia, New Zealand, Canada, Mexico, Germany, France and Switzerland. By 2010, it had sold over 10 million copies worldwide.

# Chapter 10

# Leading The Parade:
# Thousands Of Possibilities

*"We had paid our dues, shovelled the shit at Disney and now we were leading the parade."*

Taboo, 2011

*"We're chameleons. We can open up for Metallica or go rock with Justin Timberlake. Or we could go out with Busta Rhymes. We have so many different types of – I want to say 'personalities,' but then you would think we're cuckoo – but we have so many different types of suits that we could put on and still be us."*

will.i.am, 2006

The Black Eyed Peas' ubiquity was underlined by them taking part in US white goods chain Best Buy's commercial in summer 2005. A member of staff asks how it would be if the Black Eyed Peas could be controlled by a touch of a button. Presto, the group appears, singing 'Pump It'. They follow a customer onto a bus and later to a swimming pool – before the strapline is said: "The music, the stuff, it all comes together here, Best Buy – Thousands of possibilities." In a way, that strapline applied wholeheartedly to the group themselves; music, stuff, all coming together with thousands of possibilities. To further underline their omnipresence, on September 18, 2005, the group performed alongside Earth Wind & Fire as part of an opening act for the 57th Primetime Emmy Awards.

The tour that supported the *Monkey Business* album was huge and spectacular. The group had played several shows in the run-up to the tour, most notably on July 2, when they were on the Philadelphia leg of Bob Geldof's Live 8, the follow-up concert to 1985's legendary Live Aid. Second on the bill after UK-based indie stars the Kaiser Chiefs, they were introduced by Will Smith and played a four-song set – 'Where Is The Love', 'Let's Get It Started', 'Don't Phunk With My Heart' and, with Bob Marley's widow Rita and son Stephen, a rousing version of the Wailers' classic 'Get Up Stand Up'.

The *Monkey Business* tour got underway in Brisbane on September 23, 2005. It took in 137 shows, and was due to culminate in a performance at the Mandalay Bay Resort Hotel in Las Vegas on December 29 the following year, until a closing show was added for New Year's Eve at Ipanema Beach, Rio De Janeiro. After a warm-up tour of Latin America, the group was fighting fit to headline their first world tour. "We were no longer riding on someone else's wave," Taboo wrote in *Fallin' Up*. "And the tickets sold were because of what we attracted, no one else. When you've spent almost a decade in somebody else's wake it is a good feeling when the stage opens up as your own." Gwen Stefani, who had recently and successfully gone solo from her group, No Doubt, supported the group on the October 2005 North American leg. The tour then continued on to Europe.

On December 10, International Human Rights Day, Amnesty International released a version of John Lennon's 1971 hit, 'Power To The People' (pea-ple, of course). The Black Eyed Peas had recorded it to commemorate their *Make Some Noise* campaign to bring human rights issues to the attention of a younger audience. Recorded largely on the John Lennon Educational Tour Bus, it is a spirited rendition of the protest song that samples the original clumping chorus vocal, before adding new piano, beats and vocals. will.i.am sings in a quiet,

Lennon-esque drawl, with rap interjections on the chorus. Fergie sounds seductive as she croons her lines; the version works as it never rises beyond an acoustic beat, with the original record's stomping toned down. In one sense, with its slinky malevolence, it never really starts. The group performed the single on UK TV on December 10, 2005 on ITV's *Record Of The Year* programme.

will.i.am said in the days preceding the performance, "What a great way to celebrate the launch of *Make Some Noise* – with John Legend and Mary J Blige, our performance of 'Power To The People' is going to raise the roof on Saturday!" The group, who had flown in between gigs at Madrid and Munich, performed, with Blige and Legend who looked more than ever like Marvin Gaye in 1971. Standing in a line, Fergie, Legend, Blige and will.i.am all took turns to sing and rap their verses. apl.de.ap and Taboo stood at the end of the line singing chorus vocal. With Bucky Jonson supporting, this live version was more strident than the studio mix, and sent thousands of people to download the track immediately.

After a three-month break, the tour resumed in March and was sponsored by global motor car manufacturer Honda as part of its annual tour to promote its Civic range. Before the tour got underway, the Black Eyed Peas played two nights in Boston as support for the Rolling Stones on their *Bigger Bang* tour, before handing over to Maroon 5. On the Honda tour, the Black Eyed Peas played venues with an average of 10,000 seats, supported by current sensation the Pussycat Dolls, starting in North America. The band received considerable sponsorship from Honda, flying first-class for the first time and staying in five-star hotels. As Taboo was to write, "We had paid our dues, shovelled the shit at Disney and now we were leading the parade."

To coincide with the progression of the tour and as a signpost that there would be no new material for a while from the group, a mini-album of remixes of *Monkey Business* was released. Led by the album version of 'Like That', *Renegotiations* was a thumping, state-of-the art set of productions of five further tracks from *Monkey Business*, increased to seven with the addition of an edited version of 'Audio Delite At Lo-Fidelity' (without the one-minute-plus 'change' coda). Released as an iTunes exclusive for a week, and then made available exclusively to retail partner Best Buy, the album showed the Peas had none lost of their dance-floor prowess. Erick Sermon provided a simple, uncluttered mix of 'Ba Bump' without the overpowering horn riff. DJ Premier remixed 'My Style', again removing some of the extraneous production of the original, emphasising the vocals. Pete Rock turned the James Brown funk tribute into a straightforward bass-heavy floor filler, spotlighting the Chic influences of the track rather than the overt JB-isms of the original. Whereas that verged on pastiche, this is a wholly successful remodel of the track and manages to make Brown sound absolutely contemporary. DJ Jazzy Jeff is similarly successful with his re-rub of 'Feel It', sampling the opening percussion break of Sugar Hill Gang's 'Rapper's Delight', souring the track's beautiful eighties-sunshine groove. He also – unsurprisingly – throws in some old-school scratching as well. Large Professor and Max Vargas close the 31-minute album with the 'Large Pro Peas Mix' of 'Disco Club', making it sound as busy as the lyrics suggest with a beat-heavy mix of the track. The mini album's sleeve featured a close-up of the album's chimp on the front, and a superb, close-up shot of the group all screaming on the gatefold, taken by cult photographer Nabil Elderkin. The caption underneath it reads simply, "The Board Of Directors".

The *Monkey Business* tour then continued into Asia and Europe, before returning to the US. During the tour, will.i.am announced that the band would be taking a sabbatical after the non-stop grind of the past two years. In early 2006 he made his situation clear to US critic Jim DeRogatis: "The only thing we can do is wait to put out a new record in 2008. Fergie has to put out a solo record. I have to do a solo record. Then I think we have to reinvent what Black Eyed Peas is. I don't know if that's a film or redefining what a musical is... I think that's what we have to do to survive in a world of new content, gadgets, kids with PSPs, cellphones, MP3s and text-messaging. We have to redefine what it all means." The shows on the *Monkey Business* tour utilised the modern technologies perfectly, and when will.i.am asked the entire audience to hold up their cellphones and wave them around during 'Where Is The Love', as a 21st-century version of the cigarette lighter, it was a breath-taking moment.

The live performances were divided into sections – after a selection of classics and tracks from *Monkey Business*, all four members had solo freestyle sections, which would find will.i.am, apl.de.ap and Taboo dancing and rapping, before Fergie would sing a selection from her forthcoming solo album, to be entitled *The Dutchess*, as well as rock standard 'Sweet Child O' Mine'. The show's finale would begin with 'Where Is The Love', and culminate in the full-on party of 'Let's Get It Started'.

It was a feat to perform on the size of stages to be played on this tour, especially for apl.de.ap, with his sight condition. He was asked by *People* magazine how he gets by. "When I dance, I picture myself and the floor in my head," apl.de.ap replied. He prepared for the shows during rehearsals by familiarising himself with the stage and layouts for the evening, moving cautiously and slowly. "If there's a Filipino flag [in the audience], Will whispers, 'Filipinos are over there,'" he continued. "Then I wave!" The group was treated like heroes when they played the Araneta Coliseum in Manila on July 26, 2006, where apl.de.ap was treated very much as the homecoming hero, and press coverage, unlike anywhere else on the planet, was heavily skewed in apl.de.ap's favour. The venue itself had had a colourful history since its opening in 1960 as a sporting and concert venue. In October 1975, it had been the scene of the legendary Muhammad Ali/Joe Frazier heavyweight boxing final, known forever as the 'Thrilla in Manila'.

The *Monkey Business* tour closed with the date at Ipanema Beach, Rio De Janeiro, Brazil on December 31, 2006. Local legend Sergio Mendes, who had worked with the group on *Elephunk* and now on his own album *Timeless,* and long-time group friend, John Legend, joined the band. For the free concert, complete with the drum corps of a local samba school, the group expected a big crowd but nothing like the one that turned up – the organisers approximated a million revelers had come to see the group wish them a Happy New Year after a show-stopping performance of 'Where Is The Love'. In footage of the night, the group looks somewhat dazed as they stare out at the masses. As Taboo wrote, "Flashback to the days of performing to 25 people and the disbelief is obvious." The crowd surge after the gig understandably put the group on edge and they had to be smuggled back to the airport in the back of an ambulance. It had been a long, strange and ultimately fulfilling tour.

The *Monkey Business* tour was captured on a long-form video, *Live From Sydney To Vegas*, which was released on December 5, 2006, and contained material recorded at the Superdrome in Sydney on October 3, 2005 and then later their performance at the Joint in Las Vegas' Hard Rock Hotel and Casino. Directed by concert film specialist Nick Wickham, it demonstrates the size and scale and some of the excitement of the *Monkey Business* tour.

The group's involvement in promotions, marketing and tie-ins became ever wilder and more ambitious. Masterfoods, then the conglomerate name for Mars, noted that the Black Eyed Peas would be a perfect fit for its Snickers brand. It approached Adams regarding helping direct and be a key creative figure in a series of five online science fiction inspired short films ('digi-sodes'), which was to be known as 'Instant Def'. Developing the project with New York advertising agency BBDO and director Jesse Dylan, the Black Eyed Peas were to play the imaginary group Instant Def with futuristic storylines appealing directly to the teenage market.

In the somewhat unrealistic storyline, the foursome play Snickers factory workers by day, while at night they are defenders of old-school hip-hop, with superpowers granted them after they come into direct contact with Snickers at the plant. An online sign-up teaser campaign was posted in May 2006, with the episodes starting from June and playing until August. will.i.am, as always, was excited and ebullient about the process. "You know, this is fresh," he proclaimed. "You mean I can make music, incorporate it into a film that's on the Internet and wherever else we can get it played? Oh, that's tomorrow... all the way." It also provided the group with an opportunity to act out some fantasies. "I was very attracted to this project because Snickers gave me creative freedom," Fergie added. "I had always dreamed of being a comic-book character. I've always had this thought in my head of what I wanted to do with it. And so then they came to me with this idea and I said I know what I want to do."

Vic Walia, Snickers senior marketing manager, sensed that he was on to a good thing. "We knew we had to go online to reach teens because that's where they spend most of their time. But we also know that teens are very savvy consumers so we made a conscious decision to tone down our branding in an effort to build credibility with the online community. We wanted to communicate the Snickers brand message in an authentic, credible and contagious way. The Instant Def digi-sodes allow us to do that. The choice of will.i.am, Fergie, Taboo and apl.de.ap to be our Instant Def heroes was easy. They share key characteristics not only with today's young influencers, but also the Snickers brand. They are setting trends and breaking away from the clutter in the industry to really stand out amongst their peers."

The commercials were a mixture of live action and comic-book graphics. There was a 30-second trailer, which enjoyed a limited cinema run as well (in that very early 21st-century way of using conventional media channels to advertise the future). In the first digi-sode, we are introduced to imaginary group Instant Def (complete with a talking narrator dog); apl.de.ap plays 'Mag', will.i.am plays 'Nate', Fergie is 'Ella' and Taboo is 'Zap' and they rally against corporate backed MC and bad guy, Minister LP ("I'm DVD, you're just straight VHS – played out" he says after he has smashed their boom box). will.i.am stutters to get a rap out and is defeated in the street battle; a news broadcaster wonders whether Minister LP (and his supporting 'potna', Hypeman) are for real or "just a fabrication/justification of some corporation's imagination".

Other characters include the record company mogul, Mr Boo-T, played by Tony Cox, best known for his role as evil elf Marcus in the festive cult classic, *Bad Santa*. Boo-T is billed as 'super villain' (subtle this ain't) and his henchman, DeVLE. The band return to their night job at the Snickers factory, working alongside animated peanuts, when there is a huge explosion and the digi-sode ends with the four members of the group lying prone. As the saga continues over the next four instalments, the group acquires superpowers and obviously end up defeating Minister LP (who is revealed to be a record company robot) and Boo-T. The group gets to don superhero costumes, show their sense of humour and appear to be having a very good time indeed.

There is an interesting moment in the second instalment as they lie in their hospital beds and will.i.am begins 'playing' the heart monitor. Fergie gets an opportunity to wear a close-fitting rubber nurse's outfit (the clip itself became something of a YouTube phenomenon). In the third instalment there is a cameo from Bootsy Collins as Cincy, the Funky Foreman. Set in a Snickers warehouse, the group realise they have their own superpowers – Zap turns a Snickers truck into a low rider; Ella graffitis a picture of herself and suddenly it comes to life. This double makes a deal with Boo-T and knocks out Ella. All is of course resolved by the final instalment, but only after a ninja battle at a hilltop fortress, involving the band, Bootsy, an animated spider and a super hero version of Minister LP, who is ultimately killed by Ella's deadly backside shake ("looks like Boo-T forgot the booty"). It ends with the band performing their theme tune, 'Instant Def', which was, of course, available for immediate download.

It's a curious series of films and takes a peculiar slant about the group defending hip-hop from the multinationals. One can only hope that the advertising executives were indeed laughing all the way to the bank at the swathes of irony present here. It succeeded in its objective of getting the band's name as far out there, again, as possible. Blog site Rikomatic encapsulated the feelings of many viewers: "The video aesthetic is somewhere between *Grand Theft Auto* and the *Power Rangers*. The idea of one large multinational corporation sponsoring a series on the dangers of the corporatisation of the music industry is very bizarre. It's like McDonald's sponsoring television ads telling people not to wear Gap jeans. That said, I love the Black Eyed Peas and probably will tune in for the entire series." However, the review concluded with a small slap in the face for Vic Walia: "I'm not likely to run out and eat a Snickers anytime soon though." What it did do, alongside the group's various film cameos and soul performances, was to scratch their itch about wishing to appear in their own film. In the series' 30 minutes, it pastiches just about everything from James Bond to Bruce Lee and all points in between. It gave the band (alongside their videos) a chance to play out their fantasies without some appalling full-length albatross forever around their necks.

will.i.am sloughed off the criticisms: "Our videos are commercials, and the product that you're selling through that commercial is your album, and the brand that owns that product is a record company. The only difference is that the only place they play that commercial is on MTV, and MTV gets paid all the money from the ads. At some point, you've just gotta cover your ears and not listen to the he-said/she-said and the commentaries about the moves you make when you have to make those moves to survive in a business that's sinking. It has nothing to do with getting paid – it's about reaching new listeners through this new form."

A project that was dear to will.i.am's heart was *Timeless*, the album he produced for Sergio Mendes. Mendes had, at Interscope's suggestion, played piano on 'Sexy', one of the stand-out tracks from *Elephunk*. The 65-year old Grammy-winning Brazilian bossa nova legend had not made a new album in a number of years, and will.i.am, being a lifelong fan, offered to produce an album that would, in part, introduce Mendes to a younger audience, much in the same way that *Supernatural* had done for Carlos Santana back at the end of the last century. Working with the group on 'Sexy' from *Elephunk* thoroughly enlivened Mendes. "Because I'd really enjoyed the whole experience," he told *Blues and Soul* in 2006, "when I got home I told my wife that I'd finally decided to make another record. I immediately called will and suggested, 'How about if we do something where I bring all the classic melodies from Brazil, you bring the hip-hop world, and we put it together?' He told me for him that would be fulfilling a lifetime dream, and so that's exactly how our working relationship started! The idea was to try and get the new kids into these great old melodies. Because, with both samba and hip-hop/R&B rhythmically-speaking harking back to Africa and both being urban music from the streets, I think the marriage is a natural one. It's nothing forced. You know, in carnival – Brazil's biggest celebration – we have millions of people all over the country dancing and singing on the streets, and nothing is more urban than that! It's the biggest urban celebration on *earth*, if you think about it!" He added to *Performing Songwriter* magazine the contribution artist and producer brought to the record. "I brought the Brazilian stuff and he brought the urban hip-hop stuff, and that was it. Like natural combustion. He has tremendous energy, a great sense of humour and lots of creative, fresh ideas."

Taking a selection of Mendes' classics from his 40-year-plus career, will.i.am reworked them to incorporate hip-hop, funk and soul, all melded together with incessant Latin rhythms. Adams enlisted a host of guest stars to spread the love. As well as the Black Eyed Peas, Q-Tip, Stevie Wonder, Jill Scott, Justin Timberlake, Erykah Badu and India Irie were among the performers on the album. However, it is will.i.am's subtle showcasing of Mendes and his wife Gracinha Leporace that make the album special. will.i.am approached the project with all of his customary enthusiasm. "I have Sergio Mendes, Pharoahe Monch and Justin Timberlake on a track," he told MTV. "Who would have ever thought of that combination? I mean this record is beautiful. It ain't like a club record where it's like, 'Oh, oh this muffin,' and next year it's like whatever, you wait for the next club record. This is like classic beautiful melodies... It's relaxing... it's the make-love-slow record."

The album received generally positive reviews. *Music OMH* said, "This is a quality piece of craftsmanship and there isn't a weak point on the album. Not everyone will like every track, and some of them will not stand the passage of time, but for the summer of 2006 this is perfect."

Allmusic.com said: "As a producer, will.i.am means well and in general does a fine job – though he is, as would be expected, a tad overzealous in working with one of his idols." *Prefix* magazine was not happy: "Without missing a beat, *Timeless*, Mendes's attempted comeback to the American pop culture spotlight, is a predictable, oversimplified, boring mess." The album reached a respectable number 44 on the *Billboard* 200, giving Mendes one of his biggest hits in years. Mendes was delighted and put in a lot of work to ensure that the record was properly promoted. In the UK it faired very well, giving Mendes a number 15 placing. The single of 'Mas Que Nada' reached number 13 on the *Billboard* Dance Music/Club Play Singles chart, while it made number six in the UK and topped the Dutch singles chart. It success was bolstered by its inclusion in the EA Sports FIFA World Cup 2006

Video Game. In May 2006, the Black Eyed Peas appeared with Sergio Mendes on *The Tonight Show* with Jay Leno, promoting their version of 'Mas Que Nada'.

The Black Eyed Peas had become ubiquitous. "It's not like we're seen at every red carpet or going to an opening of an envelope, it's like we're performing our songs and getting out there," Fergie said. "We don't do anything that doesn't fit with the music," will.i.am added. "We kinda lend ourselves to benefits so we did the Democratic National Convention to get people out there to vote. And then we'll do a Best Buy commercial 'cause they sell music. Then we did the first iTunes commercial. We did the NBA 'cause it's like, who's not gonna do the NBA? We did the Super Bowl, 'cause who ain't gonna do the Super Bowl? And if they asked you to do two years at the Grammys, you ain't gonna do it? And then we did the Emmys 'cause they said, 'Ain't nobody ever did the Emmys.'"

The Peas work ethic was sent up by the long-running US comedy institution *Saturday Night Live* in October 2005, where their Best Buy advert was parodied by the team – with Fred Armisen, Finesse Mitchell, Amy Poehler and Kenan Thompson playing the group. As a comment on their ubiquity, it is announced that they will be available for bar mitzvahs and office parties at varying prices. The group thought it hilarious and a sure sign that they had, by now, not only arrived but were well-known enough for nationwide parody.

But the group were tired and needed a rest from their relentless schedule. "My world is all mixed up," Ferguson told *Giant* Magazine. "My body doesn't know what's going on. The Peas just keep going, going, going, like a machine." It seemed that since their re-emergence in 2003, the Black Eyed Peas had been absolutely everywhere, especially throughout 2005 when their profile rose arguably as high as it possibly could. It was time for a much-needed break. That said, being the Black Eyed Peas, all four continued to collaborate with each other to a greater or lesser extent, and there were big-money concert performances to attend to, but importantly time off provided the ability to work on solo projects for Fergie and will.i.am.

# Chapter 11

# Split Peas 1: *The Dutchess*

*"What we've accomplished as a group, it's so enormous, I'm not afraid of messing up what we do. We sell thousands of seats in every country on the planet. You can't get nervous. We're all succeeding in all different parts of our careers. Just because I produce Nas and John Legend and Justin Timberlake doesn't mean it will change the dynamic of the Peas."*

will.i.am, 2006

*"I think people will be surprised because they don't know that sensitive side of me yet. I also like to experiment with different tones in my voice, and I wanted to make the album really colourful."*

Fergie, 2006

It was finally time for Fergie to launch her solo album. Recorded throughout 2005 on the road and at a variety of studios, *The Dutchess* (sic) marked the fruition of the question that Fergie had asked will.i.am back in 2001. will.i.am, who had signed Fergie to I Am Music more or less as soon as she started working with the Peas, gave a hint about the album to MTV in December 2005: "There'll be collaborations, but collaborations that really add to the song, not just like, 'Hey, I worked with such and such just for the sake of working with them, just 'cause

117

you need like some type of publicity angle to go to radio.' That's not what these records are about." It was a long-term labour of love and was finally out, but the Peas had taken priority. "A lot of people don't realise, but I was producing her by mid-2002," will.i.am said. "Writing songs with her and, at the same time, we were recording *Elephunk*. We've been trying to figure out the release since. Should we put it out after *Elephunk*? No, we still need to work as the Black Eyed Peas. We set the anchor. No matter what happened with the individual projects, we committed to the Peas."

In fact, the two had already released something together outside of the Peas. Quietly in 2004, they had recorded a remodelled version of 'True', the 1983 hit by Spandau Ballet, for the soundtrack of the Adam Sandler/Drew Barrymore romcom, *50 First Dates*. It was on some versions of the accompanying Maverick-released album, and appeared as a bonus track on Fergie's 'Glamorous' single in 2007.

will.i.am was Executive Producer of *The Dutchess*, alongside Ron Fair and DJ Mormile, who was still very much part of the wider Peas family, since the time he passed their original demo tape to his uncle Jimmy Iovine right back in the mid-nineties. will.i.am produced or co-produced eight of the album's 13 tracks. Fergie was delighted that will.i.am oversaw the project. "He's like my partner in crime," she said. "We get in the studio and sometimes we'll disagree and sometimes we'll really agree, but we just have such a love relationship. We just understand each other... I could say something that won't make sense to the normal ear, but he'll understand." Other producers involved included beat-maker Polow Da Don, Printz Board, John Legend and Ron Fair. Fair, who had worked with and known Fergie since Wild Orchid in the mid-nineties, was delighted with the results. "Once people get this album and hear what she's capable of as a singer and writer, I think that's when the roof blows off it. That's when she's not just a little trifling pop girl doing disposable hits."

*The Dutchess* had gestated over seven years and had been recorded in numerous studios during the Black Eyed Peas career. "A lot of it was recorded on the John Lennon studio bus," Fergie told *Billboard*. "We'd go in a couple of hours before going on stage and that's how it got done. The songs span a seven-year period. Some were done before I was in the Black Eyed Peas. We just updated them, and some were done in this one-month span that we took off from touring, which is very rare for us. Will and I moved into this studio house in Malibu called Morningview. It's like a ranch. It was very serene – complete opposite to the chaos of touring."

Twenty-one tracks were recorded in total for the album, of which 13 were chosen, with the remaining songs ending up as additional material on worldwide versions, extra CD singles and download material. It's a very colourful album," Fergie said. "There's dub, there's reggae, there's stuff like the Temptations, a band that I saw when I was 10 years old in concert. There's the low rider, oldie style that we revisit that I was really inspired by in high school. There's that punk-rock aspect – that just really raw rock'n'roll, get your hair messed up, sweat as much as you want, don't feel pretty onstage – that aspect. There's jazzy. We're just crazy."

The whole project indeed seemed a little crazy – the product of having fun and being pressured on the road. The title of the album came from a sneaky joke on the former British royal Sarah Ferguson, the Duchess of York, who, since her divorce from Prince Andrew in 1996 after a 10-year marriage had – to the discomfiture of the royal family in the UK – become something of a media celebrity in the US. Her nickname was, indeed, 'Fergie'. The 't' in duchess was added for the album by the Black Eyed Peas' Fergie. "The spelling is different because I didn't want people who didn't know how to say it to call it 'the Douche-ess,'" Fergie told *Allure* Magazine in 2009. "I thought, 'Let me dumb-ify it a little bit.' Sometimes you smarten things up and get more clever with words. It's fun to go the other way, and it's always nice for people to not expect as much from me. I've always enjoyed being the underdog."

In November 2006, it was reported that Sarah Ferguson had made contact with her rather more glamorous namesake, "You know, I rang her up about that," Sarah Ferguson told *The Boston Globe* in 2006. "I said, 'Fergie, it's Fergie'... Now that you've done this, you have to sing at a concert for my foundation, Children In Crisis." Fergie went on to play concerts for the foundation in New York and London. To further the faux-royal connection, the sleeve of *The Dutchess* bore the Stacy Ferguson coat of arms.

*The Dutchess* was of enormous importance to Fergie. "I've been wanting to do this ever since I was a little girl, so it's just a beautiful thing, it's my lifetime project," she told MTV in 2005. "It's gonna be more personal and a deeper look into who I am as a person, more vulnerable than I am with the Peas." The album package reeked of quality. The Julian Peploe art-directed booklet contained seven highly stylized photographs of Fergie taken by high-class fashion photographer Ellen Von Unwerth. Von Unwerth captured images of Fergie that illustrate six of the songs (she had hoped to visualise all, but ran out of time). For example, the heavily stylized eroticism of the shot for 'Fergalicious' captures Fergie looking surprised while about to suck a lollipop; 'London Bridge' finds her looking sultry while wearing a tiara; she appears all street and streetwear for 'Voodoo Doll'. This gave weight to the album's full title, as shown on the cover – *Fergie 'as' The Dutchess*; it is clear that Fergie is playing a series of roles throughout, and will.i.am supports this, overseeing an album of infectious, sing-song sketches and nursery rhymes that was to assail the world's charts, complete with surprising flashes of maturity.

'Fergalicious' opened the album with an appropriate flourish. It was recorded on the John Lennon Educational Tour Bus as it followed the Black Eyed Peas on the *Monkey Business* tour and amply sets out Fergie's solo stall. A not-too-distant relation of 'My Humps', it is a pulsing hybrid of hip-hop and techno. It utilised two main samples: JJ Fad's 'Supersonic' – an original release on Eazy-E's Ruthless Records – reaching back to old-school hip-hop from 1987, as did its borrowing from the Miami bass classic 'Give It All You Got' by Afro-Rican (which itself sampled James Brown's 'Night Train' and 'It's More Fun To Compute' by Kraftwerk). The lyric, mainly rapped by Fergie, is delivered as if it was on a street corner; however, the first voice heard is that of will.i.am, ushering in his charge as if he were a master of ceremonies. Fergie acknowledges her role as a sex symbol and that she 'makes the boys go loco' as they derive pleasure from pictures of her. But, she is keen to stress that this is simply an image. Rapping had not come naturally to Fergie, but she was pleased with the direct homage the track made to the older MCs: "I've always been a fan of rappers like Roxanne Shante, Monie Love, Queen Latifah, Salt-N-Pepa – these were girls that I emulated growing up, but just more in private," she told *Billboard* in 2006. "BEP gave me that confidence to do it. I'm not trying to be a serious MC, that's not my goal. I'm just paying homage to everything I grew up listening to. If I didn't include that part of me, it wouldn't be a true representation of who I am." In reference to the album's variety, will.i.am said: "She'll have a song about voodoo dolls where she's talking about her past and getting over those demons, but then she'll have a song like 'Fergalicious,' where it's just being sassy and flaunting her stuff from a strong female perspective, paying homage to Salt-N-Pepa."

'Fergalicious' became the album's second single and had an amusing, childlike video directed by Fatima Robinson, who'd already helmed the 'My Humps' promo for the Black Eyed Peas. Set in 'Fergieland', with bright pink and purple candy canes – a cross between Willy Wonka's Chocolate Factory and the Land of Oz – it features dancers, possibly there to re-create *Charlie And The Chocolate Factory* author Roald Dahl's creation, the Oompa Loompas. They are working on a production line where they box 'Fergalicious' chocolates. Fergie models a variety of costumes – including a girl-guide type uniform – while people keep coming to grab her chocolates. The images are intercut with shots of Fergie in the gym, showing her super-fit body on an exercise bike in a Day-Glo-coloured Lycra outfit. She continues to flirt with personas and stereotypes of women and, in the middle eight, she bursts forth from a wedding cake. As male dancers lick their candy, the song's references to how good Fergie tastes are somewhat incongruous with the highly stylized child-like storybook setting. There is also a tremendous piece of product placement in the instrumental section, when Fergie brings out a Samsung K5 MP3 Player. The video culminates in Fergie smearing wedding cake cream all over her body and wrestling with two female dancers. Big and daft and suggestive, the video, which, by 2012, had been viewed over 34 million times on YouTube, propelled the single to the top of the US charts.

There was also a compelling – if not exactly true – rumour that the song started a spat with fellow Interscope artist Nelly Furtado, who had recently released a single from her *Loose* album entitled 'Promiscuous'. Apparently, Furtado felt that the chorus of 'Fergalicious', with its line that Fergie 'ain't promiscuous', was a dig at her. The two met at an awards ceremony where Fergie explained it wasn't but Furtado was not appeased. In her collaborative single 'Give It To Me' with producer Timbaland and Justin Timberlake, it was alleged that Furtado had directed its verses towards Fergie. In 2007, Fergie guested on 'Impacto' by Daddy Yankee, and threw in a line that if someone had a problem, they should address her directly. The story added a little more flash and controversy to the endless stream of celebrity magazines and websites feeding on spats such as this. Unbelievably, the song was to become a favourite of Sasha Obama, the youngest daughter of future US President Barack Obama. In 2009, Fergie would perform the song at the White House to complement the President's annual Easter Egg Hunt.

'Clumsy' is possibly the most appropriate title here – it is a mixture of Casiotone (the 1981 mini synthesizer at an affordable price that put technology into everyone's hands) and a sample of Little Richard's 1956 Bobby Troup-written hit, 'The Girl Can't Help It'. It sounds dippy at first, then insidiously becomes the greatest pop idea you've ever heard. Fergie wanted an old-school Shangri-Las, Supremes type song, and her monologue in the middle underlines its Sixties feel. If there were a genre called 'futuristic retro-girl group electro', 'Clumsy' would be its all-time number one.

Producer will.i.am was proud of the track: "'Clumsy' is like the Shangri-Las 'Leader Of The Pack' with a ghetto-ass beat, but then here come the guitars and her singers." The track was recorded on the John Lennon Educational Tour Bus in the parking lot adjacent to Shakeys Pizza Restaurant in the Beavertown district of Pittsburgh. The song breathlessly deals with serial monogamy, saying, "Girls like me don't stay single for long". The song's content is a microcosm of the album. Fergie insisted to the Australian press: "I'm not a promiscuous girl – like I talk about in 'Clumsy', I'm always the girl with the boyfriend in serious relationships – but I do like to play with my sexuality. I don't think that means I have to live in a morgue."

The video was directed by Marc Webb and Rich Lee and followed the style of a pop-up book. MTV described it as "an amalgam of many things we find hard to resist: Amy Winehouse style retro-nuevo beehives, free-falling, fake planes, cheesy acting, En Vogue-era little black dresses, old-school video games and, um, hot dudes". It is a stunningly well-made promo, like a state-of-the-art advert for where videos were at in 2007; using a mixture of digital and physical cardboard technology, the promo is interspersed with Fergie dressed as a fifties R&B singer, performing the 'The Girl Can't Help It' element of the song. She is cast as a catwalk model, falling off the stage when she sees a man; a Chicano-style street girl in a low rider impressing her paramour with the repeated up-and-down motion of its suspension. As the guy gets interested, the car collapses. There is a *Matrix*-style space escapade where she accidentally puts her man in an airlock and he is jettisoned out to space, and finally, during a photoshoot on a roof, she sits on the edge, takes a phone message from her admirer and then falls off the building. As she free-falls to earth in a cardboard New York, her suitor is there to catch her and the pair walk off into the sunset. And all this in one pop-up book.

However ironically, the video goes does seem to reinforce gender stereotypes, with a love-struck woman appearing frequently ditzy until a big strong man comes and saves her. MTV was concerned about the 'brand pimpage' in the commercial, with product placements for MAC cosmetics and fashion house DSquared, and, to ensure parity after Samsung's plug in the 'Fergalicious' promo, a generous brand-flash for Motorola. But despite these reservations, it was simple and well-made fun, and, when the track was released as the album's fifth and final single, it helped it reach the US Top 5. "It's a little less serious, about my high-school years," Fergie told *EDMagikTV*. "I was so boy crazy, I'd break up with one boyfriend and then all of a sudden, I was madly in love with the next. It has that LA Cholo feel to it, and that's what I wanted to go for as it reminded me of my high-school years."

The already relentless musical gimmicks briefly abate on the album's third track, 'All That I Got (The Make Up Song).' With its sample from the Commodores' 1977 ballad, 'Zoom', it sounds like it was smuggled in from a Teena Marie album from the early eighties. Written with will.i.am and Peas drummer and producer Keith Harris, it is a beautiful groove, overlaid with a lyric about true love going far deeper than the superficial. With additional vocal arrangements by Ron Fair, backing vocalist Theresa Jones Bailey adds texture and will.i.am contributes, unusually for him, a straight, love man rap. The beauty of James Anthony Carmichael's string settings for the Commodores' original being re-created by a 28-piece orchestra make 'All That I Got (The Make Up Song)' something of a special, sensitive interlude.

There is nothing sensitive, however, about the following number. Produced by rapper, writer and producer Jamal Jones, known as Polow Da Don, and crashing in with shouts and sirens wailing, 'London Bridge' was chosen as the first single to launch the album. Penned with Sean Garrett, Mike Hartnett and Polow Da Don, it is a rambunctious groove that throws in gauche metaphors for sex and concerns a strident woman at a party. It was actually surprising to find that will.i.am had had very little to do with it.

"This song is kind of like a punch in the face to let people know I'm coming out," Fergie told MTV in July 2006. Bearing more than a passing resemblance to former tour support Gwen Stefani's 'Hollaback Girl' from the previous year, it is a noisy, clattering call to arms. And from a woman who had sung about 'phunking' with her heart, here the listener was exposed to four-letter Fergie. "It's funny, because I'm a singer and this single doesn't have a lot of singing to it," she continued, "It's more of a chanty type of record, but it just seemed so obvious that it would be the first single, because it was so strong and aggressive." Chanty, strong and aggressive, it was simply unavoidable during the tail-end of 2006. The Polow Da Don hook-up suggested by will.i.am was inspired. In 2007 Polow Da Don said that in return for putting her into the urban world, "She put me on to the pop world. I can make it suitable for them, but I'm still doin' me. That's why will.i.am put me in there with her, because he knew my music was urban and hard, but was able to cross over."

The video, directed by Marc Webb, was shot on location in – unsurprisingly – the UK capital, primarily at Woolwich barracks in south-east London. "We got to use the whole cheeky London-type thing, playing with the British guards," Fergie said. "But at the same time, we were playing with the sixties London feel, with the Brigitte Bardot bouffant hair, and mixing that up with the Chola style. It's kind of a weird fusion, and it somehow just all works together." The main theme of the video was playing with stereotypes. Fergie and her female gang go into a staid London Gentlemen's Club, and finally pull the men into the toilets. The women then all return dressed as the men. "It really brings me back. People have never seen me in the Black Eyed Peas videos going to clubs and hanging out with my girls, and that's a big part of me," she told MTV. "I love to go to clubs, hang out, get buck wild, get into fashion. I probably need more girl energy in my life, because I'm around boys all the time."

With cameos from the other three Peas, the promo really is like an English Seventies *Carry On* film that has mutated into a gangsta night out. When we see Fergie dry humping a soldier on guard in a sentry box, before moving down to place her mouth adjacent to his groin, it is an example of pure lowest common denominator. It culminates in Fergie dancing on the table in the men's club wearing union flag panties – suggesting that this is indeed where the drawbridge will come down. There are cutaways to Fergie and will.i.am on a speedboat motoring up the Thames from Woolwich and passing through Tower Bridge, the bridge forever misconceived by Americans as 'London Bridge'.

The single and attendant promo were greatly discussed, with much speculation about the lyrical content. Fergie was keen to emphasise its ambiguity. "There are a couple things that you could relate with that title, but I'm just going to leave it to people's imagination," she told MTV. "And that's all I'm going to say about that." *Spin* magazine said, "Must these people invent new terminology in *every* song?" while *Rolling Stone* suggested that the song was based on "a shadowy metaphor. What exactly does 'London Bridge' mean? Is it panties? A body part? It's a sexual euphemism... It's not clear, but it's not complicated." The lyrics leave little to the imagination, and served to show Fergie as a rebellious singer, out there on the edge. *Chartattack.com* said that the single "simulates the sound of M.I.A.'s 'Galang', J-Kwon's 'Tipsy' and Gwen Stefani's 'Hollaback Girl' playing simultaneously". *About.com* added: "Take the spirit of Gwen Stefani's 'Hollaback Girl,' add some funky horns, and slather it all with puerile sexual raunch."

Cult singer and Interscope labelmate M.I.A. was reportedly less than pleased with the over-affectionate homage that 'London Bridge' paid to her work. She allegedly told Jimmy Iovine that he had encouraged Fergie to emulate her style in order to further her career. She said that when she heard 'London Bridge' for the first time she informed Iovine that, "If I don't sell records and make money for you you're just going to make them with her anyway."

Supported by a radio version that had the opening chant of 'oh shit' amended to 'oh snap', the record shot to number one in the *Billboard* Hot 100. It made number three in the UK, where it was kept off the top spot by the Scissor Sisters' 'I Don't Feel Like Dancin'' and old friend and collaborator Justin Timberlake with 'Sexyback'. Ironically, she pushed Nelly Furtado's 'Promiscuous' down a position. The video has been watched over two million times on YouTube at the beginning of 2012.

Starting amusingly with a vocal line that references the melody of the nursery rhyme 'London Bridge', 'Pedestal' – produced and co-written by Printz Board – was a reaction to some of the comments she'd read about herself in the papers and in Internet chat rooms. She wondered what these people would do if they were to get a life. Recorded at Metropolis and the Beet Market in Los Feliz, Board plays all the instruments, and it is a close-up intimate recording, in which Fergie catalogues some of the accusations levelled at her. She makes the point that she works far too hard to have the time to commit these indiscretions and misdemeanours and that all the people who make these claims simply hide behind their computer screens. The haters will soon be knocked off their lofty perch. Fergie elaborated on the matter when promoting the album with a degree of charming candidness: "I've learned to suck in my stomach when photographers are around. I used to read gossip magazines all the time, but I stopped when I started being written about in them and read incredible lies about myself."

If she was concerned about the lies written about her, 'Voodoo Doll' laid her addictions bare and was the album's most debated track. "'Voodoo Doll' is my take on dub music," Fergie told *Billboard*. "It's about my struggle with crystal meth. There's a demon part that's a completely different voice than the singing part, and it's almost like two voices. It's me battling with myself." It's a brave, confessional track, about as dark as you can get on ostensibly an up-pop million-selling record. Set against a horn-heavy upbeat dub-ska, influenced by US reggae band Groundation's 2001 Ras Michael-sung track 'Each One Teach One', Fergie catalogues her relationship with drugs and how the effects on her were like someone inserting pins into a voodoo doll. It talks about her subconscious wrestling with her consciousness, an angel and devil metaphor. She sings about being the needle in an arm, and her drug-induced paranoia. "It's kind of putting myself out there, which is scary, but at the same time it's something that I need to do just because I've always wanted to do it," Fergie told MTV. "I'm not going to air all my dirty laundry on a Black Eyed Peas record, because it's not appropriate." Fergie felt sufficiently free from her past to open up in the song: "I don't want to talk about it all the time because it's not a part of my life any more but I'm not running from it." That said, the computerized sunshine-reggae complete with Printz Board's trumpets, ameliorate the lyrical gloom. The track ends with a 30-second musical interlude which sounds like bizarre fairground music, with Fergie breathing heavily.

The album's second Polow Da Don production, 'Glamorous' was another huge hit, reaching number one in the US. Smooth, gliding hip-hop-influenced R&B, it sounds the closest to something from a Beyoncé or Mariah Carey album. The beat had actually been put together by Polow Da Don for a remix of 'Luxurious' by Gwen Stefani. The producer elaborated in a 2007 interview: "Gwen said she didn't like the remix, which was the dumbest thing I've ever heard of. And the remix was one of the best things I had done at the time. When I finished that I felt like, 'I'm gonna be the shit when this hits.' I called her and let her know it was the biggest mistake she made in her career. I was a fan of hers, and I wanted to help her out. And now you see Fergie blowing her out the water in sales, even though Gwen is the bigger star." It is a fine capture of a soulful vocal combined with a rap. It compares Fergie's life and hardships pre-fame with her current-day success, underlining that she is still indeed the same person. Many made the comparison to Stefani's Isley Brothers 'Between The Sheets'-sampling track, but in truth, they were similar only in feel. Rapper Ludacris contributes an easy-going rap that adds to the overall laid-back feel of the track.

Its video, directed by P!nk and Missy Eliott collaborator Dave Meyers, looks expensive and opulent, contrasting Ferguson's current showbusiness life with her pre-fame days, when she was told at a keg party that she didn't have enough money to be a playa, but still enjoyed herself. After she lands in her private jet, she is driven in her limousine to a fast food joint and orders food for her and her entourage, before the scenario reverts to the nineties as she drives in her Mustang to the same takeaway. It culminates in her shooting a film entitled *Glamorous* – based on the 1967 Arthur Penn-directed *Bonnie And Clyde* – in which she stars with Ludacris. The promo ends with her reviewing the pressures of fame while reminiscing about the keg-party days, emphasising that she is still the same grounded girl. It was an enormous, deserved success, and was summed up by the review posted on *ThatGrapeJuice net*, which opined, "Although the 'I'm-still-the-same-even-though-I-have-money' theme has been done to death and will undeniably continue to live on, Fergie-Ferg's take on the subject sounds surprisingly 'legit'. Trading her trademark belting for a rank, almost talky tone, she seems rather detached from that 'flossy' world that is the showbiz industry (whether actually true or not is another question)."

will.i.am takes charge again with the Motown composite 'Here I Come' that was recorded again on the John Lennon Educational Tour Bus. It is a deeply amusing, cut-and-paste early 21st-century pop song, slowing down the Temptations' greatest sixties A-side, 'Get Ready'. Retaining a little of the original's *joie de vivre* and pizzazz, it combines an autobiographical Fergie rap with its old-school beat. Adams contributes some old-school MCing to this infectious throwaway. The song was released as a single in Australia and reached the Top 30. Fergie performed the song with will.i.am and Elton John at the 2006 Fashion Rocks show with John contributing to the chorus. It was another demonstration of how far she and the group had travelled.

Fergie called 'Velvet' "very intimate lyrically and feeling-wise". She wanted it to sound "like velvet feels – very smooth – and I wanted it to be sensual". And it is. One of the older songs on the album, it was recorded at the time when co-writer and bassist Mike Fratantuno was still part of the Black Eyed Peas. Produced by Peas guitarist George Pajon Jr. and will.i.am, its sultry, bossa-nova influence supports a lyric that flips between love and lust.

'Big Girls Don't Cry (Personal)' is a not-too-distant relative of Beyoncé's 2006 number one hit 'Irreplaceable' in feel and tone. It is also a beautiful pop ballad that demonstrates will.i.am's ever-developing production skills. However, it almost didn't make it to the album as Fergie felt it was out of keeping with the album's flow. It was passed on to Bad Boy recording artist Jordan McCoy, who recorded it with a view to release as a single. Fergie heard her rockier version, and amid some acrimony from McCoy and her manager Debbie Hammond, decided to release it herself. It would have been strange for this sweet straightforward song, recorded at Metropolis, not to have been included.

As will.i.am said, "'Big Girls Don't Cry' really pushed my production skills. I did an Edie Brickell type of production – 'I'm not aware of too many things' ['What I Am'] on guitars. Its simple refreshing pop made it one of the album's biggest hits, a straightforward AOR radio-friendly smash. Co-written by Ferguson and DAS Communications writer Toby Gad (who would later pen 'If I Were A Boy' with Beyoncé), the song confronts the need for Fergie to embrace maturity, leave a bad relationship and put her house in order.

Its video was directed by Anthony Mandler, who had worked with the Black Eyed Peas in pre-Fergie days helming 'Get Original', and had recently worked with Beyoncé on – surprise surprise – her 'Irreplaceable' promo. It shows Fergie at the home she shares with her boyfriend, to whom she is writing a break-up note, while he sleeps. In a series of flashbacks, moments from the relationship are covered, including one where she clearly disapproves of an unspecified deal that happens on their front lawn between her boyfriend and some colleagues. The video ends with her packing, leaving, and driving off into Los Angeles. An extended, nine-minute version was made that follows Fergie's drive to a warehouse where her band is set up and she performs a straight version of the song again. It is interesting because this is one of the few times you really get to see Bucky Jonson – Printz Board, Tim Izo, Keith Harris and George Pajon Jr. – playing up close. The promo ends with her asking to go through the song once more. It's a touching, straightforward video, again not a million miles from the break-up-and-performance of Beyoncé's 'Irreplaceable', but it showed that Fergie could hold her own, away from the Black Eyed Peas and also the immensely stylized and extremely busy videos that she had made up to this point.

'Big Girls Don't Cry (Personal)' struck a powerful chord and topped the charts worldwide. It was only kept off the UK number one spot by the 10-weeks-at-the-top celebration that was 'Umbrella' by Rihanna. Most importantly for Fergie, the song won the Song Of The Year award in the pop category at the 25th annual ASCAP Awards in April 2008. To be recognised by The American Society of Composers, Authors & Publishers was an extremely heavyweight award for Fergie to win, considering previous recipients included Beyoncé and Lionel Richie. Fergie was also nominated for Best Female Pop Vocal Performance at the 2008 Grammy Awards, losing out to the all-conquering 'Rehab' by Amy Winehouse.

'Mary Jane Shoes' was one of Fergie's favourite numbers on the album and it featured the Wailers' backing vocalists, Rita Marley and the I-Threes. 'Mary Jane Shoes' was described by Fergie as "a breezy reggae song, and at the end I go into a little bit of punk-rock mosh music because I love to do that if you've ever seen my stage show". will.i.am also admired the song. He said that Fergie "goes from dub, doing her interpretation of roots, to some ska-punk and ends up with jazz. From a production standpoint that was fun, flipping all those different styles." It's like a four-minute compendium of genres, based around the Bob Marley anthem 'No Woman No Cry'. Ostensibly named after the single-bar flat shoes popular with children, the lyric suggests that the simple footwear makes Fergie feel that she is back, as carefree as a seven-year old. However, Mary Jane is a long established nickname for marijuana, which would explain why she sings that 'music has another dimension' and that she can dance with a 'different perception'. The presence of Marley's widow, Rita, would suggest the latter, given Marley's well-publicised use of ganja, the scared herb of the Rastafarian religion.

Produced by Rob Boldt and Ron Fair, the lyric to 'Losing My Ground' was written when Fergie was in Wild Orchid and at the zenith of her addiction to crystal meth. She told *Glamour* magazine in 2008 that René Sandstrom and Stefanie Ridel realised they had to intervene when they heard her lyrics. "I had a whole week of rock bottom. At that point I was in a writing mood and very inspired and the words were just flowing out of my pen. I really feel like I was meant to write the song because the next day I had the intervention." After many years clean, she came back to the track and it acted as a sort of Wild Orchid reunion, with Ridel and Sandstrom receiving co-writing credits. It's a big, powerful rock ballad propelled by Simeon Spiegel's acoustic guitar and begins with Ferguson muttering about not knowing what day it is, and ends climatically with chorus vocals repeating 'don't want to go back there'.

Fergie was justly proud of the album's closing track, 'Finally', an emotive piano ballad that explored her feelings now that true love, having arrived in her life, will ensure she never returns to her previous misdemeanours. Written and co-produced by long-time Peas cohort John Legend, it was tender and moderately understated, sounding not unlike a Scottish folk ballad. "It's piano, strings and vocals," she said in 2006. "It's a timeless ballad that you can play 30 years from now, and it'll still be cool because it doesn't lend to any era. And it's really stripped down. I really had a chance to sing, although I didn't oversing anything. My taste is more to bring it out at certain moments." Although not specified, it can be seen as an open letter to her boyfriend, Josh Duhamel (whom she credits on the album's 'thank yous' as her "amazing boyfriend for your love understanding and maturity in dealing with our hectic schedules"). "I've been in a lot of relationships that were exciting but unhealthy, very Sid-and-Nancy-esque," she said in 2009. "I wanted somebody I could count on. With all the craziness of this business, I know I can count on my man – and he knows he can count on me."

Fergie details how she escaped from her insecurity and how her life was ready to enter a new phase. Written also with Stefanie Ridel of Wild Orchid, it provided an emotive coda to the album. Ron Fair's string arrangement is suitably over-the-top as Fergie moves from being an innocent stumbling in a grown-up world to taking full responsibility for her actions – very much the theme of the whole record. For a widescreen populist ballad, it has a tender core and proves how accomplished a singer she is. On March 18, 2008, it became the final release from the album, marking an 18-month period of promotion and marketing for *The Dutchess*. Although the single was not a commercial success (attributed initially to there being no promotional video for it), Fergie promoted it heavily and it acted as an advert for the album. She performed it on a stage in the middle of the audience with John Legend at the 50th Grammy Awards in February 2008, her Streisand-esque long-held note inspiring rapturous cheers. It was a performance that showed she was far more than the Black Eyed Peas' eye candy, and that she could stand on the world's biggest stages without will.i.am at her side. With songs like 'Finally' and 'Big Boys Don't Cry', Ferguson proved that she could really sing, leading to the realisation of just how lucky the Black Eyed Peas were to have her in the group.

*The Dutchess* was an emotional if somewhat schizophrenic album parading in the shiniest pop finery. Fergie was discreet about who the tracks were written about but confirmed that many were about past boyfriends, who were to remain nameless. It also has that core of daftness and irreverence that courses through the best of the Black Eyed Peas' work.

Fergie promoted the album extensively. "With *The Dutchess* being my first album, I wanted to really represent who I am and what I've been through," she told *Blues And Soul* magazine, "which definitely includes my early hip-hop background. I wanted to put forth the truth and let people know that I am more than just the tomboy they see be-bopping onstage with a bunch of guys! My goal was to be honest and to let people know the thinking side of me, as well as the more aggressive side, which comes through on songs like 'London Bridge' and 'Glamorous', where I have Ludacris – one of the cleverest MCs in the business – bringing that Dirty South flavour that's so big right now. Being a white woman in a primarily black hip-hop band is definitely not commonplace. But, while it may be a new thing, I certainly don't think I'll be the last! I think more and more colour-lines will be erased because today hip-hop is everywhere! It's not just in the South Bronx any more! It's in Japan; it's in London; it's in Germany – and new boundaries are being broken all the time! And, if I have to be the first one to do things, that's fine with me!"

The album received largely positive reviews. *The Guardian* said, "*The Dutchess* is a first-class example of the modern, no-boundaries sound that throws pop, rap, R&B and old Motown into the pot." *Entertainment Weekly* suggested, "And if occasionally the lady doth attest too much to her own physical charms, *The Dutchess* proves that she's earned her Black Eyed independence – and perhaps even her new royal title." UK rock magazine *Uncut* was smitten, saying that it was "one of the most rambunctiously entertaining and high-spirited records of 2006". *The Boston Phoenix* said, "Fergie doesn't have her independent pop-star persona consolidated yet – right now she's somewhere between funky sexpot and R&B balladeer – but she's on her way." *Vibe* said that when she got it right "as she does about half the time on her genre-jumbling solo debut", the result was "strange pop that successfully blurs the thin line between annoying and alluring".

It was not all sunshine and light, however. Chartattack.com was less than impressed on the whole: "Despite a few genuinely interesting moments, including a cool Little Richard sample on the will.i.am-produced 'Clumsy', Fergie's focus group has failed to bring us anywhere we haven't been before"

The focus group theme was returned to by arch and influential UK-based site *Popmatters*. "Fergie's debut solo record, *The Dutchess*, is AWFUL. However, it's no more awful than any of the two Fergie-assisted Black Eyed Peas records, which have combined to sell seven million records in the US. So, despite any redeeming musical value, it's entirely possible that *The Dutchess* will be a resounding success... This album sounds like it was driven maybe 10% by an artist and 90% by a focus group. Fergie prances, preens, moans, talks and raps, but the result is canned and sterile." Although it is understandable how a viewpoint like that could have been reached, *The Dutchess* was deceptive, having many layers that begged repeated listening. For a piece of pop floss, it had a great deal of hidden depths.

*The Dutchess* was released on September 19, 2006 and proved a huge success for Ferguson. It reached number two in the *Billboard* albums chart, while all five singles reached the US top five, with 'London Bridge', 'Glamorous' and 'Big Girls (Don't Cry)' all reaching number one, a feat yet to be achieved by the Black Eyed Peas. The album went on to sell four million copies worldwide.

It was not just on disc that Fergie was looking to prove herself. She also bagged herself a small role in the 2006 film *Poseidon*. Directed by Wolfgang Petersen, it was a remake of the 1972 Gene Hackman-starring disaster classic, *The Poseidon Adventure*. Shot in 2005 amid the Black Eyed Peas' US tour, Fergie played Gloria, the singer in the ballroom on the New Year's Eve when the ship capsizes. In the original film the role was played by Carol Lynley, who lip-synched to Renée Armand's version of the song 'The Morning After', which won an Oscar and was a US number one hit for Maureen McGovern in 1973. Fergie sung two songs in the film, 'Bailamos' and 'I Won't Let You Fall', a dramatic power ballad co-written with will.i.am. "It will be the first time people see me as a solo artist," Fergie said ahead of the film's release. "It will give people a sense of what I can do vocally." And it was a fabulous vocal performance, dramatically staged in the ship's ballroom. The song is clearly making a play for the territory mapped out by Celine Dion on her worldwide 1997 *Titanic* smash, 'My Heart Will Go On'.

Fergie enjoyed her role as Gloria in the film, which starred Richard Dreyfuss, Josh Lucas and Kurt Russell. Gloria provided an opportunity for Fergie to glam it up. "My character is completely diva-fied – a lot more diva-ish than I am, as you can see with the big gown with the feathers," she told MTV "It's quite a fun character." She didn't survive long in the film, which despite its 21st-century twist, suffered immediate, unfavourable comparisons with its 1972 predecessor. After singing her two songs, she is seen comforting passengers after the ship capsizes, then falling to her death in the arms of the captain (Andre Braugher) as the pressure of the icy waters smash the ballroom's windows.

# Chapter 12

# Unfinished Monkey Business

*"What we've accomplished as a group, it's so enormous, I'm not afraid of messing up what we do. We sell thousands of seats in every country on the planet. You can't get nervous. We're all succeeding in all different parts of our careers. Just because I produce Nas and John Legend and Justin Timberlake doesn't mean it will change the dynamic of the Peas."*

will.i.am, 2006

2006 showed absolutely no slowing down of will.i.am's phenomenal work rate. He told Jim DeRogatis: "I'm doing three or four songs on Timberlake's record, and most all of Macy [Gray]'s new record; she's on my label, and this is the one that I think will really do it for her. I just did Busta Rhymes' new single; five songs on Nas' album; four songs for Snoop; a song for Too Short and five songs for Kelis. Oh, and five songs for the new John Legend!"

will.i.am had been working on tracks for Legend's second album, *Once Again*, a connection that was to prove very successful for him. The former John Stephens had worked with the Black Eyed Peas several times before, most notably adding his voice to 'Like That' on *Monkey Business*. will.i.am picked up a Best Male R&B Vocal Performance Grammy at the 2006 Awards for co-writing and producing the astonishing ballad

'Ordinary People'. The track, a stand-out from Legend's 2004 first major label release, *Get Lifted*, was a remarkable, plaintive ballad that started life at early sessions for *Monkey Business*. will.i.am sensed that it could be an extraordinary showcase for Legend and removed the group's contributions, making it a pure piano and vocal ballad. With its touching lyric, a rumination on the complexities of relationships, it has become Legend's signature song.

Few people realised it had anything to do with will.i.am. "It's not always about making hits. When I wrote 'Ordinary People' for John Legend that wasn't a song that I thought was going to be big," he said in 2010. "I told John we didn't write that song to be a hit. They didn't even know I had something to do with 'Ordinary People'. They just thought I only did music for Black Eyed Peas." The track is exhibit A in the case for will.i.am's defence, proving that the author of 'My Humps' could also produce sympathetically a piece of work that was so understated and emotional.

"In spring 2004, I was going to work with will.i.am at the Hit Factory, a studio on the west side of Manhattan," Legend said in the book *Chicken Soup For the Soul: The Story Behind The Song*. "We'd been writing together for the next Black Eyed Peas record. He would play me beats, see if I could come up with hooks and I'd help him write the song. We'd done it before with some success. He started playing and eventually the chorus emerged. We had a small brainstorming session but that's all the song remained for awhile – the beat and the chorus. I liked it, but the more I thought about it, I didn't think it would be a good Black Eyed Peas song. It seemed more like something for my repertoire." Legend would sing the song at soundchecks when he was on tour in Europe with Kanye West and its obvious potential revealed itself.

"When we decided that I would record the song, I had promised Will that I would let him produce it. I made a demo in Los Angeles at the Record Plant, just me and the piano. I sent it to Will and we, and everyone else who heard it, loved it the way it was. The demo was essentially the way it was when it was released."

Another of will.i.am's productions, the Macy Gray album *Big*, was released in March 2007. Gray's fourth album, it was her first in four years, and needed to be a bold, impressive comeback. And it didn't do too badly overall. Although not reaching the heights of 1999's *On How Life Is*, it performed better in the US than her previous studio album, *The Trouble With Being Myself*. Nine of its 13 tracks were tastefully produced by will.i.am and overseen by Ron Fair. It's clear that Gray and will.i.am worked very well together. Gray made that plain at the time of the album's release: "I've known Will for a long time; it's like working with my brother. He's a great visionary and really understands me as an artist." will.i.am appeared on the Dead Or Alive 'You Spin Me Round (Like A Record)' referencing 'Treat Me Like Your Money' – in which his rap nods generously to 'It's Like That' by Run DMC. Fergie appears on 'Glad You're Here', Natalie Cole guests on the smooth single 'Finally Made Me Happy' and Justin Timberlake on 'Get Out'. Most successful is the final track, 'Everybody', an only partially disguised remake of the vocal part from 'Request + Line' from *Bridging The Gap*, remade with Bucky Jonson, with a lovely, loose chorus line. 'Ghetto Love', a grafting of 'It's A Man's Man's Man's World' by James Brown to a strange hip-hop Charleston, is little short of a strange and distinctly un-beguiling mess.

The reviews were mixed – *The Guardian* suggested that it would have made a good EP and that, "As previous albums suggested and *Big* proves, Gray's scattergun talent is at its best in short bursts." *The Los Angeles Times* said it was full of "sweeping orchestral R&B, dance-flavoured hip-hop and psychedelic funk", while *Slant* said, "Gray's already weathered voice is more worn than ever; she struggles to reach and sustain notes that should be comfortably within her range, which makes guest spots by Natalie Cole and Fergie – not to mention background singer Dawn Beckman, who practically has the chorus of 'Treat Me Like Your Money' all to herself – not just a nice addition to the album, but a very necessary one." Even with the full might of Universal behind the release, and the inclusion of 'What I Gotta Do' in *Shrek The Third*, the album just made it into the US Top 40 and to number 62 in the UK. However, it proved that will.i.am could also discreetly slip into the mix. It wasn't plastered with his audio ticks and in the main – especially on 'One For Me' and 'Glad You're Here' – it was largely a sweet and gentle record.

will.i.am had bigger fish to fry and in 2006 began working on a production job that would simply dwarf everything else he was doing. He had been asked by Michael Jackson to work on tracks for a proposed follow-up to his 2001 album, *Invincible*, the only release of the 21ˢᵗ century thus far by the self-styled 'King Of Pop'. An article published by *Today's Access Hollywood* site showed a picture of a smiling Jackson sitting next to a pensive will.i.am at Jackson's studio in Ireland. Jackson looks relieved to be back behind a mixing console after a troubled period during which lawsuits were brought against him concerning his friendships with children. Although he was found to have been innocent of all the charges, the case had damaged his standing as the 'King Of Pop', and there were plenty of Princes in the waiting, ready to steal his crown.

For will.i.am, it was the ultimate accolade – Jackson had been the biggest figure in popular music for the best part of two decades with a proven track record of working with the hottest producers and songwriters. In will.i.am, he had both. Jackson was reported as saying, "I think Will's doing wonderful, innovative, positive, great music... I like what he is doing and thought it would be interesting to collaborate or just see how the chemistry worked." The project was to continue, in a stop-start manner, for the next three years.

will.i.am took every opportunity to discuss Jackson in the highest possible terms. He told *hiphopDX* in early 2009, "Here it is: the nigga that did everything first. The first dude to have a video on MTV that really impacted pop culture. The first dude that ever said, 'When you do a video, this is how you dance in it'. The first dude to say, 'When you do a Pepsi commercial, this is how you do with brands'. First dude to say, 'Yo yo yo yo yo yo yo, I'm about to sell this amount of records, and ain't anybody ever going to outpass me'. The first dude to say... 'I'm about to do these big-ass arena tours, and this is how y'all mothafuckas do that shit'. The first dude to be like... 'I'm going to leave this boy band and go solo'. He was the first to do all of that. The first dude that ever said... 'I'm the first nigga to wear one glove. If anyone else wears one glove, they're biters'. The first nigga to say... 'I'm about to do this fuckin' little curly shit at the top of my domepiece, and anybody else who does this shit, they're biting, too'. He's the first dude to do a lot of shit. So when you're in the studio, you know that. And he ain't some soft dude. Like you think you're working with Michael Jackson... He really knows what the fuck he's talking about." Whatever missteps he took in his private life, Jackson was renowned for hooking up with the very best in the studio.

In early 2007, furthering their connection with John Lennon, the Black Eyed Peas added their version of Lennon's 1971 hit 'Power To The People' to the Amnesty International-backed album, *Instant Karma: The Amnesty International Campaign To Save Darfur*. It was a benefit for the aid campaign for the crisis in the Sudan, where the Sudanese government and government-backed Janjaweed militia committed acts of genocide against the population in a brutal civil war. Yoko Ono said: "It's wonderful that, through this campaign, music which is so familiar to many people of my era will now be embraced by a whole new generation." The Peas keep stellar company on this album of Lennon cover versions: U2 perform 'Instant Karma', R.E.M. – reunited with original drummer Bill Berry – do a folk-influenced '#9 Dream' and, interestingly, Jakob Dylan and Dhani Harrison perform a suitably angst-ridden version of 'Gimme Some Truth' with Harrison playing a solo that is so like his late father's work, it is chilling. Sequenced in between Green Day's 'Working Class Hero' and Jack Johnson's take on 'Imagine', 'Power To The People' again showed that the Peas could more than hold their own in this company.

Of course, it wasn't just about the music. To coincide with his forthcoming solo album, *Songs For Girls*, will.i.am announced that he was launching his own denim line, in association with Blue Holdings, Inc. Publicised in March 2007 to hit the shelves in August the same year, the 'i.am Antik' line was to be a premium collection. will.i.am explained, "I produce and write my own music, and the same creativity, energy and imagination I put into making music is the same creativity, energy and imagination I put into designing clothes. I am excited to collaborate with Antik to create a fresh remix of denim." It complemented the Antik range, and acted as a springboard for a relaunch of will.i.am's own clothes line, i.am, which had been in existence until 2005. Blue Holdings employed PR Agency aLine Media to ensure the best coverage possible for the launch and the clothing line was well received.

At the Grammy awards on February 11, 2007 the Black Eyed Peas won a Grammy for Best Performance by Duo Or Group With Vocal for 'My Humps' and presented a lifetime achievement award to Stax instrumental legends, Booker T & the MGs. The following month, Taboo had something of an epiphany. A fun-loving adherent of rock'n'roll excess, Taboo had partied hard right since the days of the Black Eyed Peas' first recording contract, and had enjoyed his fair share of drugs and alcohol. On March 27, his luck ran out. He was arrested for driving under the influence of drugs, and thrown into prison. He described his incarceration in some detail in his 2011 autobiography, *Fallin' Up*. "On Hollywood's surface, life could not have seemed sweeter. But demons lurk beneath that glossy exterior, and they are never satisfied with mere achievements and happiness. Inner demons want your dream just as much as you do – but they just want it realised so they can fuck it all up. I am the Hollywood cliché. The textbook example of someone ill-equipped for the success he wished for."

He had smashed into the back of a woman driver on the LA freeway. "I was sitting in the jail cell thinking about all the people I hurt and disappointed like my wife, who was then my fiancé," Taboo told Holly Stafford at *Hollywood Dame*, "my family, and the Peas. I got out and called my manager and said, 'I want to change'." Although this was not the first time he had said such a thing, he realised he had to focus to move on. Taboo was finally to conquer his addictions and has remained clean ever since.

In this busy year of transition and epiphany, Fergie also had another high-profile acting cameo in Robert Rodriguez and Quentin Tarantino's B-movie film compendium, *Grindhouse*. Fergie was full of praise for Tarantino, the strange and mercurial director who had broken through in 1992 with the cult classic *Reservoir Dogs*. "He came to the set and ran lines with me," Fergie told *Maxim*. "In one scene Quentin got really into the character and bit me. My manager has it on his camera. I'm not going to sue him or anything, but I wanted documentation. It was crazy cool." Fergie played lesbian Tammy Visan, a one-time paramour of Dakota Block, played by Marley Shelton, in the Rodriguez-directed segment, *Planet Terror*. She is fairly quickly killed by zombies after her car breaks down on a Texas highway on the way to meet her former lover. "It's not a big part, which is how I prefer it. I didn't want to be the lead and not be able to handle it. Robert asked me if I had a problem playing a lesbian, and I was like, 'Hell, no!'" The film was released to mixed reviews and poor box office in April 2007. It was quick, it was fun, and it maintained her profile.

The Black Eyed Peas convened sporadically throughout 2007 to play key live dates. In July 2007, they were involved with two prestigious gigs at London's Wembley Stadium, just across the road from where they had supported Macy Gray in the Wembley Arena back in 2001.

On July 1, Fergie played solo at *The Concert For Diana*. The show, which had been partly organized by Princess Diana's sons, William and Harry, fell on what would have been Diana's 46th birthday. That August marked 10 years since her death in a car crash in Paris. Fergie was among a star-studded bill that included Elton John (who had memorably sung a new version of 'Candle In The Wind' at Diana's funeral), Duran Duran (long known as her favourite group), Rod Stewart, Kanye West, P. Diddy, Tom Jones and Take That. Fergie sang 'Glamorous' and 'Big Girls Don't Cry (Personal)' in between short sets by Lily Allen and the Feeling. Playing with Bucky Jonson, she delivered sweet, stadium-filling performances. Supported by a swathe of male and female dancers during 'Glamorous', she was dwarfed by the size of the stadium during 'Big Girls Don't Cry (Personal)', standing on stage on her own in a short white puffball dress. The show was broadcast to 140 different countries and Fergie's performance was largely deemed a success.

On July 7, the Black Eyed Peas performed at the *Live Earth* concert at the same venue; one of 12 concerts undertaken on the same day. The Live Earth project was set up by former US Vice President Al Gore and producer Kevin Wall in an attempt to raise awareness of the global environment through the power of entertainment. The group played a 25-minute set on the stellar bill between Paolo Nutini and John Legend, which included Genesis, Duran Duran, Metallica and Madonna. Aside from their usual showstoppers, 'Pump It', 'Let's Get It Started' and 'Where Is The Love', Fergie sang 'Big Girls Don't Cry (Personal)' and will.i.am debuted 'Help Us Out', a song about the state of the planet.

In September and October 2007, the group played the 24-date *Black, Blue And You Tour* which started in Ethiopia and took in Russia, Argentina, India, South America and China, before closing in Sydney on October 30. The group declined to play North America, for, as will.i.am explained, "There's no Black Eyed Peas record out and America's weird like that. If you ain't got nothing in the marketplace, (the fans) ain't showing up." The tour – which was sponsored by Pepsi in alliance with its Dorito corn-chip division – was the biggest multi-million sponsorship in which the band had been involved.

The *Black, Blue And You Tour* set lists featured a range of material from across the group's career, and regularly featured a solo showcase for Fergie, performing 'London Bridge', 'Big Girls Don't Cry (Personal)' and 'Glamorous'. will.i.am performed 'I Got It From My Mama' from his forthcoming *Songs About Girls* and the group included the Sergio Mendes collaboration, 'Mas Que Nada'. The set also included snippets from the White Stripes' 'Seven Nation Army' and Fergie's rock showcase, 'Sweet Child O'Mine'.

The band delivered a new song, the rock/rap hybrid 'More', which featured in a new Pepsi commercial. The ad featured a man trying to get his can of drink from a vending machine. As he stomps the floor, he falls through it, to where the Black Eyed Peas are playing – and then the group continue to fall through various floors into various parties, until finally the group and the purchaser of the drink are united on the ground floor. The final shot shows the vending machine falling through also – and his drink finally arrives. "From the very beginning The Black Eyed Peas have thrown themselves into working on this campaign with us," a spokesman for Pepsi said. "Shooting the commercial was no exception, with will.i.am and the rest of the group performing many of the stunts themselves." The group also donated previous stage outfits for the launch of the tour to be auctioned off with money raised being split between a variety of children's charities including, of course, their own Peapod foundation.

After the tour finished, the group, who had not had an album of original material together for over two years now, dispersed again to their solo projects. Bucky Jonson – Printz Board, Tim Izo, Keith Harris and George Pajon Jr – their faithful band, also recorded an album. *The Band Behind The Front* was released on BBE in June 2007. Described as "four musicians from different backgrounds, making one unified sound. Bucky Jonson is the best band you have already heard", it was a fine collection of soul, funk, jazz, blues and reggae, with guest appearances from Taboo and Fergie. The Black Eyed Peas collectively would not appear again together significantly until 2009.

With all this variety of activity happening within the Peas camp, the time was fast approaching for will.i.am, whose vision had launched the group and its empire, to finally have his own solo moment.

# Chapter 13

# Split Peas 2: Songs About Girls

*"Music is my therapy, so I let it out."*

will.i.am, November 2007

*"These songs are not for business, I didn't do these songs to get on the radio."*

will.i.am, 2008

Recording for will.i.am's third solo album, *Songs About Girls*, continued throughout the remainder of 2006. At the end of 2005, Adams was pondering what course the album would take. "There's three ways I could go about it," he said. "I could pick my favourite producers and just have 'em produce me as an MC and a singer/songwriter. Or I could do everything myself. Or I could hook up with like a Lalo Schifrin-type of orchestrator and really do some mind-boggling type of stuff, like, 'Did you hear that one record will.i.am did, it was kinda crazy?' I might wanna make it real theatrical and orchestral." One thing he knew was that unlike his first two albums, unless he was to release it pseudonymously, this would be no recorded-in-a-week series of jams like his first two low-key releases on BBE. Released in September 2007, it was, if you will, his first 'proper' album and maintained the standard of his intermittent solo career. In an interview on French radio at the time, he said as much, calling his BBE work 'side projects'. *Songs About Girls* is full of sincere sing-song raps and at times nursery-rhyme house. However, unlike the majority of his previous work, it has something of a dark, disturbed heart.

Released in September 2007 with a simple headshot of will.i.am by fashion and music photographer Joseph Cultice adorning the packaging, *Songs About Girls* is a loose concept album about love and relationships. will.i.am told *Billboard* that it was, "where all the songs could tell a story of falling in love, falling out of love, trying to get back in love, destructing love and destroying love and then starting a new situation. That journey is what makes this unique." He alluded to the fact that the album chronicled the break-up of an eight-year-long relationship that ended around 2003. For a man so ready for an interview on most subjects, he'd kept the relationship close to his chest. "I first fell in love when I was 20. We went out for eight years and I learned a lot about relationships. When things got hard, we went to a counsellor, who inspired us to do activities to work out what was wrong. To cook together – that's why I know how to cook now. And I read a lot, about the destructive relationship we were in. It wasn't abusive, it was just destructive emotionally. I learned in counselling that me and my ex-girlfriend both have a fear of abandonment from not having a role model in relationships." will.i.am made it clear that his love was from outside his world. "She doesn't care about entertainment, or fashion, she's just a real person. As I went this way, towards fame, she went even further the other way. Love isn't a sexual commitment. I will always love my ex-girlfriend. She'll get married, but that love we had, regardless of exclusivity, is beyond that. Love lasts forever."

Talking about the album, he said that it was "real personal, talking about the relationship I was in. Most of the songs are about that relationship. The title of the album is the opposite, it's not personal, it's songs about girls." As the album was "digging deep, a journey to who I am," will.i.am was also clear that he did not want to fill the album with superstar cameos, especially after *Monkey Business*. To that end, there is only one guest appearance across the album's 16 tracks. He stands alone.

*Songs About Girls* has a very clean, uncluttered production, shorn of the trickery that he had overseen on the last two Peas albums and Fergie's *The Dutchess*. It seems like a reaction to the glitz and glitter of those records; shot through with sadness, regardless of its many upbeat moments. Although using all the synthetic mediums that he came to make his own, it is almost will.i.am's unplugged record. Samples were kept to a minimum, and he was clear that he wanted to construct something "from the ground up".

As the album opens, it is clear that the relationship is terminal. The relatively downbeat 'Over', is based on a sample from 'It's Over' by English pomp-rock group Electric Light Orchestra's 1977 album *Out Of The Blue*, with writer Jeff Lynne billed on *Songs About Girls* credits as 'Jeffrey Lynne'. will.i.am had already used an ELO sample when he produced the track 'Beep' for the Pussycat Dolls' 2006 album *PCD*, which used a string interlude from 'Evil Woman'. will.i.am had nothing but respect for ELO, telling the BBC: "Those guys were pretty freakin' crazy, dude! I don't know if anyone can touch that type of production. Electric Light Orchestra. I mean, wow!" Also using a break from T/ Ski Valley's old-school rap hit, 'Catch The Beat', 'Over' first details will.i.am's lost love. Although some critics wrote that will.i.am actually delivered the rap in a manner that suggested he didn't care, his down-played shtick is a refreshing contrast to his usual gaudy style. The ending repeat of "I heard this on another song, don't know what you've got 'til its gone" references 'Big Yellow Taxi' by Joni Mitchell. By featuring the whole mournful coda of the ELO original, 'Over' sets a morose tone, unusual for an individual usually so upbeat.

will.i.am suggests that he was to blame for the relationship's collapse with the next track, 'Heartbreaker', which maintains the downbeat feel. With its heavily synthesized beats and guitarist Josh Lopez's best Nile Rodgers impression, Adams (with Cee-Lo Green) provides call-and-response vocals before the song dissolves into an Ennio Morricone-style guitar figure. A rumination on how Adams had become devious in love and broke his girl's heart, the phrase 'fucking jerk' gained will.i.am his first ever 'Parental Advisory' sticker on the album's sleeve. 'Heartbreaker' had something of an afterlife. It became the album's second single in the

UK and featured a vocal from UK singer Cheryl Cole. Cole, who had first found fame in TV-talent show assembled girl band Girls Aloud, had become a media superstar in Britain, not least because of her troubled marriage to English Premier League footballer Ashley Cole.

She first met Adams when filming a TV show called *The Passions Of Girls Aloud*, in which the group members learned skills and pursued their ambitions. Cole auditioned for and was successful in getting a role in the 'Heartbreaker' promo. An executive at their shared UK label, Polydor, which oversaw Interscope in the UK, suggested they record together and Cole added her vocals to the single for the UK release. "I hung out with her and I was like: 'Wow – she's cool,'" Adams told the BBC. "I heard her sing and I was like: 'Wow, she's dope'; I saw her dance – 'Wow, she's fresh.'" Adams liked the fact she had been through personal issues. "She's going through the things she's going through. I've been through that, and that's what the song's about. So I said: 'It's perfect. Let's do this.'" The video, directed by Toben Seymour, which was also featured in *The Passions Of Girls Aloud*, portrays will.i.am standing in front of dancers dressed in black wearing suits of lights. Various dancers depict the women whose hearts will.i.am has broken. Cole is one of the dancers and there are frequent cut-aways to her singing. The single re-record hit the UK Top 5, spending 26 weeks in the charts, a result of the publicity surrounding Cole after revelations that her real life husband had cheated on her.

For some, the downbeat opening to *Songs About Girls* killed the rest of the album, but it can be seen as a prologue to the uptempo 'I Got It From My Mama', which was selected as the album's first single. Described by will.i.am as a "lighter record, a fun record", it featured vocal back-ups from singer and actress Kat Graham, who was to sing with the Black Eyed Peas on the *Black, Blue And You Tour*. It is based on a sample of 'Don Quichotte' by French dance group Magazine 60 and, as the song progresses, it incorporates the oft-used percussion break from Bob James' version of 'Take Me To The Mardi Gras'. A crisp, propulsive groove with ringing sampled rhythm guitar, its lyrics basically update the old and somewhat chauvinistic adage that a man should look towards the mother of his prospective partner to ascertain if she will retain her looks. It is, like most of the material on the album, an elaborate sketch as opposed to something more substantial.

The song went into Black Eyed Peas set lists and had a relatively straightforward video to accompany it, directed by Rich Lee. It is shot like an expensive holiday home movie and features will.i.am on a Brazilian beach, mainly sitting in a deckchair, surrounded by a bevy of glamorous women in bikinis. He plays with perspective with his fingers, pretending to hold the girls in the distance between his thumb and forefinger. It's a very romanticised and stylized image – the sky is blue, as is the sea, while the girls cavort around a beach bar, drinking Campari. A mirror effect sees the girls dancing with each other, before the screen is split into four in a giant, kaleidoscopic effect. The final shot is that of will.i.am framed in a postcard from Brazil, with the simple and well-known vacation chestnut, 'wish you were here'. Like the phrase itself, the video was something of a cliché. The track reached number 31 in the US and a lowly 38 in the UK.

will.i.am was clear that although he was going to do most of the work himself, he also wanted to be produced on his album. After the brief glimmer of faster beats, 'She's A Star', produced by Polow Da Don, drops the tempo one more time for a wistful discussion of a new girlfriend. Largely sung throughout on Auto-Tune, it's fairly moving and will.i.am stresses that in this new relationship, they don't need drugs or alcohol because the love that he and his paramour share is better than ecstasy and that they are capable of indulging in "automatic sex, like triple X movies". A simple video was shot, in black and white with Adams walking along a shore pointing out constellations, which then appear superimposed in computer graphics.

'Get Your Money' was one of the first examples of will.i.am's increasing interest in fast, uptempo Euro-house music. Using a sample of the minimalist Euro-techno of 'Body Language' by M.A.N.D.Y. and Booka Shade, which had been a break-out Ibiza hit in 2005, he constructs a groove-heavy tune, singing largely in falsetto with his first traditional rap performance on the album. Written about a stripper that will.i.am used to date after he'd split with his long-term partner, without any apparent irony it urges an intelligent single-mother stripper to get her money from the floor. The attitude seems a touch prehistoric, and that if she is not 'strippin'', will.i.am is not 'trippin''. It seems out of character for such a usually thoughtful lyricist to be dealing in such obvious and dubious subject matter.

This precedes the album's only guest appearance – by Snoop Dogg – on 'The Donque Song'. Produced and co-written by Mexican house producer Fernando Garibay, it has a clean, repetitive snare, reminiscent of Michael Jackson's 'Billie Jean'. There is vocal sparring between will.i.am, Kat Graham and Tara Ellis. However, Snoop provides such a low-key restrained cameo that it's hard to really feel his presence as he joins in the paean to 'donques', street slang for, as *Urban Dictionary* puts it, a 'woman's fine ass'. will.i.am said it had no further meaning than "paying tribute to girls with nice asses". Snoop actually manages not to sound like himself on it, which, given he has one of the most distinctive voices in rap, is quite an achievement.

One track was destined to have a life far beyond the confines of the album. 'Impatient' – will.i.am's favourite track on the album – is largely instrumental aside from the nagging, much-repeated vocal refrain, 'I can't wait'. It acts as a palette cleanser after the anguish evident on the rest of the album. It owed, in equal measure, a great deal to French house and the early Nile Rodgers and Bernard Edwards' production and co-write, 'Saturday', by original Chic vocalist, Norma Jean. will.i.am told French radio that he wanted to make a song that reminded him of going to clubs in Europe. With Josh Lopez again providing a choppy rhythm guitar and long-term associate Dante Santiago on backing vocals, its filtered breakdowns and vocodered vocals show an obvious debt to French dance maestros Daft Punk. When will.i.am does sing, it is buried in vocal effects. The following year, will.i.am was approached by Atlantic to produce some tracks for UK R&B star Estelle's second album, *Shine*. He took 'Impatient' off the peg and used it as the main sample for 'American Boy', which, with the addition of Kanye West's unmistakable rap, becoming a UK number one and a US number six. His other contribution to Estelle's album, 'Wait A Minute (Just A Touch)', was a sprightly rap based entirely around Slave's jazz-funk classic, 'Just A Touch Of Love (A Little Bit)'.

Produced and co-written again with Garibay (who would soon make his name as Lady Gaga's producer), 'One More Chance' became the third single from the album, and is arguably its most commercial track. Opening with a keyboard homage to Duran Duran's 'Save A Prayer', it breaks into an infectious, sunshine house, with will.i.am finally rapping at full stadium strength. As he pleads for another opportunity with his lover, she agrees on the grounds that he should protect their love. Influenced musically by what will.i.am heard while touring in Europe, the song is one of the very few on *Songs About Girls* that actually feels as if it could be part of a Black Eyed Peas record. A video was shot by arty LA production house collective Self Aviary, who shot the clip entirely on a Nokia N93i camera phone in LA. will.i.am sings to his love, who is on the opposite side of the road to him. As he crosses, he is hit by a Dodge, but then rewinds the footage to give himself another chance. Its homespun guerilla-style feel and its added-on graphics thoroughly enhance the track. It is little surprise that it was also used as a Nokia commercial. Even with this innovative approach to filmmaking to support it, the record only reached number 97 in the UK chart and failed to make the US charts at all.

'Invisible' uses a Prince-like drum sample and again produces another crepuscular, downbeat groove. Co-written and produced with old-school LA rapper Paperboy (Mitchell Johnson) and also with the assistance of the Bullets production team (will.i.am had been executive producer on their member Spitfiya's album), it is acoustic guitar-driven soft rock, which again deals with the wreckage of a failed romance. No matter what will.i.am does, he appears simply invisible to his lover. It falls in line with his statement that the album was about "love, heartache, but not regret, because I learned from it, but I apologise for breaking her heart and she broke my heart, but I forgive her". The vocal effects of the chorus of 'she can't see me' work well, but it can't disguise the fact that it is not one of the greatest tracks on the album. will.i.am said that this song, alongside 'Heartbreaker' and 'One More Chance', were all intensely personal and that he wasn't prepared to give them away to other artists.

'Fantastic' however, is, um, fantastic. It highlights will.i.am's magpie production tendencies. Undoubtedly inspired by his ongoing work with Michael Jackson, the song utilises David T. Walker's lazy, sunshine-infused guitar figure from the Jackson 5's 1969 debut hit 'I Want You Back'. With it, he creates another repetitive infectious pop classic. Reflecting again on the doomed relationship that runs throughout the album, will.i.am reminds his ex-lover that he is doing so well, he's fantastic. It teeters along a tightrope of unbearable self-pity, and is the musical equivalent of an ex-partner losing weight and having a new hairdo to suggest that everything is OK after a break-up. Yet will.i.am's lethargic delivery undermines his words.

'Fly Girl' begins with George Pajon Jr. strumming electric guitar chords, before Keith Harris' live drums kick in. Again, it looks at faithfulness in a relationship, with will.i.am stressing that he doesn't wish for anybody other than his lover, no matter how many pretty girls come around and tempt him. There is a brief minute-and-a-half of the sleek groove and grinding electric guitar of 'Dynamite Interlude'. It is one of the album's most successful tracks and slithers away just as interest is gathering. Again produced by Polow Da Don, the following 'Ain't It Pretty' is a work of staggering accomplishment; it's hard to believe it's almost thrown away on this album. Over a beautiful, languid summer groove, it has layered vocals and guitar, sounding like something that will.i.am would have delivered for the BBE label half a decade earlier.

The rap in 'Make It Funky' is very reminiscent of DJ Casper's 'Cha Cha Slide'. A moderately insubstantial, relentlessly uptempo groove with synthesized horns, beatboxing and a vocal from will.i.am's protégé Marii G, it comes and goes without any great élan. It again falls into will.i.am's growing repertoire of ready-to-party songs, requesting that the DJ make the night's records funky. The tempo changes for album closer 'SOS (Mother Nature)', which featured a sample of the Steve Gadd-performed drum track from Paul Simon's '50 Ways To Leave Your Lover'. Out of context with the rest of the album, this eco-friendly tune was inspired by the request for the Black Eyed Peas to play the Live Earth concert in London, and it was performed at the show, under its working title, 'Help Us Out'. With its clipped guitar played by old Peas cohort Ray Brady, will.i.am bemoans the state of the planet, saying the new threat for the world was 'the weather'. *Rolling Stone* voted it 12th in their list of '15 Corniest Pro-Environment Songs', saying that "will.i.am's brooding (if occasionally less than fluid) rhymes do have a respectable snap of urgency. The drum part lifted from Paul Simon's '50 Ways To Leave Your Lover' is less effective, as is the equal-opportunity praying to Jesus, Buddha, Mohammad and basically everyone but L. Ron."

There were two fairly inconsequential bonus cuts added to the UK edition of the CD. 'Spending Money' is an uptempo rap about lavishing money on a lover, while 'Mamma Mia' ends the disc with an overt nod to 'Gold Digger' by Kanye West. Whereas West used 'I Gotta Woman', 'Mamma Mia' uses a sample of Ray Charles' 'What'd I Say.' And like West's track, it is fairly irresistible because of the strength of the original track, with a primitive drum machine and a loud electric guitar.

will.i.am said that he was "really excited and nervous at the same time" about the release, which he described as "painting emotions about the past". *Songs About Girls* received an exceptionally mixed press, especially as will.i.am was now synonymous with grand, tricksy productions and the, at times, undercooked feel left reviewers scratching their heads. While *Rolling Stone* said, "*Songs About Girls* isn't a hip-hop record, but a pop R&B album of mellow head-nodders that veer between chilled-out soul and lite-electro funk," the BBC argued that, "Hardcore Black Eyed Peas fans will consider this a useful form of escapism but casual users will be left disappointed. The soulless record would have benefited from will.i.am tapping up contributors from his extensive list of heavyweight contacts and adding some bite to its bark." *Entertainment Weekly* was suitably unimpressed: "Still, by naming the album as he did, will.i.am draws attention to the fact that the 'girls' of whom he sings are, in his most generous estimation, gossamer ideals to be pined over after he breaks their hearts in unspecified ways. Primarily, though, they are steady-shimmying, modern-day Hottentot Venuses in need of badonkadonk appraisal."

While *Slant* magazine approved of his dabbling with a variety of styles, especially the Euro-house of what was to come for the Black Eyed Peas, it concluded that, "Unfortunately, will.i.am's lyrics are almost appallingly bad enough to retract my impending endorsement of the album. Evidently, his mama never told him that lines like "I know you want more than a dick in ya" aren't exactly the kinds of things that make girls with 'beautiful buns' swoon." *Vibe* magazine was scathing: "With a thin vocal range and punchy delivery, will sings and raps his way through half-baked funk vamps like 'She's A Star', failing to effectively update the sizzling '*Thriller*'-isms to which he's clearly in thrall." Importantly, the album did not create any huge single successes.

will.i.am undertook an interview with *The Observer* in which he opened up a little about his personal life and outlined just what kind of ladies' man he was: "These days I'm a masseuse and a cook. Then I become a cuddler, and a spooner. I'm a conversationalist. I just like to talk – to have random conversations about odd things, like dance music and jogging. If you don't talk about a girl's interests, then forget it. You need to inspire them to achieve all the things they want to achieve. As well as just saying, 'You look hot today'. And in a good relationship, time is nothing. You've got to always keep your phone on, you've got to get Skype, get a webcam, get MSN, get Yahoo; get 'em all. You know? So you're always available. That's hot. And you've got to try your hardest not to lie. But you can't say you're never going to, because then you're lying."

*Songs For Girls* was to have additional online promotion. will.i.am had just become involved with Musicane, which was a 'widget' (an expandable screen) that was embedded in artists' websites as a means of selling product. It could be uploaded to fans' social networking pages and blogs and, although his record label was involved, will.i.am looked to share monies earned from Musicane product sales with fans who embedded the store. will.i.am became the Head Of Marketing at Musicane and announced, "Musicane is a new platform where the artist has the ability to go straight to the user; from band to the fan, from the fan to the fan, no one in between... from me to you." will.i.am saw the album as an ongoing work that could be added to digitally. "If I have an album filled with songs about girls, what happens if tomorrow I write another song about a girl?" he said at the time of the album's release. "So something that started off just with 15 songs, in the next

10 years could have 100 songs. Having 12 songs on a record? That day is done."

Even with this new development, although reaching the Top 10 in Russia, *Songs About Girls* only made number 38 in the *Billboard* Top 100, which considering the number 14 placing for *Elephunk* and the number two position for both *Monkey Business* and *The Dutchess*, was disappointing. Although greater single success was achieved in the countries, *Songs About Girls* made only 58 and 68 respectively in Australia and the UK, the Black Eyed Peas' two key overseas markets. It was a great shame as, although flawed, it is one of the best works from the entire Peas output. The album feels somewhat unfinished, underplayed, with the tracks never really rising above sketches, albeit extremely interesting ones. The world wanted to see, and indeed, had become accustomed to will.i.am as the gregarious ringmaster, not the skulking malcontent. will.i.am mused on the album in 2010 at the time of the release of *The Beginning*. "It would have changed everything within the Black Eyed Peas if that album had been successful. Because that album did not succeed, it taught me what to do with the Peas and what not to do."

# Chapter 14

# Yes We Can:
# From Obama To X-Men

*"I was inspired by Obama, and when inspiration calls, you don't send it to voicemail; you answer it. You pick it up. You have a conversation with it."*
will.i.am, 2008

As it became clear that Barack Obama was in a good position to run for the presidency, will.i.am got behind his campaign after a long period of not discussing his politics. Travel had broadened his mind. "The spark was travelling outside America and seeing it from a distance, seeing the way people viewed us," will.i.am responded to a questionnaire in *Time* magazine. "America went from this beautiful country to 'Oh my gosh, you guys are so stupid.' But America tomorrow could still be the light of the world."

Inspired by Obama's progress, will.i.am recorded the song and its attendant video, 'Yes We Can', taking the speech that Obama made in defeat to Hillary Clinton in the New Hampshire Primary on January 8, 2008. will.i.am had been asked in 2007 if he would be interested in supporting Obama, but he wanted to see how the campaigns progressed before committing himself. He knew emphatically that he wanted a

Democrat in office. Taking Obama's speech as the background, will.i.am went into Ethernet and the Record Plant in LA on January 31 that year and recorded a variety of voices singing the phrase "yes we can" as well as a variety of lines from Obama's speech. "When I did it, it gave me the chills," will.i.am said. "I was inspired by Obama, and when inspiration calls, you don't send it to voicemail; you answer it. You pick it up. You have a conversation with it."

The video, directed by Jesse Dylan, with whom will.i.am had last worked on the Snickers 'Instant Def' digi-sodes, became a viral phenomenon. It featured a host of guest stars singing along to Obama's speech; from Scarlett Johansson to Herbie Hancock. John Legend, Common, Nicole Scherzinger and Eric Christian Olsen were also among the plethora of entertainers appearing in the video. By the end of February 2008, the clip had been watched 22 million times via all the various repostings through YouTube. The video gained a momentum all of its own: "The 'Yes We Can' video... It all came together like it was supposed to, like it was already destined to exist." will.i.am told *Time* magazine. "One person found out, told another person, and it all happened in four days. It was just a beautiful time. People were just pouring into the studio." The track was one of three that will.i.am contributed to the compilation album *Change Is Now: Renewing America's Promise*. His second track, 'We Are The Ones', was released as a video and single in February 2008

will.i.am was clearly on a roll in his support for Obama. When Obama was elected, will.i.am, like many African-Americans, was in a state of disbelief. Democrats had seen Al Gore 'win' in 2000 only to have the Florida count change how America would be run, ushering in George W. Bush. "It was a beautiful thing," will.i.am told Oprah Winfrey, after he had spent election night in Chicago. "I can't really explain it. I think of my grandma. I think of all the people who paved the way for that moment... like the invisibles who pushed the movement forward." He added later that, "Now that Obama's President, it changes inner-city youths. They can now not just dream to be Lil' Waynes and 50 Cents, but they can now dream to be Obamas. And that's dope." His final track from *Change Is Now: Renewing America's Promise*, 'It's A New Day', was released on November 8, 2008. will.i.am was asked what was the best thing that Obama ever said to him. He replied, "He told me that he likes my style and he likes the way that I dance."

will.i.am performed at one of the many inauguration events for Obama in January 2009 and then on February 25 that year he joined Tony Bennett, Diana Krall and many more in the presidential mansion's East Room for 'Stevie Wonder in Performance at the White House: The Library of Congress Gershwin Prize', when Obama presented Wonder with the Gershwin Award.

With his love, grasp and understanding of all facets of multi-media, it seemed inevitable that will.i.am would move into acting. A seasoned contributor to various soundtracks, he took part in two big-budget Hollywood blockbusters during 2008. Firstly, he voiced the hippopotamus Moto Moto in the animated DreamWorks blockbuster *Madagascar: Escape 2 Africa*. Directed by Eric Darnell and Tom McGrath, it featured the voices of Ben Stiller, Chris Rock, David Schwimmer and a cast of talented and well-known performers. It was the follow-up to 2005's box office success *Madagascar*.

The hippo, a neat parody of all the seventies soul love men with a low, gruff voice, meets Gloria (voiced by Jada Pinkett Smith), the main female hippo from the original film. After he performs his song, 'I Like 'Em Chunky', he sweet-talks Gloria: "You must be Moto Moto?" "The name's so nice when you say it twice". Melman the Giraffe (Schwimmer) is distraught because he secretly harbours feelings for Gloria, and the romance between her and Moto Moto is doomed when she realises he only wants to be with her for her large body. will.i.am got the nod for the role when Justin Timberlake recommended him to DreamWorks CEO Jeffrey Katzenberg. will.i.am had left a growly Barry White type voice on Timberlake's answering machine, and Timberlake, then voicing the part of Artie for the 2007 film *Shrek The Third,* told Katzenberg that he should think about using will.i.am in the future. Released in November 2008, *Madagascar: Escape 2 Africa* was a roaring success, and went on to top the US box office, and to date has grossed $603 million dollars from a budget of $150 million.

will.i.am also collaborated on the soundtrack to the film with established film composer Hans Zimmer. The soundtrack was released on November 8, 2008 and featured five new will.i.am tracks: the rocky 'The Travelling Song', the aforementioned hilarious parody 'I Like 'Em Chunky', the sweet calypso-influenced 'She Loves Me' and the sunshine pop singsong, 'Raindrops Keep Fallin' On My Head'-styled 'Best Friends'. He also sang the film's main song, 'I Like To Move It', the 1994 Erick Morillo-produced hit for Reel 2 Reel featuring The Mad Professor. The rest of the soundtrack was made up with Zimmer's score and classics such as 'More Than A Feeling' by Boston and 'Copacabana' by Barry Manilow.

'The Travelling Song' had a particular poignancy for will.i.am, as it conflated the life of animals taken away from their habitat with the nomadic lifestyle of a group out on the road. "It's about being stripped away from your home, and not knowing really where you come from," will.i.am told the *LA Times* in 2008. "But wherever you are – because of your friends – that is your home now. Those lyrics really sum up my life, a black guy in a Mexican neighbourhood, and apl.de.ap's life, being giving up for adoption at 14 and coming to America not knowing English. We made it our home because of our friendship, and that's what *Madagascar* is about." The soundtrack album was well-received and contained an appropriate amount of will.i.am's kid-friendly whimsy, further making the case for him as hip-hop's Paul McCartney.

Around the same time, will.i.am was approached by director Gavin Hood for a role in the next edition of the successful *X-Men* series. The film was to be a prequel to the three already released films, showing the early days of Hugh Jackman's ever-popular Wolverine character. will.i.am was delighted to be approached, being a fan of the Stan Lee-Jack Kirby Marvel cartoon series.

will.i.am was keen to stress his credentials when he met Christine King and Debra Zane, the film's casting directors. "I went to the casting right, and they asked me if I knew about X-Men," he said. "I was like, 'Pssh, I know X-Men.' They were like, 'Yeah, you know, you're gonna play a teleporter.' And I was like, 'You mean like Night Crawler?' 'Night Crawler wasn't a teleporter.' 'Yes he was a teleporter!

The dude was a teleporter! He would be on the walls, and he was in the Presidential office disappearing and people couldn't really hit him. He was like, disappearing, poof poof. I was like, 'Yo, I'm telling you, homey.' I'm a fan of *X-Men*."

Squabbles about teleportation aside, he was cast instead as John Wraith, aka Kestrel, a character that first appeared in the comics in 1991 in *X-Men Origins: Wolverine*. Kestrel had been part of the Team X project alongside Wolverine, Silver Fox, Mastodon, Maverick and Sabretooth. Something of a paranoid character, he had a love for explosives.

will.i.am was also delighted that his first major foray into film was not as a stereotypical character: "I love black films, I love 'em, but I want to see black films other than, like, barbecues, barber shops, and *Fridays*," he told MTV. "The fact that I'm in this film, that's super dope because you could've had me in a film, like, on a corner. I'm in a rap group. Cast him and have him play this thug, which is all great. But I'm saying as black people we need to do some other stuff. So I'm super, super, super, super blessed and proud to be a part of *Wolverine*." Filming began in Australia in early 2008. will.i.am got fully into the part; he showed an MTV reporter his scar, and stated that "I'm a newbie when it comes to big action films and stuff... It was my fight scene. I was real into it, and then I missed my mark, and I punched the camera and broke the lens!"

Released in April 2009, *X-Men Origins: Wolverine* received decidedly mixed reviews, yet performed strongly at the box office. The *Austin Chronicle* said, "If you're a longtime reader of the Marvel series, you'll likely laugh at Reynolds' portrayal of Deadpool, you'll dig will.i.am's Wraith, and you'll already know enough about Logan/Wolverine's back-and-front story to wonder how on earth an *X-Men* film could be so... bland." *The Guardian* said, "In these straitened times, Hollywood likes nothing better than a sure thing, so in creeps this frankly redundant fourth effort, purporting to tell us how Wolverine, aka Logan, got his metal skeleton and fancy retractable claws." UK film magazine *Empire* was also unkind, "Time is dedicated to rubbish mutants Wraith (rapper will.i.am) and The Blob (*Lost*'s Kevin Durand), who belong in another film or Sky1's *Gladiators*." The film grossed $373 million from a budget of $150 million. It was enough success to prove that the franchise still had its superpowers.

Something finally emerged from the ongoing will.i.am/Michael Jackson collaboration. For the 25th Anniversary Edition of *Thriller* that was released in February 2008, two extensive overhauls and mixes that will.i.am did for 'PYT' and 'The Girl Is Mine' were included. Adding a layer of insistent electronics to Quincy Jones' original production, both have additional raps from will.i.am. By far the most successful is 'The Girl Is Mine', which removes Paul McCartney's rather saccharine vocal and leaves Jackson's vocal and will.i.am's rap. The tracks gave further proof that will.i.am was the go-to producer and remixer, proven by his exhaustive work rate elsewhere. He worked extensively with Nicole Scherzinger on her debut solo album, Flo Rida, Estelle, Usher, Mariah Carey (who amused will.i.am by turning up to the studio 'late-on-time', being exactly the time that her people told him she'd be late and wearing a diamond dress after an awards ceremony), John Legend, SMAP and Usher.

will.i.am also found time to work again with Sergio Mendes for the album *Encanto*, after the success of their 2006 collaboration, *Timeless*. "*Encanto* is a beautiful word in Portuguese, which in Brazil means 'enchantment' or 'charm'," Mendes told *Blues and Soul*: "And I think it pretty much describes the music that's in the album – the beautiful melodies, the sensuality, the rhythms, the diversity... You know, going to Brazil to make this record, because I hadn't recorded there in a long time, brought a whole new vibe that's very different from the last album. Because, while Will at first went to Brazil with me – I felt taking him back to my roots was very important – he ended up having to go back to the States before we'd finished recording. So, with me then producing the rest of the album myself down there, it did bring a fresh, more Brazilian-oriented flavour to the party. You know, there's a very special, musically creative environment in Brazil which does inspire me tremendously." will.i.am and Mendes worked on a deeper, more traditional jazz and Latin album than the showmanship of *Timeless*.

In June 2008, a collection of will.i.am's productions was released only in Japan. *The Black Eyed Peas Family Best* was an intriguing 18-track CD round-up of his work in and outside of the Black Eyed Peas since 1998. It played like a précis of 00s chart R&B. Aside from the Black Eyed Peas, Fergie and material from *Songs About Girls*, it included tracks from Justin Timberlake, Nas, Common, Nicole Scherzinger, Mary J Blige and John Legend. He had the opportunity to work with U2, for whom he co-produced 'I'll Go Crazy If I Don't Go Crazy Tonight' for their forthcoming album *No Line On The Horizon*. Although will.i.am had been circumspect about this – every new U2 project is shrouded in a good deal of secrecy – Kanye West blogged "WILL I AM IS PRODUCING ON U2's NEXT ALBUM. I'M SURE IT WILL BE DOPE AS SHIT JUDGING FROM THE CRAZY BEATS HE'S DONE IN THE PAST 3 YEARS!" The result was one of the most critically well-received numbers on the album. will.i.am forged a close friendship with Bono. "Bono leads all the conversations," he told *Interview* magazine. "He's like the walking Wikipedia. Ask him anything and he'll tell you all about it. He's a wonderful dude. I had the Bono 'talk', hell yeah, and it was the first time I had Irish whiskey. That dude is the coolest."

Fergie also had the opportunity to work with director Rob Marshall and the ensemble cast of *Nine*, the musical remake of Fellini's legendary film *8 ½*. Fergie, playing alongside Daniel Day Lewis, Nicole Kidman and Judi Dench, plays the part of Saraghina, a prostitute whose speciality is introducing young men to the joys of sex. "She's almost animalistic," Fergie told *Allure* magazine. "She's not the sharpest tool in the shed, but she's very physical, just very intense... Saraghina is all woman." It was an interesting part, which she played in flashback, as she was the woman who introduced the film's principal character, film director Guido Contini, to sex, singing the song 'Be Italian'. She also had to gain 17 pounds to have the Mediterranean curves required for the part.

Taboo and apl.de.ap did not release the solo albums that will.i.am predicted to complete the full complement of individual BEP work. Both had other priorities: on July 12, 2008, Taboo married Jaymie Dizon in Pasadena, becoming the first group member to get married. will.i.am and apl.de.ap both served as his ushers. With his striking looks, it was obvious that he, too, should dabble in film. He'd played a small part in the 2007 independent film *Cosmic Radio*, and during 2008 he'd filmed a part in the Andrzej Bartkowiak film, *Street Fighter, The Legend Of Chun-Li*. Taboo played Vega in this franchised spin-off from the video game, which filmed in Thailand. Although the film was something of a failure at the box office on its release in June 2009, Taboo received positive notices that left the door ajar for future film roles. "Acting is my first love," Taboo told *IGN*. "If and when this music stuff settles down, that's what I want to do. You know, I'd like to do more action and even more challenging roles. My favourite actor is Johnny Depp, and he's all over the board – it's like he can play anyone. That's what I'd see myself as."

Taboo had finally found an inner calm, away from the crutches of drugs and alcohol that had supplemented his success. He and Jaymie have two children together to date, a boy, Jalen, born on July 19, 2009 and a daughter, Journey, born in April 2011. This gave him the stability he required and he ensured that the children would enjoy a more settled relationship with their father than his eldest son, Joshua, who was born in October 1993, when Taboo was a struggling 17-year-old dancer.

apl.de.ap worked tirelessly for his home country. In 2008, he established the apl Foundation, to give back and support children throughout the Philippines and Asia. Affiliated to the Peapod Foundation, it focused on education, culture and environment. The programme's initial aims were to provide computers to schools, look at creating an international Filipino network and to protect the environment. "Through the apl Foundation, I will be able to give back to my community back in the Philippines." apl.de.ap said. "The Foundation's aims were simple: that there... be no separation between gender, class or race, and that all children deserve homes, food, education and healthcare. The AF would select new projects on a yearly basis, and some of the money raised was to be set aside as a contingency for disaster relief." apl.de.ap worked hard at building his Foundation. It was also at this time that tragedy struck again for apl.de.ap when his younger and favourite half brother, Joven Pineda Deala, was shot dead in Porac, Pampanga.

On January 10, 2009, Fergie marrried Josh Duhamel after a year-long engagement. It was, according to *Marie Claire*, a "lavish gardenia-and-crystal studded ceremony" at the Church Estates vineyard in Malibu. It was a suitably star-studded affair, too. Aside from her fellow Peas, among the 367 guests were Kate Hudson, Slash, Kid Rock and Duhamel's *Las Vegas* co-star James Caan. The event gained huge attention from the celebrity paparazzi, to the extent that the photographers' helicopters circling overhead shook the chandeliers in their wedding marquee. The pair opened the dancing with the 1994 Rolling Stones track 'Sweethearts Together'. "It's funny," she told *Marie Claire* soon after, "because at work I have to be a very strong, tough. woman. But when I'm with him, I just turn on this baby girl voice because... he's my big tall man!"

Elsewhere on the domestic front, on will.i.am's 34th birthday in March 2009, he bought his grandmother a house as he had done for his mother before her, so she could move out of the Estrada Projects. Filmed for the Oprah Winfrey television programme, it shows his grandmother and will.i.am overcome with emotion as he takes her to her new smart, detached house. will.i.am's family remained at the absolute heart of everything he did.

But he also had a lot of work to finish. will.i.am had, of course, been busy working on material for the next Black Eyed Peas' masterwork. While working in Europe and Australia he'd become seduced by the big, glitzy techno that he'd heard in local clubs and that hadn't quite ignited in his home country. It gave him ideas and inspiration that the other Peas eagerly and happily took on board. With a working title of *From Roots To Fruits*, the first musical hints at this inspiration on *Songs About Girls* would now wholeheartedly be developed.

# Chapter 15

# Construct It As Architecture: The E.N.D

*"I'm so caught up in the raw essence of how hard the beats are now. Right now, we're in this edgy electro space. We're taking it back to the days of Afrika Bambaataa sampling Kraftwerk to the Jungle Brothers when they did 'Girl I'll House You' to Technotronic's 'Pump Up The Jam'. That's what we're reliving – the late 80s, early 90s hip-hop."*

Taboo, *Entertainment Weekly*, 2009

*"2008 was an interesting year. I was filming X-Men, campaigning for Obama, dedicating a lot of my time to inspire the youth to go out and vote, and now in 2009, he's president. And then, all the while when I was doing that I was going out to... electro underground dance clubs. And now we have the biggest record in the world. That's pretty crazy if you think about it."*

will.i.am, 2009

Alongside Beyoncé's ambitious double CD *I Am... Sasha Fierce*, few albums encapsulated the feel of late 00s party and paranoia as *The E.N.D (The Energy Never Dies)*. With this album, the group really flew at its audience. The album was recorded in a variety of studios between

Ethernet and Jeepney Music in LA, Square Prod studios in France and again at Metropolis in West London. The original *From Roots To Fruits* had become *The E.N.D*, its title a homage to Leaders Of The New School's *T.I.M.E. – The Inner Mind's Eye,* the album which included 'Bass Is Loaded', the sample for which 2003's 'Let's Get It Started' was based. It was as much a critique of the current state of the music industry as it was a music release; every track was made available as a single-track download as well as being released as a physical album.

Musically, it was influenced squarely by what will.i.am had heard in Europe and Australia, a love affair that started with Fedde Le Grand's techno-heavy club and chart smash from 2006, 'Put Your Hands Up For Detroit'. will.i.am talked about the album as early as 2007, when on the *Black, Blue And You Tour* he was telling an interviewer in Stockholm that the music – at that point the bones of the instrumentals – would be the sort of music that you would play if you'd just robbed a bank and wanted to drive the getaway car at full speed. When sessions began, the group were refreshed and ready to work again; Fergie spoke of the joy of the four of them and their team being together in the studio again.

After recording the majority of the album at LA's Record Plant with Padraic 'Padlock' Kerin, will.i.am worked with engineer Dylan '3D' Dresdow to create the album's unique sound. Although there had been no plans to do any additional recording, Dresdow made sonic suggestions to will.i.am that he gladly incorporated into the mix. "I think Will's main vision is for *The E.N.D* to be a little like a DJ spinning records in a nightclub," Dresdow told *Sound On Sound*. "DJs don't stop in between songs, they keep the music going, non-stop. So *The E.N.D* is sequenced in a certain way, with short or no spaces between the songs. Will also was really adamant that he wanted it to be on a par with many of the electro-influenced sounds that are out there now. The main bass in 'Boom Boom Pow' is an 808, for instance, there's no bass guitar or keyboard bass. As a mix engineer, I had to treat some elements in very unique ways."

It was imperative to will.i.am that the album was absolutely right, that it had a unity of sound and wasn't dogged by the extreme eclecticism of *Elephunk* and *Monkey Business*. "There really was no final stage that one would call the mix stage with any of the songs on *The E.N.D*," Dresdow continued. "We jumped around until the very last hour. We even did tweaks to songs after they came back from mastering!" Dresdow also gave a fascinating insight into how will.i.am works: "will.i.am is travelling quite a lot – one day he's with Oprah Winfrey, the next with Bill Clinton – so instead of sending him MP3 mixes I can use Source Element's Source-Live. It's a plug-in that broadcasts audio over the Internet. Let's say Will was sitting in a green room before doing an interview with Oprah, and there's a change he wants me to do. I send him a link, and he clicks on it, puts in his password, and he can listen to the mix, hopefully on a decent set of speakers or headphones. With artists that are often on the road, it's impossible for them to always be in the room with you. It's a godsend for international collaboration."

This new music, which was the spirit of international collaboration itself, came as a shock on first hearing. In the UK, initial reaction from Peas-watchers was muted. The frenzied house beats had been well-known to European ears for many years and represented little that was new. For a group so associated with a mix of hip-hop, funk and increasingly pop, it seemed too radical, and arguably a retrograde direction for the group to be travelling in. However, first impressions were misleading, for when the tracks are heard over and over again, some profound depth charge within becomes embedded in your brain and creates that deeply familiar, hands-in-the-air vibe.

The album sounds incredibly progressive, and although not making any claims for parity in stature, *The E.N.D* could be as influential to the next generation as Kraftwerk were in the past. Asked what the future held for the Black Eyed Peas at this time, will.i.am responded with: "Better question: what does the future hold for music as a whole? If I tell my seven-year-old cousin when she's older, 'Hey, you know Virgin?' She'll be like, 'Yeah, I'm still a virgin.' She's not going to know that at one point in time Virgin was a record store, because everything is changing. The future of the Black Eyed Peas is to wrestle with the state of the declining music industry and make content that lends itself to different formats." And different formats were exactly where the

171

group were at. Even on the record, a disembodied voice suggests that, "There is no longer a physical record store." The album was all about the possibilities for music in this new age.

The group loved the title of *The E.N.D*, partially as a dig to all of those who thought they were about to break up. "There was a lot of speculation that the Black Eyed Peas had broken up when Fergie did her own thing, when Will did his own thing and me and apl did our own thing," Taboo told *liveDaily.com*. "We just ran with it. It was so funny because people were always saying we had broken up because we did solo projects. So we thought, "Why don't we entitle the album *The E.N.D* so people will talk about it and be like, 'Oh, this is the end of the Black Eyed Peas'. No, it's not the end of the Black Eyed Peas. It's the end of the rumour that we had just broken up."

The deeper meaning was one of intense reflection on the seismic shifts within the music industry. "It's also the end of the era of music," Taboo continued. "Before, here in the US, you were able to go to Sam Goody, Virgin Megastore. Those places don't exist any more. It's the end of going to a CD store and getting a tangible CD. Now, you have to go online or to Best Buy to get it. We felt like it's the end of that era. Where there's an end, though, there's a beginning."

Taboo expanded upon this theory for *beatweek.com*: "*The E.N.D* is the end of an era as far as conventional ways of selling music... the days of going to get a tangible CD and having that in your hand... You have iTunes and all these different programs on the internet that will take you into a different way of looking at promoting your record, and how to get your record out there. It's not just about having a CD no more, it's also about creating components on the internet or on our site dipdive. com so that we're not just giving people the CD, we're actually creating opportunities for people to remix songs and to upload different ideas and content."

The first music from the new album, 'Boom Boom Pow', was just, um, weird. Released to iTunes on March 30, 2009, there really had been little like it in mainstream pop before. Written by the group and produced by will.i.am with long-term associates Jean Baptiste Kouame and Poet Name Life, it was inspired by will.i.am's voracious appetite for the new. "That's a fusion of Miami bass, Chicago house, and European zombie music," he said in 2009. "That was inspired by... the whole electro scene in Australia – that breakdown. I was like, 'Dude, I want to have a song with not a lot of words.' I just want a beat. That's the hardest thing to do, is minimalism, when you have to take away and still make it feel full. Anybody can put a whole bunch of stuff on a plate. But how do you put the right things on the plate where you're not hungry afterward? That's the hardest thing to do. Anybody can take an elephant and put it in the room and fill it up. But how do you put a chair and a table in a big room and have it look finished? With 'Boom Boom Pow' that's what I tried to do. Construct it as architecture, with its own space. It's more sound design that it is traditional song structure."

will.i.am stated at the time that he made the song purely for underground clubs. Had he been aiming at the radio, he would have made it differently. The track is minimal, skeletal even, with a nagging, robotic beat, a reliance on Auto-Tune and a repetition of the phrase 'gotta get get'. It features all of the members of the group trading verses. When you consider the ornate-plus kitchen-sink productions of *Monkey Business*, there's hardly anything to it. It also features one of Fergie's most gutsy vocal performances on record so far. will.i.am's rap extols the virtues of satellite radio, which caused some conventional channels to edit this section out. With a synthesizer solo that sounds like a Theremin, and a whooshing, rushing noise at its close, in one sense, it never really gets fully underway, but in another grooves like little you've heard before.

The single raced to the top of the US charts. After its new entry in March at number 71, it then shot up from number 39 to number one and stayed at the top of the chart for 12 weeks. It sold 465,000 downloads in its first week of digital release and seemed very much an anthem for its time in the digital age. It gave the group their first UK chart-topper since 'Where Is The Love' in 2003. Owing a great deal in style and feel to Afrika Bambaataa's 1982 anthem 'Planet Rock' (itself basically Kraftwerk and hip-hop blended), it smuggled techno fully into the US mainstream. Its call for moving forward lyrically and musically struck a chord.

Its video, directed by Mathew Cullen and Mark Kudsi, was all computer graphics and robotic dancers swathed in green neon suits, which looked as if they had been inspired by the outfits worn by Kraftwerk during the encores on their 2004 world tour. In fact, the video can be seen as a homage to Kraftwerk's 1986 video, 'Music Non Stop'. It is set in 3008, the date mentioned by Fergie in the record, and finds Taboo scrolling through negative images such as a gun and a mushroom cloud, which are turned into positives as the promo progresses. A computer head, which was to be the cover of *The E.N.D*, is seen throughout – it is an amalgam of the faces of the four Black Eyed Peas.

"It's just amazing. The fact that 'Boom Boom Pow' took off blows me away because it's such a left-field song," Taboo told *Artist Direct*. "If you think about our previous work, it's very different. We came out with 'Where Is The Love' and it was a phenomenal monster, but 'Boom Boom Pow' is so different from what people have heard from us that it was even a bigger monster than we ever imagined it would be."

Released on June 9, 2009 on the head of steam created by 'Boom Boom Pow', the album's second single truly rammed home the new message of the Black Eyed Peas. This seemed now like a completely different group under the same name. 'I Gotta Feeling' was more than just a single or anthem; it became almost an unavoidable worldwide behemoth. It was written by the group with DJ David Guetta and French house producer Frédéric Riesterer, who for purposes of the LA and world music scene was known under the somewhat less Gallic soubriquet of Fred Rister. It samples the electronic pulse from Rister and Joachim Garraud's remix of 'Love Is Gone', the 2007 record Guetta made with US pop gospel singer Chris Willis. But this song is no mere rendition of a rap over an extended sample. The team twisted and turned the original to create something altogether new, a commercial realisation of the grind and bleep of 'Boom Boom Pow'. "I met David Guetta at Ibiza," will.i.am told *The LA Times*. "I had a gig at Pacha on a Friday and went to his gig on a Thursday and met him there... and that's how it all came together. And, actually, it was our first true band/DJ collaboration – no middleman, no management."

174

David Guetta was a huge fan of the group and was more than happy to collaborate. "Will is a really big producer and he could have taken a bit of that sound and incorporated it in his music," he told *HipHopDX*. "Instead of [that], he called me and went like 100% for it... It's [got an] insane guitar sound, and I came with a little bit similar [sound]. I sent him a few tracks, and he selected some of them and then I went to the studio to finish with him." Guetta knew an enormous hit record when he heard one and was full of admiration for the set-up: "When [will.i.am sings] 'I got a feeling,' it's like a hook on a hook. It's crazy... it's just perfect, and I think also the fact that they came with something so positive, you know, probably in a difficult time. That's a big element of such a huge hit. I think people needed a little bit of that positive message. In the music I make, it's always very positive, so it was just perfect. And, you know, working together, we were like screaming, dancing, going crazy in the studio because we were feeling like kids, you know because we're so different, but at the same time, it was making so much sense."

'I Gotta Feeling' *was* different. It did not course with any deep or hidden meaning. It was a simple call to arms for the party faithful. will.i.am wrote on his dipdive blog in May 2009 that the song was "dedicated to everyone who is getting ready to go out. It's the song to listen to when you drive to the club or party. It's the song to listen to after a long day or week at work. It's the song that makes me wanna throw my stress away... tonite's gonna be a good good nite." This was made explicit across the variety of remixes that accompanied the single, such as Guetta's own FMIF mix (his club brand, 'Fuck Me, I'm Famous'), Laidback Luke's and Printz Board's own mix. If it was hard not to like it, it was simply harder to ignore it. *The LA Times* said, "It's reminiscent of the Five Stairsteps' soul classic 'Ooh Child', emulating that song's use of a repetitive, warm vocal line to signify a good mood coming on. That sunlight-coloured hook is interrupted by silly raps; by the time Will and his mates are shouting 'Mazel Tov!' it's impossible to begrudge the high."

will.i.am expanded on the single on the eve of its release for *Marie Claire* magazine: "It's dedicated to all the party people out there in the world that want to go out and party. Mostly every song on the Black Eyed Peas record is painting a picture of our party life. It was a conscious decision to make this type of record. Times are really hard for a lot of people and you want to give them escape and you want to make them feel good about life, especially at these low points."

Its video caused some controversy by seemingly being an advert for going out and getting drunk, as well as containing scenes of overt lesbianism. Directed by Ben Mor and Mikey Mee, the clip centres on the group getting ready for a night out on Hollywood Boulevard. The video starts with three girls heading towards a party; then we see the Black Eyed Peas about to do the same. apl and Taboo check their messages, will.i.am combs his 'fro; Fergie smoothes her legs and squeezes into her bra, and then we are off to the party. Taboo and will.i.am are frequently seen suspended in mid air. At two and a half minutes there is a passionate lesbian kiss, and soon after we see Fergie using a feather duster on a masculine-looking woman.

As the beat builds, the room of party goers – which includes friends and stars Katy Perry, David Guetta and Kid Cudi – start daubing themselves in fluorescent paint. The video ends with the three girls we saw in the first frames stumbling out into the night, looking exactly like the teenagers that are shown as examples of the effects of alcohol, prone on inner-city pavements. In some respects, the video was like a behavioural manual for a certain type of youth.

The record went to number one on the US charts on July 11, 2009, replacing their 'Boom Boom Pow' which had been at the top spot for 12 weeks. They became only the fifth group in US chart history to do so, joining a select club of the Beatles, Boyz II Men, OutKast, Usher and T.I. The record remained at the top of the charts for 14 weeks, meaning the Black Eyed Peas were the biggest-selling group in the US for precisely half of 2009. It gave them their second UK number one of the year as well, becoming the first single ever to sell a million in download sales alone. Martin Talbot, the head of the UK's Official Charts Company, described the feat as a landmark that "represents a coming of age for digital downloading, six years after music downloading moved into the UK mainstream... and underlines the enduring, and growing, popularity of legitimate digital music today." The group had learned so much since their Napster experience back in 2000.

With two killer fanfares such as these, there was a great deal of anticipation for *The E.N.D*, the group's first album in nearly four years. Understandably opening with 'Boom Boom Pow', signifying their new direction, the album is an hour of cutting-edge dance, with unmistakable Black Eyed Peas touches. Before 'Boom Boom Pow' there is a computerized voice welcoming the listener to the project – "Welcome To *The E.N.D*. Do not panic. There is nothing to fear. Everything around you is changing. Nothing stays the same. This version of myself is changing. Tomorrow I will be different. The Energy Never Dies... This is the end and the beginning."

Recorded in Paris and at Metropolis (where virtually all of Fergie's vocals for the album were recorded), 'Rock That Body' is another Guetta/ will.i.am production. Although it charts more conventional territory, it stays very much with its French/Euro house flavour, featuring wild Auto-Tune, with Fergie sounding akin to Alvin The Chipmunk, and filtered breakdowns. It borrows the breakdown from Rob Base and DJ EZ Rock's 'It Takes Two', as well as elements of Lyn Collins' 'Think About It'. *Spin* said, "Regardless, the Peas keep it exuberantly funky. Witness the trance-y 'Rock Your Body', which sounds like would-be stripper music for suburban Bratz doll collectors." It became the fifth single to be taken from the album in January 2010, and gave the group a Top 10 US hit. *Digital Spy* summed up the exuberance of the track: "It's got plenty of pounding beats, synths that sound like they've been filled with Red Bull and more twisted vocal effects than an MP3 of Akon cutting loose in a vocoder factory."

'Meet Me Halfway' was an enormous hit single that followed up the techno punch of the album's debut releases. It was more of a straightforward 'song' than 'Boom Boom Pow' and 'I Gotta Feeling', but still had enough strangeness coursing through it. It is like a track from *Songs About Girls* finished off with a proper tune. The tune was very special to will.i.am. He wrote on his dipdive blog that "this song is dedicated to lovers in relationships that have sacrificed so much... love hurts... and love makes you crazy... but love will only last for ever when you make it last... listen to the lyrics on this song... it's about compromise, dedication, responsibility, effort, and of course, dreams...love is nothing without dreams...in this song the woman in love has gone as far as she could for love...and she needs her man to meet her halfway." Fergie's emotive vocal channelled her childhood: "I transported myself back to 1985, when I was 11 and saw Madonna in concert for the first time on the Virgin tour. I took on her persona in that song as a homage." It's true: Fergie evokes the frothy pop spirit of not just Madonna: there are echoes of Debbie Harry and Cyndi Lauper in there as well.

Although swathed in synthetics, it is one of the foremost acoustic tracks on the album, with all four members of Bucky Jonson playing. It was co-written by the group with Jean Baptiste and Sylvia Gordon. Gordon was signed to Downtown Music, the publishing house that handled the Black Eyed Peas' songs. She was from the New York trio Kudu, who'd recently written for Moby. The record starts with Fergie before, unusually, apl. de.ap takes the lead vocal, before will.i.am and Taboo appear. Discernible in the mix is a soupcon of the guitar and drum parts of 'Maps' by New York post-punk group the Yeah Yeah Yeahs.

will.i.am oversaw the artwork for the single release. The picture of a road leading into space was supposed to depict two people travelling on "the path of love". One takes the road and the other, the stars. They have to meet in the middle, which is reflected in the promo for the song. Directed by Ben Mor, it contains more fantasy than the futurism of its predecessors. That said, it does involve will.i.am riding an elephant on a moon of Venus, and Taboo orbiting the sun. The main story involves all three men, who appear to be potential suitors, trying to get to meet their love on earth. apl.de.ap levitates on a desert planet, dressed as a Bedouin, and Fergie, the only one not in a far-off galaxy, appears as some kind of flower-nymph in a wooded glade. 'Meet Me Halfway' was released as a single in September 2009 and topped the charts in the UK and Australia, and reached number seven in the US charts, giving the group three Top 10 hits in a row.

The fourth single from the album, 'Imma Be', was again strange as it mutates from hip-hop into a strand of mid eighties funk. Co-produced with Bucky Jonson drummer Keith Harris, it is based on a sample of 'Ride Or Die' from Staten Island Daptone-signed funk revivalists, the Budos Band. It also manages to be a four-minute track that feels as if it's been on for about an hour. It starts as a slow drum-machine and vocoder-led number with Fergie dominating the vocals. It suddenly shifts gear into a full-on stomping sensation. *Slant Magazine* suggested, "Halfway through, the pulse gets an upgrade, the tempo hustles up to a strut, the rudimentary synth hits explode into a chunky-funky rush, and before you know it, will.i.am has transformed a deliberately lazy self-parody into a heated club-floor burner."

And it does what *Slant* says – and just as attention has been grabbed it peters out. That said, it mattered not and gave the group their third number one from the album in the US. will.i.am keeps his rap topical when he refers to the then recently collapsed Lehman Brothers bank, the first domino that had fallen as the world raced towards economic turmoil. He suggests that if he were a bank, he would be "loaning out semen". In many ways the track emphasises that no matter how many bleeps and pings or how much will.i.am's rapping, it is Fergie's album. *The LA Times* said about Fergie's performance: "Whether she's being weepy in 'Meet Me Halfway' or superbad in 'Imma Be', she takes her part to its logical end. Her obviousness once seemed to reflect a lack of skill, but by now it's clear that it's a strategy. As a means of grabbing attention from a hopelessly distracted audience, it works." Fergie, strengthened by her solo success, now seemed invincible within the group. All four were fully firing, a situation no doubt enhanced by all four members enjoying four-way writing credits on every track.

The video for 'Imma Be' encapsulated the Black Eyed Peas' retro-futurism perfectly. Filmed on January 10, 2010 in Lancaster, California and directed again by Rich Lee, it is set in the desert, and opens with Fergie lying prone next to a motorbike on the road. An iguana's eye blinks in time to the repeated use of the phrase 'Imma Be'. In the distance we see a city. Could it be Oz? With her long train billowing behind her in the wind, and in a silver-plated swimsuit, sun visor and silver ankle boots, Fergie begins her march towards the city. She is also wearing a silver-plated 'roboglove', not at all dissimilar to the one designed by Lorraine Schwartz for Beyoncé for the 'Single Ladies (Put A Ring On It)' promo.

It is a full minute before we see any other members of the group: she goes into a diner where will.i.am is repeatedly pouring a drink, as if stuck in a loop. As she enters the diner, however, a *Predator*-style monster descends from space. The setting is classic fifties B-movie. The pair get into a jet- powered hover car and take off towards the city, with the monster in tow. They arrive at an apocalyptic trailer park, where they meet apl.de.ap at a computer, seemingly monitoring monsters. As another monster assembles itself from the junk in the trailer park, it is joined by eight other smaller robots that appear to be made out of speakers. However, if the junk monster appears benign, he and his strange metallic crew begin dancing in time. Taboo's torso is found strewn among the junk, and the trio locate his legs to put him back together. The group continue their walk to the city with the dancing robots following, watched over by the gaze of the original monster. This ultramodern mumbo-jumbo helped the single reach the US top spot, thus making the group the first act since Wilson Phillips in 1990/91 to have three number one singles from the same album.

The rush of 'I Gotta Feeling' continues the breathless standard of *The E.N.D.* Before moving any further, the listener has just enjoyed five stellar hit singles. This front-loading means that the rest of the album suffers somewhat by comparison, but little matter – the Black Eyed Peas' stall is firmly set out – this new formula works. 'Alive' is a lower tempo moment, with will.i.am singing the chorus and Fergie emulating her vocal line from 'My Humps'. With Josh Lopez on guitar and Caleb Speir on bass, it sounds as if it is a leftover from *Songs About Girls*. will.i.am's Auto-Tuned vocal sounds like Daft Punk's 'One More Time'. "'Alive' is a song about love," will.i.am wrote on his blog. "It's about a relationship... when the person makes you feel new. When the one you love makes you feel like nothing negative in the world matters." It is cute, un–gimmicky, and maintains the quality established on the album.

'Missing You' is another Fergie showcase – a downbeat love song, co-written with Printz Board and Jean Baptiste, it rattles along at a breezy pace, complete with computerized breakdown. Despite its futurism, it's a classic lovesick song. The protagonists may be living the high life but they are apart and no material gains can substitute for their love. Released as a promotional single, 'Missing You' became an airplay hit in France.

Joined to 'Missing You' by a synthesizer riff, 'Ring-A-Ling' is minimalist hip-hop about a booty call. With all four members rapping, it could be the continuation of the previous song, talking about phone sex across the miles. Produced by Keith Harris, the synthesizer motif becomes a little distracting as the song progresses. After these moments of introspection, we begin to head back to the dance floor for 'Party All The Time', which looks at the possibilities of living a hedonistic lifestyle 24/7. Its anthemic chorus is reminiscent of one of will.i.am's recent production charges, U2. The group want to party 'like Ibiza', but they 'don't need no visa'. The song owes a debt to Adam Freeland's 'Mancry' from his 2009 album, *Cope*, which was initially uncredited on *The E.N.D*'s sleeve. Again, the song changes mood towards the end with a vocal breakdown. Had the album not had such a welter of commercial riches, this would have made a perfect single – with Fergie stating, in a southern accent, that she feels tipsy at the song's close, it leads seamlessly into 'Out Of My Head'.

When Caleb Speir's bass leads the track off, it comes as a great relief to hear an acoustic instrument. Again reflecting a party night out, 'Out Of My Head' sounds like some great lost early eighties groove classic – owing something to T.M. Stevens' bass part on Narada Michael Walden's 1979 disco classic, 'I Shoulda Loved Ya'. Fergie is clearly about to lose it, and wishes to have a wild party night; she's hitting the bar to drink vodka and Red Bull. When she mentions the phrase 'steppin' out', some very Kool and The Gang-type horns come in, and will.i.am's otherworldly rap references 'Gypsy Woman' by Crystal Waters. Sampling Dave Barbarossa's drum pattern from the 1982 hit 'I Want Candy' by Bow Wow Wow, 'Electric City' is heavily synthesized ragga, which manages to namecheck serial killer Jeffrey Dahmer, dildos and UK dubmaster The Mad Professor.

'Showdown' is another rap-led song emphasising the role of the group

– to get the audiences ready for the showdown that the group are about to bring to the world. Produced by apl and DJ Replay, it actually has quite a tender vocal line amid all of the slamming machines. The Black Eyed Peas' wholly capitalist message is inserted as the song closes as a celebration and a warning – while lauding the energy of youth (the most powerful force on the planet, no less), it can stimulate the economy but if it decides not to buy things, what will happen? The author's message couldn't be clearer – stealing music (as had happened to the group with *Bridging The Gap* in 2000 and also more recently with an early leak of 'Boom Boom Pow') is not the way forward. This leads into the straightforward rock/punk 'Now Generation', which was called by *Slant* magazine, "calculatedly crass pop-cultural-cum-garbage disposal word-slinging... an admittedly tongue-in-cheek but still unremittingly vapid name-check on MySpace, Facebook, Google, Wikipedia, Macs, and PCs." It talks about kids getting exactly what they want, when they want it, somewhat ironic for a group who have repeatedly aligned themselves with the forefront of technology and luxury consumer products. With a Prodigy-like vocal from both will.i.am and Fergie, it gave the group a remarkable opportunity to rock out on the tour that was to support the album.

As the album comes to a close, there is room still for their now customary 'Where Is The Love' and 'Union' moment. 'One Tribe' makes a call for a united world, a universe in harmony. It encourages the Now Generation to remember that they are all, indeed, one tribe and urges a collective amnesia to forget all the evil around the world. With its harmony vocal introduction, it is a dose of the old Peas passing through this new filter. It demonstrated that their message of unity remained strong, no matter how it was dressed and how powerful a tool the Internet was to bring the planet together.

We hear the computerized voice again: "There is no longer a physical record store", but, we are assured, the group will continue to "let the beat drop". 'Rockin' To The Beat' ends the album in full synthesized house mode once more, as the group head off into their own orbit – utilizing a 'Billie Jean' drumbeat, Daft Punk-style keys and Nile Rodgers inspired-guitar, the track is like a neat summation of dance music over the past four decades.

The group arrive at the 2005 MTV Video Music Awards held at the American Airlines Arena in Miami.

The big time: backstage at the 47th annual Grammy Awards at the Staples Center, Los Angeles, after winning Best Rap Performance By A Duo Or Group, with 'Lets Get It Started'. MIKE BLAKE/REUTERS/CORBIS

Playing with their heroes (and future will.i.am production charges), Earth, Wind & Fire before the start of Super Bowl XXXIX at Alltel Stadium in Jacksonville. JOHN ANGELILLO/CORBIS

Fergie at the Superbowl. MIKE BLAKE/REUTERS/CORBIS

Still got the moves: will.i.am on the Honda Civic tour in Norfolk, Virginia, April 2006. JASON MOORE/ZUMA/CORBIS

Promoting *The Monkey Business* Asian Tour in Hong Kong, July 2006. ANDREW ROSS/CORBIS

Fergie, New York City. 2006. Her model looks, vocal ability and down-to-earth personality put the group on magazine covers around the world. JAMES PATRICK COOPER/RETNA LTD/CORBIS

EXTRA ONE: Tonight's gonna be a good night: Fergie holds up three fingers to celebrate the group winning three Grammys, Los Angeles, January 2010. EPA/CORBIS

Fergie and husband Josh Duhamel.
DALE WILCOX/WIREIMAGE FOR UNIVERSAL PICTURES

will.i.am in award mode.
DAN MACMEDAN/WIREIMAGE FOR THE RECORDING ACADEMY

Casual styles no longer appropriate. The band promote *The E.N.D.* at the 2009 Victoria's Secret Fashion Show.
SCOTT MCDERMOTT/CORBIS

Shut Up! will.i.am and Fergie onstage at the Stravinski Hall at the 43rd Montreux Jazz Festival, Switzerland, July 2009.
JEAN-CHRISTOPHE BOTT/EPA/CORBIS

Taboo and will.i.am at the HP Pavilion, San Jose, April 2010 on the seemingly never E.N.Ding tour to support The E.N.D.
TIM MOSENFELDER/CORBIS

With a total viewing figure estimated at 162 million, and before an audience of 80,000, the group perform the biggest concert of their career during half-time at the Super Bowl XLV in Arlington, Texas, February 2011. RALPH LAUER/EPA/CORBIS

"This is a group that redefined a style of musical performance and presentation" – David Saltz, promoter of the final Black Eyed Peas concert (to date, maybe ever), at the Sun Life Stadium on November 23, 2011 in Miami Gardens, Florida. LARRY MARANO/GETTY IMAGES

With another apl track, 'Mare', as a bonus on UK editions of the album, *The E.N.D* was released on June 3, 2009. As it was their first new group recording since 2005, it attracted a great deal of column inches: *Rolling Stone* said, "As often as not the results are dumb. And that's an awfully good thing." *Entertainment Weekly* thought that the album was fuelled by "by some mysterious slurry of dance-floor plutonium and diet Red Bull", while suggesting that it was all "pure Top 40 nirvana". Caroline Sullivan writing in *The Guardian* said that "electronic clicks and buzzes are used lavishly, and the mood is as positive as ever. Just don't expect to love it immediately." The *LA Times* wrote, "This is a sloppy party. But it's one where you're welcome. So come on in." *Vibe* magazine said "While *The E.N.D* may be the farthest the Black Eyed Peas have ventured outside traditional hip-hop, the final product proves the group is best at creating their own conventions." *Prefix* magazine, however, questioned its artistic merit, and said, "All that matters is that this thing sells a few copies, ends up in an iPod or Miller Lite campaign and gets a few spins on the radio. And in those endeavours, *The E.N.D* will probably be a resounding success," *Slant* said there were some sparkling bits of production wizardry from will.i.am, who, "when freed from the self-sabotaging stupidity of his crew, proves himself an adequate dance-pop beatsmith".

The group loved *The E.N.D*: "This album is about celebration and a transition," apl said. "We are in a time of transition. We want to bring together all cultures and remind them how to find the joy in celebrating, even when there is a lot of fear and unknowns. We have infused music and influences from all over the world." *The E.N.D* was huge. It topped the US charts, as well as those in Australia, France, Canada and New Zealand and became the group's biggest album, selling three million copies in the US by March 2011. Although those numbers were down from the four million plus of *Monkey Business*, the world of the music industry had turned significantly since then, with the vanishing of worldwide record retail outlets and the prevalence of single track downloads as opposed to full album sales. In the UK, it reached number three in the albums chart and their trio of number one singles ('Boom Boom Pow', 'I Gotta Feeling' and 'Meet Me Halfway') made them the first group to achieve that feat since Blondie in 1980.

In a way, the album is not a million miles removed – although completely different in delivery – to will.i.am's 2003 curio, *Must B 21 (Soundtrack To Get The Party Started)*. It is all at a certain pitch to enliven an evening; however, whereas old school hip-hop was the mode in 2003, here was something very different, in tune with the changing times.

# Chapter 16

# "A Cross Between An Alien Insect Exoskeleton And A Time Machine"

*"It felt like we were opening for Bono in my back yard."*

Taboo, 2011

Less than three weeks after the release of *The E.N.D*, on June 25, 2009, Michael Jackson was found dead in his rented mansion at 100 North Carolwood Drive in the Holmby Hills area of Los Angeles. In the very public outpouring of grief that followed, will.i.am was called upon many times to speak about the artist with whom he'd been working for the past three years. He recorded an emotional, from the heart piece to camera for his blog, telling the world of the closeness of their recent relationship, and the fact that Jackson called him up on Father's Day in 2007 as will.i.am didn't have a dad. He talked about how Jackson inspired him to dance, and talked, through genuine tears, about the talent Jackson had. He spoke about the impact of "evil, wicked" journalists on Jackson, who have "nothing better to do than criticise".

will.i.am also reflected on Jackson's role in the music industry, how he presided over its rise and fall. He wrote, "I am so blessed to have worked with him. I am so proud to have witnessed and been a part of his last interview. I am so proud. And I am so sad to have lost a friend. We have all lost a light. He was a true gift to the world."

"I am so grateful to have worked with the King," he told MTV. "He is a bright light, and I wouldn't be surprised if the world stopped spinning tomorrow." Although the world remained on its axis, questions were soon asked about the material that will.i.am and Jackson had recorded together. At the time of writing, it has still to see the light of day.

will.i.am was also busy updating and promoting his clothes range. In September 2009, he launched a new line for the i.am range, with a new tagline, "I am me, you are you, feel good about it". He said at the time, "Music is my first love, but I've always been into fashion... I've always designed my own clothes for music videos, and I've been the stylist for the group. I'm just a creative individual and clothing is just another outlet for that creativity."

The celebrity perfume business was big news by the middle of the 00s. It seemed wholly appropriate that while other stars were launching their scents in Macy's and Bloomingdale's, Fergie should try something a little more of-the-people and struck a deal with Avon, the legendary door-to-door selling company that had been founded back in 1886. As the Avon website proclaims, Avon Founder David H. McConnell offered women a rarity in 19th-century America: a chance at financial independence. In 1886, it was practically unheard of for a woman to run her own business. Only about five million women in the United States were working outside the home, let alone climbing the ranks of any corporate ladder. That number accounted for just 20% of all women. From that moment on, Avon has been a metaphor for neighbourhood capitalism. No matter how many brand revamps it has had, it is still seen as a symbol of cheap-as-chips cheeriness. Its direct selling has inspired many women to become their own bosses.

Avon spoke to Fergie in 2009 about launching her own scent. "They approached me, and what girl doesn't want to have a fragrance?" she told *Billboard*. "What was interesting to me was that my grandma was an Avon lady. My mom used to help her package all the Avon stuff and have these little parties, so for me it was just a sign. I also love all the work they do with breast cancer and cancer survivors." Avon worked closely with Fergie to develop Outspoken over two years. Asking for her favourite smells of childhood, she replied, "Besides my mom's lasagne, one of the things I thought of was my old rock'n'roll leather jacket – I love the smell of that, and it matched my personality as well. So now there's a hint of leather in Outspoken. I toughened it up a little bit."

The press release suggested that Fergie is the living embodiment of the scent. It screamed, "Uninhibited. Feminine. Floral. Exclusively for Avon! Outspoken is for the woman who needs no introduction. With her fearless confidence, she lets her true personality shine through. True to herself and her beliefs... she is Outspoken. Sexy. Fearless. Unexpected."

The Black Eyed Peas' new level of popularity was clearly evident on September 8, 2009, when the group performed on the Oprah Winfrey show. To mark the start of her 24th season as America's prime-time chat show host, they played at an outdoor concert in Michigan Avenue, Chicago. With the brief to make it something special, the group left the organisation of the event to the producers and choreographers of *Oprah's 24th Kick Off Party*. Although the group was aware that something unusual might happen, Taboo thought this entertainment meant "12 to 15 dancers doing something rare". They began to perform 'I Gotta Feeling', with modified lyrics to 'today's gonna be a good day' and references to Winfrey as the performance was in the afternoon.

Unbeknownst to the group, the production team had organised a 20,000 strong flash-mob that broke out in sections, until everybody in the crowd was performing a choreographed routine to the song. There was a look of incredulity on the faces of the group and Winfrey as first one woman, then around 20 people, then sections of the crowd and finally, the entire throng, danced stylized actions to the song. Best of all, during the final major breakdown of the song the masses bent down lower and lower before repeatedly jumping up and down as the beat came back in, accompanied by cannons of dry ice from the stage. Even though choreographed, it is deeply moving; a perfect capture of the transformative power of music, turning a crowd into a collective whole.

The day after the Oprah performance, with 'I Gotta Feeling' at number one in the charts, the group renewed its association with the John Lennon Educational Tour Bus. Visiting the vehicle while on a promo tour in Seattle, they gave three teenagers from a local youth club the opportunity to interview them. The group seemed genuinely moved to be there, continuing their association with the project. "Coming on this bus brings back so many memories," Fergie told reporters. "I wouldn't have been able to release *The Dutchess* without this bus coming with us on tour, and going before shows, after shows, doing vocals here and there. It's such a great chance for people who may not have lived in LA or NY or Atlanta, to have a chance to show their skills. It's an amazing tool." After posing with the children, will.i.am, who had been present also in 2008 when a new bus went on the road, added, "I think it's great that the John Lennon Educational Tour Bus goes around America on tours like Bumbershoot and the Warped Tour. Especially now in America, when a lot of money has been taken away from music in schools. The Bus teaches music, lets kids learn and helps fill the void of the lack of funds that are allocated for music and arts."

*The E.N.D World Tour* was a huge undertaking, and aimed to be more than a concert. The group had prepared by making a summer of festival appearances, including headlining the Glastonbury Jazz World Stage on June 28 and the Auditorium Stravinski at the Montreux Jazz Festival in early July. *The E.N.D World Tour* expanded the group show, built around solo spots by each band member and made it more like a full-on club night. The band acted almost as their own comperes between their solo turns and will.i.am performed at least a 10-song DJ set in the middle of the show. "It's going to be the biggest tour, production-wise, that we've ever done," Fergie told *Billboard* in June 2009. "We're actually planning for that now, which we've never done before – actually plan for a tour. It's usually just learn the songs by performing at festivals and that's our show. But now we're stepping it up. We had some visuals before, but now we are going to have a lot more, and we're really excited about that." She had every right to be excited. It was a huge multi-media entertainment with the latest state of the art HD visuals, lasers and dancers. The tour was sponsored by BlackBerry, and Bacardi, which created its own Black Eyed Peas cocktail – the V.I. Pea – was the key media partner hosting the concerts' after parties.

The tour began in Hamamatsu Auditorium in Japan on September 15 before 14 further dates in Japan and the Antipodes. After this leg finished in Auckland on October 13, the group reverted to being a support act for a handful of dates. But this was no ordinary support slot – they had been asked by Bono to support U2 for five nights on their gargantuan *360° Tour*. The band were delighted, playing on the enormous hydraulic staging entitled 'The Claw', a set-up so big and revolutionary that it enabled the audience not only to surround the band, but some could actually stand within the stage. Three separate versions of it were made so they could be set up and dismantled in sequence as the tour moved from city to city. The Black Eyed Peas and U2 got on famously, with the Irish superstars frequently meeting up and chatting with them. will.i.am had, of course, already worked with them, but all were impressed with the level of intimacy the headliners shared with their support act. The show at the Rose Bowl in Pasadena had special resonance for Taboo, as it was just a few miles away from his home. "It felt like we were opening for Bono in my back yard," he wrote in 2011. Most of U2's 96,000 fans – a record for the National Historic Landmark venue, which opened in 1922 – were already there when the Black Eyed Peas did their nine-song set.

The relationship with U2 continued when the group guested during U2's star-studded set to celebrate the 25th Anniversary of The Rock And Roll Hall Of Fame at New York's Madison Square Garden on October 30. The Black Eyed Peas came onstage during a version of 'Mysterious Ways' before it blended into a complete hands-in-the-air version of 'Where Is The Love'. Fergie remained on stage while, as *The New York Times* said, "U2 started playing a limpid, meditative but still recognizable version of 'Gimme Shelter', with Fergie singing the introductory oohs, before Mr. Jagger strode onstage and took over, answering Fergie's vampy body language with his angular rock-scarecrow moves." The night's guest appearances underlined the stellar company the group was keeping, but more importantly it's clear to see how much the Peas were respected by U2 and the Rolling Stones, two groups at the very zenith of the rock establishment. Although it is commonplace for older, established artists to dally with current, hot pop stars, to keep re-establishing contact with them shows there is not only sales potential, but genuine respect and affection.

After the U2 experience – a relationship that would be ongoing as will.i.am went on to produce further tracks for the group with Danger Mouse – the Black Eyed Peas finished what had been a tumultuous 2009 by playing the Mandalay Bay resort hotel in Las Vegas on December 29 and 30. The Vegas shows were followed by a $300-a-ticket club performance at the LAX Club at The Luxor. *The E.N.D* tour started again in earnest on February 4, 2010, when its North American leg began at the Philips Arena in Atlanta. All the requisite flash and pizzazz was present, with enough moments of nightly unpredictability to ensure that there were very human elements among the slickly choreographed performance.

The set was designed by Bruce Rodgers, in tandem with production manager Tim Miller and long-term Peas cohort, creative director Fatima Robinson. The brief handed to Rodgers was simple – the group wanted "a cyber-tron music experience from the future. They wanted a design that matched the intensity and energy of the music. It was a great way to start a design process, so I went about sketching and came up with a design fully inspired by the Peas' music and ended with a concept that looked like a cross between an alien insect exoskeleton and a time machine."

It truly did look like something from the future: huge plasma screens would form the set, with various raised platforms for Bucky Jonson and tour DJ, DJ Poet (sometimes DJ Ammo) to play on. The band emerged from pods and would appear on stage through springboards. A huge runway went into the crowd to accommodate will.i.am's DJ booth, which would rise from the floor and then, during his set, be raised up on hydraulics. The dancers would dress in the mosaic bodysuits as seen in the 'I Gotta Feeling' video and on the Mark Kudsi, Matthew Cullen and will.i.am-designed sleeve for *The E.N.D.* They would also wear the silver speaker robot costumes from the 'Imma Be' promo. Interestingly, it was the first tour where the group played no material from before *Elephunk.*

will.i.am would still do his freestyle and rather spectacularly dress in full robot outfit with face mask to DJ. Fergie showcased *The Dutchess* songs, Taboo sang his solo, 'Rocking To The Beat', suspended above the crowd on an illuminated motorbike as well as freestyling, and apl. de.ap performed 'Bebot' and 'Mare'. Such was the embarrassment of riches and plethora of hits that 'Boom Boom Pow' and 'I Gotta Feeling' were held back to the very final encore.

The tour was full of celebrity drop-ins on stage and in the audience. The John Lennon Educational Tour Bus joined the tour for 19 of the dates on the North American trek, starting at the Philadelphia gig on March 3, 2010, running through to the final US date in Tacoma. The show was running like a well-oiled machine. Prince was in attendance at the Xcel Energy Centre in St Paul on March 22. He rang will.i.am afterwards to say just how impressed he was with 'I Gotta Feeling.' "I remember we played the song in Minnesota, and Prince was at the show, and he called me on the phone afterwards. He said, 'Congratulations,'" will.i.am said. "He says, 'You know, those songs don't come all the time. You're blessed to have one of those songs. You know, they're gifts.' I was like, 'Wow.' For someone like Prince to tell you that, that's bigger than a Grammy for me."

The group's March 30 performance at Los Angeles Staples Center was beamed live to US cinemas in 3D. There was talk of this performance, *The Black Eyed Peas: The E.N.D. World Tour Live Presented By BlackBerry,* being released commercially on DVD, but so far it has only been available on Dipdive and YouTube. It was a very emotional night and captured the group performing at the peak of their career, with all the robotic trickery. The euphoria during will.i.am's DJ set when the crowd sang along to Journey's 'Don't Stop Believin'' and Eurythmics' 'Sweet Dreams (Are Made Of This)', reflected how much of a music fan he is. The unmistakable guitar riff of 'Sweet Child O' Mine' was played by its writer, Slash, as Fergie, in her leather leotard with silver plating, did her best Axl Rose impression. The look of joy on Bucky Jonson guitarist George Pajon Jr's face was priceless. will.i.am's passionate speech before 'Where Is The Love' and the song's extended outro when he encouraged the whole crowd to turn their mobile phone screens to the stage to create a huge sea of lights was another highlight. The crowd was full of old friends, family and associates, right back to characters such as Eclipse, Taboo's old bandmate from Rising Suns in the mid nineties. When will.i.am gave his shout out to 'East LA' and Taboo saw a sign saying 'Viva Mexico Taboo', it added to the overall sense of this strange emotional theatre.

After a short break at the end of the US tour in April, the band began their European dates on May 1 in Dublin. The support act was Cheryl Cole, with whom will.i.am had formed a close bond and recently produced her *3 Words* album. will.i.am's relationship and professional guidance of Cole was "the one good thing" that came out of *Songs About Girls*. "She's great company to be around, she works hard, she loves music and she's not all diva'd out. Cheryl is really down to earth." The production and co-write of '3 Words' for Cheryl Cole is one of his greatest works – co-written with George Pajon Jr, it is a strange minimalist piece of acoustic-guitar-driven house. Although Auto-Tune threatens to cloud the song at times, it is a refreshingly low-key opener to the much-heralded debut album by the Girls Aloud singer. Pajon's double-tracked and heavily sampled guitar creates a distinctive sound. will.i.am added some depth and sophistication to Cole. *The Guardian* described the single perfectly: "Her showcase is the album's title track, built on dark loops of treated acoustic guitar and building into a claustrophobic dance track. It's as brave and novel a song as anything Cole's group have released, and shows how good she can be given a more imaginative setting."

will.i.am became linked romantically with Cheryl Cole after producing her single, '3 Words'. Taboo was sufficiently impressed with her to write in his autobiography that, "This girl is a superstar in the UK, and I couldn't believe the amount of press attention she got on a daily basis, and so it was impressive to see how unaffected and down-to-earth she was. It almost felt like she was in awe to be in the Black Eyed Peas tour – that she almost didn't believe it herself – and I liked that humility in her." The Peas and Cole criss-crossed the continent taking in the 02 Arena in London's Docklands, the venue where Michael Jackson had been planning his much-trumpeted comeback shows the preceding year. This was the venue where actor Tom Hanks joined the group on stage for the encore of 'I Gotta Feeling.'

One of the most significant events on this momentous tour was their concert in Johannesburg on June 10 for the opening ceremony of the 2010 World Cup. The group played at the city's 30,000 capacity Orlando Stadium on a bill that included Alicia Keys, Shakira, Hugh Masekela, Angelique Kidjo and John Legend as well as local artists. Jerome Valcke, from FIFA, football's governing body, saw the concert as of supreme importance. He was thrilled that a show of such magnitude would open the first-ever World Cup held in Africa and that the concert would be a "testament to the universal and unifying power of football and music".

The band played early in the show, which was broadcast live around the world, giving a compact, glittering hits set: 'I Gotta Feeling' received special love from the Portuguese fans in the crowd, as the national team had used it as a pre-match anthem during their qualifying rounds. Much was made of Fergie's outfit, the same she had been wearing throughout the tour, but it was now being discussed on the world's fashion pages. UK tattle-rag the *Daily Mail* proclaimed that she "poured her figure into a leg-baring black, gold and silver number, complete with bejewelled breast plates and structured shoulder and hip panels". Taboo also later guested during Latin superstar Juanes set. The whole group joined the assembled cast for the finale of Sly & The Family Stone's 'Everyday People'. The biggest cheer of the night came when Archbishop Desmond Tutu introduced a filmed message from Nelson Mandela.

The Black Eyed Peas headlined the T In The Park festival in Scotland, playing the Radio 1 stage on July 9, in a bill that included Muse, Faithless and Florence + The Machine. It demonstrated that even with their new pop sheen, the group was still very much in tune with the festival scene. The tour returned to North America in July with LMFAO and Ludacris as support, taking in Canada and Mexico, before the final 12 concerts in South America in October, playing Brazil, Argentina, Chile and Peru, for which the group had their own private jet with their name emblazoned on the exterior. The tour had been momentous. Director Ben Mor captured some of the mayhem from the South American leg for the video for their 2011 single 'Don't Stop The Party'.

Thanks to the commerciality and innovation of *The E.N.D*, the Black Eyed Peas became regulars at awards ceremonies throughout 2010. In February, they picked up three Grammy Awards, after being nominated for six at the ceremony in the Staples Center on January 31. Although it was widely seen as Beyoncé's night – she won six awards – after the group performed 'Imma Be' and 'I Gotta Feeling', they won Best Pop Performance By A Duo Or Group With Vocals for 'I Gotta Feeling', Best Pop Vocal Album (*The E.N.D*); and 'Boom Boom Pow' won Best Short Form Music Video.

In September 2010, things came full circle for will.i.am as he was honoured at the BMI 10th Annual Urban Awards at the Pantages Theater in Los Angeles. The award was presented by none other than David Faustino, who had provided such encouragement for will.i.am back in the early days at Balistyx on Sunset Strip.

Another voice from the past, Kim Hill, broke her long silence about the Peas at this time and was asked in an interview for her thoughts about their success: "It doesn't make sense to me... The Black Eyed Peas, to me, it's like going to a restaurant, if I ordered fish and someone bring me a pork shark, I'm gonna do: 'Hold on a second, I've ordered fish'. To make the analogy make sense, I was in the Black Eyed Peas and I feel like what they are now is another product, like now they're potatoes. I'm not trying to make fun of them, but they're not the BEP any more to me, it's the same name, but it's a completely different product. So if I saw who they are now, without knowing the back history where they came from, it would be a little easy for me to accept... I do feel that the Black Eyed Peas have accomplished something really unique; they've been able to go from underground hip-hop to this kind of electronic dance music, and still sell a lot of records and they pleased a lot of different people, that's what's beautiful about it." Although Hill spoke for a dewy-eyed hardcore that longed for another day, by 2010, the group had gained their biggest audience ever.

# Chapter 17

# Stylishly Avant Garde:
## *The Beginning*

*"That's what we're doing – we're connecting the pixels."*

will.i.am, 2010

*"Pop's reigning peddlers of dumb fun are actually starting to sound stylishly avant-garde on their sixth album."*

*Spin* Magazine, 2010

*"If you do wish to escape it, please avoid bars, open windows, doctors' waiting rooms, sporting events, sitcom montages, preschool graduations and your grandma for the next year or so, because it's gonna drown 'em all in rhythm and sound."*

*Rolling Stone*, 2010

In early 2010, will.i.am announced that, alongside the forthcoming Peas material, he would start recording work suitable for his next solo releases. Working under the pseudonym Zuper Blahq, he released the collaborative single 'I'm In The House' with electro house producer Steve Aoki, which reached number 29 in the UK singles chart. He also guested later in the year with Nicki Minaj on her single 'Check It Out' with backing vocals provided by Natalia Kills. Talk of his solo album would continue intermittently throughout the next year. By the middle of 2011, will.i.am began talking about releasing two – *Black Einstein*, which would be a more traditional 'hip-hop' release, while the other, at present without a title, would make further adventures into the electro/dance field that will.i.am had been so contented in making of late. But all of this was in the future; there was still much Black Eyed Peas business to attend to.

*The Beginning*, recorded during breaks on the gargantuan *The E.N.D World Tour* (indeed the album was released a mere 13 days after the final show in Lima, Peru), was the next step forward for the group. Released on November 26, 2010, it was another relentlessly modern piece of music, just over an hour of which was released on a physical CD. Not atypical for a Black Eyed Peas release of this period, it garnered enormous sales. *The Beginning* was mainly written by will.i.am around the world while mailing tracks back to long-term contributor Jean Baptiste in California. For the first time since *Elephunk*, the group did not record in London, and much of the recording took place at Glenwood Place in Burbank, Ethernet, The Record Plant, Germano Studios in New York, the Stewchia and on location in a variety of hotel rooms by will.i.am in Ireland, Canada and Ibiza.

To illustrate how close-knit the BEP family was, *The Beginning* also marked a return to the camp of original Atban Klann member Mooky Mook, who had been off with his group, Burning Star. The group summed up the intention of the album thus: "These are all the type of songs that tap into everyday feelings of everyday folks; they evoke the anxious moments before a great night out; the memories of best times spent with friends; or the butterflies of ambition."

*The Beginning* was written as a continuation of all the themes on *The E.N.D*, and in a way, it is more adventurous, as the mould had been broken and it was now time to explore further possibilities. will.i.am and the band were now seen as party arbiters, and the after-party at every show on the tour was almost as important as the gig itself: "When you have that interaction with the fans there's no other greater inspiration in the world," will.i.am said on the Black Eyed Peas site. "You see them rapping the lyrics back to you or dancing to your joints, it's energizing. And at the after parties, when we DJ, you can experiment with different sounds and see how people react, it's not a pretentious environment in the clubs and they embrace you with an open mind. It becomes like a laboratory. And so that whole experience of being on tour and that interaction, all of it just drives us to want to make the best and most creative music we can." And the album did feel like something of a lab.

*The New York Times* questioned will.i.am about its unashamed party direction: "It's electro," he replied. "Electro is today's disco – making electronic music not for the sake of selling it but for sharing it and touring around the world DJ'ing... Right now in the world, clubbing is needed. It's a time when people want to rub shoulders against people they don't know and share, even if the sharing is expressing your like over a beat."

will.i.am was also clear how much the album was a tribute to the progressions that began in the eighties: "The eighties was very unique – it launched humanity into hyper mode," he told *Spin* magazine. "From then to now, we've transcended to a totally different culture, like, 'What?' Now we have high-definition, 3-D animation whereas the beginning was *Tetris* and *Space Invaders*. How did *Space Invaders* become *Madden NFL?* That's what we're doing – we're connecting the pixels."

Whereas *The E.N.D* had made a statement about the dwindling and near extinction of older technologies, *The Beginning* was just that: "*The Beginning* is symbolic of adopting new technologies, such as augmented reality, 3D and 360 video," will.i.am said. "It's also about being experimental, taking songs we've liked from the past and playing around with sick, crazy beats. It's an amazing time to be creative right now and I think people are open to that."

Whereas 'I Gotta Feeling' had been bold in its reclaiming of styles, the first listen to the lead track from *The Beginning*, 'The Time (Dirty Bit)', felt like the Black Eyed Peas were actually having a laugh at their audience's expense. Written and produced by will.i.am and tour DJ, DJ Ammo (Damien LeRoy), it seemed rather easy, taking one of the most popular songs of the past 25 years, the Bill Medley-Jennifer Warnes sung

'(I've Had) The Time Of My Life' from the ever-popular *Dirty Dancing* movie and building a series of futuristic beats around it. *The Guardian* said that it "excavates the 1987 hit... and drapes it in Casio keyboard effects for an easy shot at the Top 10." But again, as with all the biggest tracks in the group's repertoire, it is elegantly deceptive; thudding beats and atonal synthesizers with will.i.am's Auto-Tuned rap breaking up the repetitive chorus of the original hit and after a while, it becomes another Black Eyed Peas earworm, impossible to shake out of the listener's head.

Fergie said that the song was "a celebration of this amazing time in our lives. We've been on tour all over the world, and looking out at stadiums full of people who came out to see us – that's as big as it gets. After the shows, we go out to the clubs and meet the fans; those are moments that we have to remember." apl.de.ap mentions that his 'swagger' is like 'Jagger's' – a year later there would be two records that glorified Mick Jagger's onstage posturing – Cher Lloyd's 'Swagger Jagger' and Maroon 5's 'Moves Like Jagger'. He also includes a great pun by suggesting that the listener "download their app", a reference to the new worldwide craze of download applications for mobile devices. *The Independent* called the track a "textbook blend of the over-familiar and the electronically treated, though their use of Auto-Tune and digital-stutter vocal effects is a touch more restrained than usual." Nathan Rabin, writing for the online review service the *AV Club*: "It's as if will.i.am is once again begging us to call his bluff and banish him from the world of music, as opposed to the land of cross-promotion and jingles that is will.i.am's natural habitat... He's Slim Pickens in *Dr. Strangelove*, waving his cowboy hat and screaming 'Yee haw!' as he drives a nuclear bomb straight into the heart of pop music." Exactly the sort of track which would irk serious music scholars, it was another deeply silly instalment of Peadom. The track was released as a download on November 5, 2011, and although only reaching number four in the *Billboard* chart, it made number one in 10 countries.

The video, directed by Rich Lee, is probably the ultimate capture of the group in their bizarrely futuristic cartoon caricature. After seeing will.i.am perform at a party, a great deal of the action pixelates; the dancers, the drink poured, the headphones, even, rather tastefully, a party-goer's vomit, which falls in a blocky,white pixelated pile. Halfway through the video, the group morph into animated walking computer avatars, as an iPad screen is shown to billboard posters of its members. It was an image that was included in the album's artwork as well – they were now universal caricatures. There is much freaky dancing, which culminates in at least one couple emulating the Patrick Swayze-Jennifer Grey routine from the original film, *Dirty Dancing*. It was another rip-roaring call-to-party and became the group's most viewed promo on YouTube, with over 175 million views by February 2012. So many millions being aware of your work illustrates just what a global phenomenon the group had become.

The party continued with 'Light Up The Night'. It features additional synths by DJ Ammo and, bizarrely, guitar from Alain Whyte, who had played on 'Yes We Can', but was most known for being the guitarist for glum British indie legend Morrissey. It is like an Auto-Tuned version of Salt'n'Pepa's 'Push It', the 'uno-dos' a reference to 'The Bottle' by Gil Scott Heron and the samples from Slick Rick's 'Children's Party' suggest that no matter how far the group have travelled musically, they have no intention of leaving their hip-hop routes behind. It has great vocal breakdowns, and backing voices that recall UK dance outfit Basement Jaxx's 'Where's Your Head At'. Released as a promotional single, it is another extremely serviceable, radio friendly piece of chart pop. UK writer Gavin Martin picked up the underlying joie de vivre of the entire operation, and said, "The band mixing past, present and future is fun."

'Love You Long Time' is interesting. Built around a keyboard figure reminiscent of KC And The Sunshine Band's 1983 hit, 'Give It Up', it takes the phrase that suggests a superficial relationship and turns it into a futuristic love duet between Fergie and will.i.am. She echoes his repetition of the chorus but the location of their romance, 'the velvet lounge', suggests that it is about the words suggested in the moment of passion at a nightclub, with no longer-term prospects. It is like an interlude that never fully gets started before we head back to more conventional dance-floor territory with 'XOXOXO'.

Taking its title from textspeak for hugs ('O') and kisses ('X'), 'XOXOXO' is a strange, dislocated and disconnected modern love song with a synth riff and handclaps introducing the individual raps and eccentric, staccato vocals. To maintain his dance-floor credentials, will.i.am namechecks both DJ Tiësto and Paul Oakenfold's Perfecto label. The use of Auto-Tune makes the vocals sound completely surreal as the long-distance relationship is being enlivened by text sex, which will soon turn into full-on 'knock boots'. "We wanted to use the combination of our voices, which is unique," will.i.am said of the track. "It's not about who's singing what part. A lot of times, people fall short in the studio worrying about who gets to sing which part." It is a true team effort. The song was released as a promo single at the end of the album's life and had a dreamlike video to accompany it. Directed by Pasha Shapiro, Ernst Weber and Huan Nghiem, it follows the animations who were first seen leaping off the advertising hoardings in 'The Time (Dirty Bit)' promo.

It seems strange having such a surreal, child-like, cartoonish promo for a song about sex. The three male Peas take off in the space shuttle; when will.i.am begins his rap, he transports to India when he talks of the Kama Sutra. A record spins when techno is mentioned; he waits outside an Ibizan building for his lover, and then goes underwater; these are all the places he is sent after he receives a text from his lover (the cartoon Fergie, sitting on planet earth). By the time of apl.de.ap's verse, apl is chasing the cartoon Fergie around a platform computer game. There is then a neat simulation of various arcade games from throughout the years. The viewer then learns the outcome of the space mission – the three Pea astronauts were putting the final section into a space station, which forms the shape of an 'X', which, when set alongside planet earth, becomes a huge 'XO'.

The futuristic clicks and glitches of the track give way to 'Someday', which is a cross between muscular U2-style guitar (again played by Whyte) and pumping house. It is wholly successful upbeat pop, with will.i.am singing of the realisation of dreams and the redemptive power of the dance floor. With will.i.am's synth and Moog bass, the clash of a rock beat and a dance rhythm, the anthemic backing chant, the breakdown with breathing and the heavily chorus-pedalled guitar make this one of the most intriguing tracks not just on the album, but of the group's entire career. apl.de.ap continues the theme singing through Auto-Tune, again telling his story of coming to the US with nothing, leaving his family. It departs long before its welcome is outstayed. *Rolling Stone* singled out the track: "[In the] gracious 'Someday,' apl.de.ap gets personal, singing about his blue-collar work ethic and Filipino-immigrant background as Edge-like guitar shimmer suggests boundless promise."

'Whenever', written by will.i.am and Fergie, is an intense Euro-influenced high octane chorus-heavy pop duet between the group's leaders. A showcase for Fergie, with will.i.am as a distant Auto-Tuned voice, almost akin to that of a Greek chorus, it begins as a soft-rock ballad, with a sweet melody played on synthesizer before the pounding Euro-trance influenced beats kick in. With Whyte on acoustic guitar and Bucky Jonson's Keith Harris on piano, at just over three minutes long, it was released as a promotional single in France. It again illustrated the group's all-round appeal.

'Fashion Beats' is basically a new Auto-Tuned rap over Chic's 1979 hit, 'My Forbidden Lover'. However, it is a perfect example of how will.i.am's work can penetrate even the most resistant skins. Co-produced again by DJ Ammo, once Fergie begins her Estelle 'American Boy' inspired vocal, before breaking into a French rap – which owes a great deal to another record of the Chic era, 'Rapture' by Blondie – you're swept away. Josh Lopez provides his best Nile Rodgers-a-like guitar, and by its end you have little option but to participate fully in the groove and infectious passion of the record. The track meanders on, and by the fifth minute, with the instruction of 'to the beat' by Fergie, it goes into mechanical Franz Ferdinand-style riffing. Like everything about the group, the path least obvious is often evoked when you are not expecting it.

*Spin* said 'Don't Stop The Party' was "a buzzing, hot club jam that features whooshing synths and slap-funk bass grooves. Will's lyrics are some of his funniest yet: dude manages to rap 'lyricals' and 'digital' with 'aboriginals' and 'genitals' in a thick, Caribbean patois." will.i.am was particularly delighted with the tune and played it to Jay- Z. "I would go to Jay's studio and play this, be like 'Boom! Check it out!'"

he told *Spin*. "Then I go dirty Caribbean on him on the last verse." Co-written and produced with DJ Ammo, it showcases Caleb Speir's slippery bass over wild sequencers. Released as the album's third single, it maintained the standard of the single tracks, yet did not have any great commercial resonance, peaking at number 86 in the *Billboard* charts and at number 17 in the UK. Its video was assembled by Ben Mor from footage of the South American leg of *The E.N.D World Tour*. It is an ever relentless groove, marching forward on its mission to fill the dance floor, complete with a huge injection of euphoric house breakdown five minutes in, playing out with Speir's bass following the 808 synth's repetition. However, rather than the groundbreaking lead singles of *The E.N.D*, it feels as if the brew is getting rather laboured.

'Do It Like This' is both minimal and stomping, almost skeletal techno and was released as a promotional single at the start of the album's campaign to flag that the Black Eyed Peas were still very much on the ultra-modern dance floor. It's grimy and atonal. "I don't care if you've shot a billion people and I don't care if you've sold crack to the Pope," will.i.am told *Spin*. "That beat is harder than any attitude or any freakin' mug-shot face. It goes to a place no hip-hopper would go to right now."

And will.i.am was probably right – a lot of those characters were unlikely to venture into Ibiza-style party clubs. Working again with DJ Ammo overseeing the song's glacial synthesizers and mixed loud Moog bass, it moves from a ragga-influenced lope and after a climactic synth build and rise turns into a wild, off-kilter electronic stomper. All three men take verses, apl making a claim that the group are, indeed, 'underground Beatles'. It is a banging, wild song, which lyrically references its ancestor, the 1997 Fatboy Slim hit 'The Rockafeller Skank'. The influence of underground dance production outfit Major Lazer is evident. A video was made to complement the single edit featuring all four members caught in an early eighties computer game, with deliberately naïve graphics showing the lyrics, as the band – in their pixilated icons from the front sleeve of *The Beginning* – scramble through the various platforms.

The immediate thought when hearing the opening of 'The Best One

Yet (The Boy)' is that the group has returned to straight ballad territory. Not so. As soon as Fergie appears 40 seconds in, David Guetta adds his warm, pulsing synthetics, and this sweet-centred pop song is one of the lower-gear highlights of the album. With Keith Harris on grand piano and Josh Lopez on guitar, it has an organic feel amid the electronics. Celebrating a positive relationship that's going forward into the night, although Fergie sings little more than the repeated chorus, it acts as a marvellous showcase for the emotional power she injects into the album.

'Just Can't Get Enough' is the continuation of 'The Best One Yet (The Boy)' looking at the development of the relationship that started in the heat of the moment. It was based on a song written by Julie Frost and Rodney 'Darkchild' Jerkins and then worked on by the group, and became the second single from the album, released in February 2011. Again, it starts as a relatively straightforward love song before the rhythm shifts to another stomping dance-floor moment. It's almost as if there are too many ideas at play. Produced by DJ Ammo, the song features a 12-piece string section, and creates a successful blend of orchestra and synthetics.

*The Wall Street Journal* called it, "a big ballad in which Fergie shares the vocal with hip-hop toasting; an orchestra enters quietly under the swooshing synths, then becomes more assertive until the tempo and texture suddenly change". About.com was tired of the familiarity of the Peas' output: "Listen to the wistfulness in Fergie's vocals here, there are seeds for something more exciting. Her voice can carry an unvarnished sweetness that cuts through all of the electronic studio trickery with a palpable warmth. However, here, with all that surrounds it, that sweetness begins to sound like just another processed loop. The opportunity for real warmth is lost."

Its video was especially emotional. It was shot in Japan by Ben Mor when the group were on a press tour for *The Beginning*, just before the tragic earthquake and tsunami that claimed many lives and prompted the nuclear reactor to shut down at Fukushima in March 2011. The opening still is white lettering, out of black: "This video was filmed in Japan one week before the earthquake and tsunami. Our thoughts and prayers go out to all the people of Japan. We love you." The video's final frame gave the Red Cross text number. The promo was a wonderful advert for Tokyo, with Fergie singing her wistful lines high above the city, and will.i.am returning his in the back seat of a car driving down a neon-drenched thoroughfare. apl delivers his rap in a club, as the record's progression from ballad to screeching dance-floor futurism accelerates. The group, like the rest of the world, was stunned at the scale of the natural disaster.

Fergie told *Entertainment Tonight* that, "It was the easiest video I ever shot because it was us living our lives. I love that it's showing a true perspective of how it can sometimes be lonely on the road away from our loved ones. It also demonstrates the love and connection we have with Japan. Our heart goes out to all of the Japanese people who have been affected by this natural disaster." The video has a poignancy, not just for what was to unfold in the country where it was filmed, but for the way it captured the group, who, for once, seemed to be simply going through the party motions. 'Just Can't Get Enough' was released as a single in February 2011, and bolstered by an appearance on *American Idol*, it reached number three in the *Billboard* Top 100, a position equalled in the UK.

The final track, 'Play It Loud', sounded like a summation of the 15-year career of the Black Eyed Peas. Co-written with Alain Whyte, Michael McHenry and Jean Baptiste, with its swathes of guitar, muted drum machines and wistful vocals, it feels somehow valedictory. Effectively a will.i.am solo performance, he swears his allegiance to the music that has shaped his life (John Lennon and Bob Marley are "his presidents"). Although this is something he had done on virtually every Black Eyed Peas album before, here he was a multi-millionaire much moved on, but in his heart, he's still playing it loud and loving the tune. *The Independent* said that it "features the most poignant, soulful melody on the entire album, with something of a Radiohead quality about it". The song ends with will.i.am's voice simply supported by Whyte's chiming guitar, repeating the track's refrain of pledging his loyalty to 'rhythm and sound'. It was a superb closer to an album that although patchy, captured exactly the mania of the Black Eyed Peas as they toured the globe. In many ways it reminds the listener of *Rattle And Hum* and *Zooropa*, the two albums that U2 made when they were caught in the middle of worldwide tours promoting other records, and released relatively quickly afterwards.

With the six bonus tracks dotted around the running order of the disc ('The Situation' is especially good, with Fergie sounding like late seventies new wave diva Lene Lovich), there is almost too much to take in, and tracks like 'Someday' and 'Whatever', although as good as anything the group have ever done, are overshadowed by the bigger, dafter, dancier numbers. *The Beginning* was less of a wild ride than *The E.N.D*, and its sales were lower. It feels more mellow and measured, likened in the *Wall Street Journal* as having a "tone and temperature that suggest it's music to accompany the last dances that give way to dawn". "With *The E.N.D* we were saying don't wait for someone else to give you the answers," will.i.am told the journal. "I don't want to wait any more for solutions from people who only care when things go wrong – let's change our perspective. 'Tonight's gonna be a good, good night.' When it's over, you go, 'I had the time of my life.'" There was a feeling, certainly in light of the announcement the following year that the band were about to go on hold again, that *The Beginning* was a long, loving farewell note.

*The Beginning* actually demonstrated that the press was finally getting the hang of what they were dealing with when they wrote about the Black Eyed Peas. Their very diversity was their strength, and if you had to sit through a song that was below par, another one would be along shortly afterwards to tickle your fancy. *The Guardian*'s review summed it up perfectly: "It's modish to disparage the Peas, but consistently coming up with stuff that's this infectious is harder than it looks." *Spin* said: "Pop's reigning peddlers of dumb fun are actually starting to sound stylishly avant-garde on their sixth album." *Entertainment Weekly* said: "Every song is piled high with sticky pop melodies, slick hip-hop rhythms, bright synth parts, and vocals that have been diced and processed to high heaven, all furthering the goal of maximum catchiness... nothing here quite reaches the euphoric heights of *The E.N.D*'s 'I Gotta Feeling' or 'Boom Boom Pow'. Still, standouts like 'Don't Stop the Party' come close. The Peas may not have dramatically outdone themselves this time, but they've succeeded at keeping the good times rolling yet again." *Billboard* saw the group's never-ending, amazingly commercial sensibilities: "It's official: No lyric or synth, sample or influence exists that can't be finessed into a dance anthem by will.i.am." The final word on *The Beginning* came from *Rolling Stone*, which defined the sometimes infuriating appeal of the group: "This much serotonin in four humans can only mean they'll get carried away all over the place, and *The Beginning* bubbles with the kind of slobbering excess that drives Peas haters bonkers... If you do wish to escape it, please avoid bars, open windows, doctors' waiting rooms, sporting events, sitcom montages, preschool graduations and your grandma for the next year or so, because it's gonna drown 'em all in rhythm and sound."

To promote *The Beginning*, the Peas appeared on the semi-final results show of the Simon Cowell-devised UK TV phenomenon, *The X Factor*, in December 2010. will.i.am had been instrumental in assisting Cheryl Cole, who was on the judging panel, with the selection process for her acts on the show, and the programme, which routinely clocked up audiences of 10 million, was the most-watched Sunday night show in the UK. Introduced by Peter Dickson's hubristic voiceover and clips montage, the facts tumbled out across the screen. "SIX GRAMMY AWARDS ... THREE MULTI PLATINUM ALBUMS ... FOUR UK NUMBER ONES ... 30 MILLION WORLDWIDE ALBUM SALES ... THE BLACK EYED PEAS." Playing on a futuristic set in their cartoonish space outfits, the group was backed by a selection of dancers with flashing green–lit cube heads as they romped through 'The Time (Dirty Bit)' just as it was about to top the UK charts.

*The Beginning* came with all the prerequisite support media and technology furore. The group became the first to have a mobile 4D 360 Music video as an application through iTunes. Released on January 24, 2011, the application had been developed in tandem with Talent Media LLC and copyrighted by the very amusing 'will.i.apps'. The aim, as the iTunes blurb read, was to enable you to 'be dropped into the party with the world's first 360 party video'. By holding an iPhone you are able to view a 360-degree view of the Rich Lee-directed video, placing the viewer in the centre of the action. In addition, if the iPhone or iPad is pointed toward the cover of *The Beginning*, the pixilated characters pop up and dance to the beat, just like in the video of 'The Time (Dirty Bit)'. The app was completed with a link to the Peas' Twitter feed, enabling users to see Tweets visualised and a puzzle game that owed something to Tetris. The app sold very well, placing the group high in the iTunes download charts.

will.i.am was now synonymous with the latest in technology. On January 25, 2011, he was named Director Of Creative Innovation at Intel, consulting on developments in smartphones and laptops. The global leader in chip making issued a statement. Marketing Director Deborah Conrad said: "It's imperative that Intel and our innovations are kept in front of the global youth culture that embraces new devices and new forms of communication and entertainment." will.i.am added: "It's official. I just became the Director of Creative Innovation for Intel. Every beat I make is made with Intel. And now we're partners."

He had come a long way since borrowing Stefan Gordy's DAT machine back in Palisades High School.

# Chapter 18

# The End?

*"We always have two cycles of records and then we take a break. When we take breaks you know, we work on side projects and get our personal stuff in order then come back and make beautiful music. We think beautiful music."*
will.i.am, 2011

*"Who else would even think of such a wonderfully batshit idea?"*
Rolling Stone, 2011

The group were asked to perform the prestigious half-time slot at the Superbowl XLV in 2011, the first non-traditional rock act to perform there since 2004. That year Justin Timberlake presided over Janet Jackson's legendary 'wardrobe malfunction', during which one of her breasts was exposed during their performance. will.i.am. was suitably overawed. "They could have picked anybody," he told *Rolling Stone*. "They could rock a million and get Cheap Trick. I love me some Cheap Trick, those motherfuckers is dope. But it says something that they picked us." He said at the official press conference to launch their performance that, "Even though football is an American tradition and an unofficial holiday, we're taking football places where it is not part of their culture but this is part of our culture and I am so proud. It's a dream come true for us." The group didn't disappoint.

Taking place at the 80,000-capacity Cowboys Stadium, the home of the Dallas Cowboys, in Arlington, Texas on February 6, 2011, the final was between the Pittsburgh Steelers and the Green Bay Packers. For the game, the 2009-opened stadium increased its standing capacity, so a total of 103,000 people saw the Black Eyed Peas playing in front of the enormous high-definition television screen. After performances from Keith Urban and Maroon 5 pre-game, and Christina Aguilera performing the national anthem, the group played a medley of 'I Gotta Feeling', 'Boom Boom Pow', 'Pump It', 'The Time (Dirty Bit)', 'Let's Get It Started' and 'Where Is The Love'. Slash joined Fergie again as he had done on selected tour dates to play on a cover of his former band's 1988 anthem 'Sweet Child O'Mine', while Usher joined will.i.am to perform 'OMG', his incredible song and production that topped the US and UK chart in 2010. The show was a 12-minute blast for the senses: a non-stop journey through their hits with all the requisite bangs and crashes. Slash's appearance was unkindly written about in terms of it softening up Peas fans for a future rock direction. The sound was not brilliant and cut out at times, but it succeeded in importing their enormous tour into the single most prestigious gig of the modern day. Such a high-profile appearance produces as many critics as it does fans.

The show, broadcast worldwide by Fox, became the most-watched US television programme ever at that point (ironically it would be superseded by the following year's Superbowl where Madonna performed and M.I.A.'s middle finger caused so much controversy). According to Nielsen Media Research, it acheived just over 100 million viewers at prime time, and a total viewing figure of 162 million people. Some critics were sniffy. *The Chicago Tribune*'s Greg Kot said: "Coming in short minute-long bursts, the Peas' songs actually benefited from the nervous, jump-cut energy of the medley, exiting long before their repetitiveness and triviality could become apparent." *The New Jersey Star-Ledger*'s Jay Lustig wrote: "While it's true that when there wasn't something spectacular going on, visually, they didn't offer much in the way of vocal dynamics, it's also true that there was usually something spectacular going on, visually – those hordes of glowing dancers really were pretty cool – so the 12 minutes passed very quickly," he added. "It was a solid 'B' performance – but nowhere near an A." The *Los Angeles Times*' Christie D'Zurilla wrote: "Regarding the music... was being three-sheets-to-the-wind drunk a requirement to enjoy this Super Bowl halftime show? Are the folks who said it's still cool to like the Black Eyed Peas eating their words? Do you sympathize with the not-an-old-fart-at-all editor who sent me a frantic note about that 'horrific caterwauling by Fergie', proclaiming her ears had been violated?" *Blast* magazine was the most vitriolic: "Although this performance in every definition of the word, sucked, I am happy to see risks being taken by allowing the Black Eyed Peas to perform. Hopefully in the years to come we will see better and more relevant artists perform the halftime show, more risks being taken, and more collaborative efforts like we used to when MTV produced the show. Either that or we will be doomed to never have good entertainment during the Superbowl ever again – one or the other." The negative criticism mattered little to the group; they had just been seen by their biggest audience ever.

When promoting *The Beginning*, will.i.am was frequently asked about President Obama's performance as president, and whether 'Yes We Can' still rang true. "I don't want to hope any more," he told the *New York Times*. "I don't think we should hope any more. We hoped enough. Now we have to do. We all have to do now. I don't feel disappointed [in Obama]. I feel like, 'Argggh! Speak louder!' I feel like, 'Do something!' I feel like jumping in."

It was obvious that *The Beginning* wouldn't be as groundbreaking as *The E.N.D* as that had broken the mould, but it did maintain their success. Before they worked the world on another tour, they relentlessly took all key promotional opportunities and paid special attention to the UK, the country that had so taken them under their wing all those years ago. There is footage of them backstage at the Radio 1 Big Weekend in Carlisle, Cumbria, on May 14, 2011. Sitting in the back of their trailer on a windswept day (all part of the BBC's fervent desire to demonstrate that they are a truly national and not London-centric station), the Peas look tired but still ready to promote and do yet another ident for another TV and radio station. Fergie welcomes everyone to Newcastle, the city 52 miles away on the other side of the country. She clearly needed a rest.

The worldwide tour to support the album, a natural continuation of *The E.N.D World Tour,* was brief. *The Beginning Stadium Tour* comprised 18 dates that took in Europe, Asia and North America, commencing at the Stade De France in Paris on June 22, 2011. That gig was a phenomenal party opener, with David Guetta supporting in full FMIF mode. will.i.am had frequently turned up at his DJ nights around the States, most recently earlier in the year in Miami. To continue this party theme, there is footage from Paris of the crowd dancing to the White Stripes' 'Seven Nation Army' played by DJ Ammo before the Peas' set, to show the crazy eclecticism of the whole operation. They headlined the Wireless Festival in Hyde Park, London on July 1, heading a bill that included Tinie Tempah, Plan B and Example and Bruno Mars. Guetta headlined the second stage, and joined the group during their set.

In the middle of their 2011 tour, the group announced they would be taking another sabbatical. That said, the pace of the tour was so frenetic, it found Black Eyed Peas scaling up their shows to the widest possible degree, playing huge open-air venues. The news failed to arouse a huge reaction, probably because this was very much conforming to a pattern they had established after *Monkey Business.* As ever, their detractors had a field day. Arch critic Nathan Rabin wrote on the *AV Club* that, "Hologram Man, Meth Lady, The Other Guy, and the Other Other Guy could concentrate on sucking separately." Those who got the group loved them, and for those who refused to dig deeper, here was another opportunity to sharpen their knives.

One of the underlying reasons for the sabbatical was Fergie's desire to start a family. "It's all about Black Eyed Peas; there's no room in my schedule to have a child," she said in 2011. "Even if I wanted to get pregnant, there's no way I could perform on stage and be pregnant. I would feel too guilty. Once I have children, the kids come first. One thing at a time for me. Women can have it all, just not all at once. It's too much if you're doing everything at once."

As *The Beginning Tour* reached its climax, they performed another show in the UK. Playing the enormous Alton Towers theme park in the Staffordshire Peak District in front of a 17,500 audience on July 6 seemed wholly appropriate for the Black Eyed Peas. Although the castellated towers themselves had once been the principal attraction at the park, they had long been superseded by a spiralling and bewildering selection of rides such as the vertical drop coaster Oblivion, the extreme Nemesis and the floating-through-air coaster appropriately named Air.

Fergie confirmed their sabbatical from stage. "This is a very special show for us because it is the last time we're going to be in England for a long time. We want you to know that we love you and thank you for the support you've given from the beginning." will.i.am added: "We're going to be taking a break just like we did after we released *Monkey Business* in 2005 until we came back in 2009." He then, of course, stressed, "But this isn't going to be the last time you'll see us." The group delighted the audience with the show that by now was well-honed – featuring solo slots and the now obligatory DJ set from will.i.am. The encore showed how the group could now ramp up their performance to absolute snapping point with the encore of 'Boom Boom Pow', 'The Time (Dirty Bit)' and 'I Gotta Feeling'.

Their status sufficiently established to withstand another lengthy break, there was still a great deal of business to finish, and 2011 became something of a giant victory lap for the group. They were determined to make their mark before they receded into solo careers and family life. On September 3, they played a benefit concert at the North Dakota State Fair in Minot for the victims of flooding by the Souris River that devastated the surrounding area in June 2011, displacing 12,000 people. Fergie's husband, Josh Duhamel, a Minot native, was the chairman of the Minot Area Recovery Fund. The concert raised more than $1.3 million for flood victims and broke the attendance record for a concert at the State Fair that had been set by Kiss in 2010, when 15,800 attended their performance. "The Black Eyed Peas and their band, Bucky Jonson, rocked the house on Saturday night and raised a ton of money for the flood victims of Minot," Duhamel said. "We will never forget what they did."

On September 30 the group performed a concert in front of 60,000 people in New York's Central Park, with many thousands more watching through live web stream. Supported by a variety of media houses, the proceeds went to the Robin Hood fund, which supports disadvantaged youth by providing music and artistic education. The group worked with the charity to ensure 'text-to-donate' programmes and Twitter was used to bolster funds. Fergie said, "I choked up just the other night at Central Park when we did that show. These are great celebrations of our friendship, and we know it's going to be a while before this happens again, so we're just taking it in right now and just really enjoying each moment."

The following night, Sting performed a similar concert for the Fund at The Beacon Theater for his 60th birthday and 25th year celebration of being a solo artist. will.i.am appeared onstage with him alongside other guests the calibre of Billy Joel, Lady Gaga, Bruce Springsteen and Stevie Wonder. Between the two concerts, and in between the two concerts, more than $7 million was raised. The band's association with Earth Wind & Fire also continued when EWF played at the Black Eyed Peas' now annual Peabody event at the Music Box Theater, Hollywood on October 2.

On November 21 the group were at the launch of their first fully-fledged computer game, *The Black Eyed Peas Experience*, put together with the group by Ubisoft, and released on wii and X-Box versions. It seemed a perfect fit as the interactive games world had gone dance crazy with the advent of updated technology. Players are guided through dance moves to 24 of the group's post-2003 classics with different levels of difficulty. Fergie was delighted to promote the product, yet another extension of the Black Eyed Peas' brand: "It's based on all of our choreography and what our dancers do during our shows. We're all doing the moves together in this with some of our freestyle because it's more of a flash-mob choreography game but you'll see different moves from different songs, different videos, and the numbers that our dancers do as well." Reviews of the game were largely positive: *The Belfast Telegraph* said, "Born of the same well that gave us *The Michael Jackson Experience* and *Just Dance*, if you love the Peas, you'll enjoy the BEP Experience as an excuse to shake a leg to their choons."

The Peas' final concert of *The Beginning Tour* was at the Sun Life Stadium in Miami, Florida on November 23, 2011, home to the Miami Dolphins. The group chose it because Miami was a city that knew how to party: Taboo told the *Miami New Times*: "Miami's always been a great fan base for us. I remember doing the Carnival tour with Wyclef and Aaliyah and Timbaland and all these artists. We were opening up, and it felt good because those were the first instalments of understanding what the Miami lifestyle was and getting a read on the fan base coming to support the Peas. Then we started to do the MTV Awards, and when we got our chance to do our own tour, Miami was pretty fresh. I'm excited about it, and Miami is always a great place to party."

The Thanksgiving celebration was a suitably stunning affair, with a strong feeling of the end-of-an-era. The Peas were promoted by David Saltz, a specialist promoter for major outdoor venues, who had first encountered the group when they scaled up their operation; he was struck by how their music leant itself to major sporting occasions. "This is a group that redefined a style of musical performance and presentation," he told the *Palm Beach Post*. "They added musicality to dance and club music. Their shows are a new kind of show and presentation – going to a show with the Peas is electrifying and pulsating... What they do has made them very exciting and good friends of stadiums." It was to be a full extravaganza. The group was joined by actor and hardcore Miami Dolphins fan Marc Anthony onstage, and were supported by Jason Derulo, old friend and collaborator Cee-Lo Green, T-Pain, Rick Ross, Jordan Hollywood and Sean Kingston.

However, not all reports of their swansong were glowing. The *Miami New Times*, which had so supported the group in the past, was a trifle dismissive: "In the history of final live performances by outrageously popular bands, last night's Black Eyed Peas show stands out for an unusual reason. The group's time onstage outlasted the audience's interest in them. Yes, the audience stayed through all the songs. But the band could not (and would not) discontinue babbling and just let everyone go home and remember them fondly. A six-hour concert isn't fun. It's like spending a full day in elementary school." The fan forums were even more scathing – for those who had come to see a conventional

Black Eyed Peas concert, this was not to be it – with all its prolonged speeches and DJ sets, it tested their loyal fans' patience. One such fan, ES, said on the *Palm Beach Post* website: "I know it's Thanksgiving and all, but I did not come to see a group therapy session."

Veda Jo Jenkins for the *Palm Beach Post* too commented on the length of the show and how it tested the patience of even the hardiest fan, but felt "will.i.am was a show in himself, even delivering a DJ set solo on a platform that rose out of the stage. There was so much going on I didn't know who to watch. Even Taboo and apl.de.ap, who may not be the group's big names, were entertaining. For the men, Fergie was gorgeous, sexy and seductive, making them drool and even the women, myself included, were amazed at how beautiful she is. Although the night was long, the Black Eyed Peas did deliver. I assumed they were going to play a shortened set of their best hits, but they played 18 songs and Fergie pleased the audience with her wardrobe change...Taboo had a touching moment when he brought his mother out on the stage."

And that was it. The Black Eyed Peas were put into storage, like the androids that their personas had become. The Peas were frozen.

Before the show was over, will.i.am wasted no time in issuing his first solo download. 'T.H.E. (The Hardest Ever)' was the first release from his forthcoming album *#willpower*. Again, it continues with the futuristic minimalism established on *The E.N.D.* The music sounds like the sort of tune that *Wall-E* would have made. Sequencers and synthesizers abound, with will.i.am delivering a cutting-edge rap. He seems to have re-created the Peas around him, with Jennifer Lopez singing the female parts and then, three quarters of the way through, Mick Jagger kicks in with his trademark squall, this time sounding exactly how you'd expect Jagger to, mentioning the word 'trigonometry'. Produced by Audiobot, Dallas Austin, and, making his return to the recording studio, to record Jagger, for the first time in years, Jimmy Iovine.

The single was originally going to be a duet, and will.i.am and Iovine discussed who could be a suitable vocal collaborator. will.i.am mentioned Jagger's name as a joke, not thinking for one second the ennobled Rolling Stone would agree. Iovine contacted Jagger and the vocal was duly recorded. Amazingly, the two had never worked together previously. "He produced Mick's vocals, and this was the proudest moment of my life," will.i.am said. "Winning a Grammy is cool, but the guy who helped you out – and then you got to see him execute one of his dreams – that's just the dopest ever." *Rolling Stone* was quick to comment: "Who but will.i.am could get Mick Jagger to rap – yes, rap – over a glitzy Ibiza beat in 2011? Who else would even think of such a wonderfully batshit idea? It all feels a bit perfunctory – except for Mick's guest verse, a kitschy delight delivered in a 'Midnight Rambler' snarl."

The video, directed by Black Eyed Peas stalwart Rich Lee, was filmed on October 17, 2011 in Los Angeles, with Lopez adding her contributions at the end of the month. It's little wonder that will.i.am was rumoured to have injured himself during its making. It takes the form of a real-life video platform game, filmed on a giant runway, starting with him running at a wall. As he comes through it, he is on a bicycle; towards him is flung an enormous piece of what looks to be kitchen furniture. It is clear that a stunt double takes over from this juncture: he gets on to a superbike and then jumps over the next wall. The wall turns into paper and a car motors through it. By the time huge posters of J-Lo appear through the floor of the runway, will.i.am smashes through the final one in what is now a bullion truck, which is soon bombarded by debris... and suddenly he is singing in the open roll-on carriage of an airplane. Jumping out of the plane, he lands on top of a high-speed train; which then turns into a bomber and becomes... a rocket. As will.i.am and J-Lo continue into space, they encounter Mick Jagger who appears as an asteroid-surrounded spectral presence, upping the Jagger quotient to around a thousand. It's a spirited performance that, although marking the resumption of a solo career, kept just enough business as usual to ensure continuity with the recent Black Eyed Peas output. It's clear that there is nothing *Songs About Girls* downbeat about this.

The song made its debut on the American Music Awards on November 20, 2011 at the Nokia Arena in Los Angeles. On a bill which included live performances from David Guetta, Justin Bieber, Pitbull, Katy Perry,

LMFAO and Maroon 5, Adams introduced his new sound and look to American audiences. Performing on a blacked-out stage, with risers, Lopez appears in white singing her refrain. In a truly disquieting look, will.i.am appears with his head blacked out, just signing in a fluorescent white jumpsuit. The 13-piece US dance troupe Fighting Gravity, whom will.i.am had first encountered on the 'Heartbreaker' promo, offer the visual buffet.

Using a maximum of four dancers, they appear in white, with the rest of the troupe in darkness to provide the illusion of lights and objects floating behind the main performers – and then they lift the performers in white to give the illusion that they are floating in space. Like most things associated with will.i.am (and the Black Eyed Peas), it is part future and part something you would see on *The Muppet Show*. Nevertheless, it is extremely effective, especially when Jagger appears on an enormous side-screen singing his rap and throwing his classic moves. His head was also projected on to one of the dancers. MTV raved about it: "will.i.am delivered a complete glow-in-the-dark performance that included floating dancers, a headless will and even a blink-and-you'll-miss-it disappearing act."

The track was released to iTunes in the USA immediately and was downloaded 70,000 times, enough to make a showing in the US Hot 100 at number 36, while debuting at number 10 in the Canadian Top 40 and at 68 in the Australian charts. It served as a fabulous introduction to the new album. The single was not to be released in the UK until February 5, 2012. In the meantime, a cover version by Kings Of Pop reached the UK Top 40. On February 12, 2012, it entered the Top 40 at number three. It garnered much attention from the media as it gave Mick Jagger his first appearance in the UK Top 10 since his duet with David Bowie on 'Dancing In The Streets' in 1985. The will.i.am juggernaut rolls forever forward and with such an enormous statement of a single as this, he declared he was not about to deliver another *Songs For Girls*.

# Chapter 19

# Outro: Mazel Tov!

*"If The Black Eyed Peas are still selling these songs in 20 years (see Marvin Gaye, the Temptations, Pink Floyd, the Beatles, etc...), then we'll know it's great stuff. If not, they'll be blissfully forgotten along with countless other fad groups whose music traded heart and soul for the gimmick of their day."*
650Dad, Cracked.com, 13/11/08

*"Try to stay humble... I stay humble because the place where I'm at now I won't be 10 years from now. Ten years from now, I can be much, much bigger. So I'm humbled about how I have been able to grow. I've gone from playing colleges to playing stadiums."*
will.i.am, 2010

There is a saying about the Beatles that as a group, the Fabs are overrated by those who love them and underrated by those who don't. The Black Eyed Peas are no Beatles, but the statement holds true for the gang of East LA misfits who hit the big time. For those who dare to get beyond the prejudice that surrounds them, there are some untold riches to savour.

The group's 2012 onwards sabbatical comes after a period of remarkable growth and development. It is hard to notice their absence due to the ubiquity of their performances across the Internet, their records in clubs. The European charts are awash with US R&B artists applying European house beats and achieving enormous success, something that was looked at with a great degree of puzzlement when the Peas began fusing R&B and techno back in 2009.

All four members of the group are busy. "I'm glad to be able to sit back and do my thing," Taboo said in 2011. "The Peas' legacy will keep living on no matter what, because each individual doing their thing will bring awareness to the Black Eyed Peas. Some people are going to be like, 'Thank God the Black Eyed Peas are gone. They're everywhere.' It's cool. There are some people that are glad and some people that are sad. At the end of the day, we love all our Peabodies, and we're grateful to be a strong family."

One by-product may be that the spirit of the original group resurfaces: will.i.am never stops being in the studio. "Every time he's in the studio, me and apl.de.ap will stop by," Taboo added. "It's all positive things. I hate when people say, 'Oh, it's the end of the Black Eyed Peas. The Black Eyed Peas are breaking up.' No, it's not a break-up. It's just a little break, giving people some time to rejuvenate and then come back strong and compete."

Part of the reason for the sabbatical is to give Fergie an opportunity to spend time with Josh Duhamel. "The Black Eyed Peas taking a little break is something that we respect and we all agreed upon," Taboo said. "We have to respect Ferg. [She] is our sister. She definitely wants to have a family, and we're happy for her. And we're going to keep being a strong family being there and supporting her."

Although, of course, it wasn't all about settling down with a family. In January 2012, Fergie became the owner of Californian-based Voli Vodka, a spirit that was between 25 and 40% less calorific than other vodkas. For someone who had loudly proclaimed French rival brand Gray Goose on 'London Bridge', the wheat-based drink, aimed squarely at the sophisticated party market, seemed to fit with Fergie's increasingly grown-up good-time persona.

The company's CEO, Adam Kamenstein, said in a statement: "As a brand that appeals to women as well as men, it has always been our goal to align with a vibrant, fun, and sexy female, such as Fergie. We were thrilled at Fergie's passion for Voli and interest in an even larger role with the brand as a partner and owner."

"I'm excited about my new partnership with Voli Light Vodka; a company that understands the modern girl on the go," Fergie said. "A fit and active lifestyle can now happily co-exist with a sexy night on the town with your girlfriends or your man... Voli's innovative and delicious low-calorie vodkas mean I can have my workouts not be ruined by a night out. J'adore Voli!"

With Fergie taking time out, apl.de.ap doing ambassadorial work through his *We Can Be Anything* project for children in the Philippines alongside his apl. Foundation, and Taboo out on a DJ tour in 2012, there is little question that the last has not been heard of the Black Eyed Peas. One persistent rumour was that Fergie could be replaced with singer and group friend, Ashanti. After all, they have done it once, surely they could do it again. That said, this unfounded rumour seems just wild speculation and frankly, at the moment, it would be hard for will.i.am to find the time.

will.i.am remains ubiquitous. His fourth solo album *#willpower* is soon to be released at the time of writing. He took part in the BBC TV talent show, *The Voice*, as one of the panel of judges, further enforcing his close relationship with the UK. He told the BBC: "I'm proud to be doing *The Voice UK* because the UK was the first place I saw success. It's the place I'm the most creative outside of home." will.i.am added a benign, mercurial presence to the programme – on a panel with Jessie J, Danny O'Donoghue from the successful indie pop band the Script and industry legend Tom Jones. The show has been adapted from a successful Dutch talent show which first broadcast in 2010, and had an American adaptation in 2011. It presents itself as a higher-brow alternative to ITV's successful *X-Factor*, itself a show that will.i.am was no stranger to. Though nominally cast in the 'bad guy' role that popular television talent shows demands, will.i.am seemed happy to share his knowledge and came across as very fair and measured. Aside from his obvious showbusiness, will.i.am has been most astute at playing the music industry to his favour. He reminisced in 2011, "Our whole thing was college kids, because we rocked with a band. College, college, college," he told Steve Stoute. "Then the Internet came and the college kids got our shit for free. I was like, 'Yo, why is it that we sell less records but we sell more tickets? So, I didn't hate the Internet. I met Shawn Fanning and started going to Silicon Valley all the time trying to figure it out. So then when we finally started touring..., I noticed that people started watching the shows differently. In 2002, they watched concerts [just watching the stage]. In 2003, they watched concerts [through the camera on their phones]... The introduction of the camera on your phone changed your behaviour at events. You no longer record the memories in your mind. That wasn't good enough. Now you want to record on your piece of hardware. I came home and I was like, 'Yo, Jimmy! I just found something out. We need to get into hardware." Hence the constant stream of endorsements, board seats, Internet channels and boundary-pushing. It seems wholly appropriate that they became the first group to sell a million downloads of a digital single in the UK with 'I Gotta Feeling'.

will.i.am's grasp of the 'new' music industry and the challenges faced by current groups is astute. In 2006 he was already casting a beady eye across what was happening and looking for the best methods to stay ahead. "It's just about new media outlets. I have a lot of ideas about that! When you go get your money at the bank and there's a TV screen right there on the ATM, at some point somebody is going to infiltrate that and make a deal to play their music while people are taking their money out. When you're pumping gas and watching the numbers go by, it takes 10 minutes; you might as well listen to a song." No doubt about it, he is one of the smartest men in popular music.

To dismiss him as a cartoon-like buffoon is to both embrace and miss the point entirely. will.i.am's low-key, humble approach to his success is refreshing. "I fly both first class and coach. When you become one of those artists that always fly first class you lose your touch with the people and yourself. I get my own bags when I'm at the hotel. I stay humble because the place where I'm at now I won't be 10 years from now. Ten years from now, I can be much, much bigger. So I'm humbled about how I have been able to grow. I've gone from playing colleges to playing stadiums." And that sense of humility is never lost in his work, no matter how swaggering it sometimes may be.

will.i.am, certainly at his mid 00s peak, was able to look back while looking forward: "I love music. I was inspired by artists like Earth, Wind & Fire, Bob Marley, Peter Tosh – and they would fuse social issues into their music, so I don't think of it as political activism but social activism. I don't like politics." will.i.am remains a riddle wrapped in an enigma. He has publicly stated that he doesn't like politics, yet was instrumental in putting together one of the most significant popular campaigns for a political leader in US history. What is true, however, is that will.i.am comes from the tradition of Sylvester Stewart, Prince and Nile Rodgers – he is a musical innovator, simply working in another time.

Few groups split the crowd quite as much as the Black Eyed Peas. There can be no question that they know their way around a pop song but the brush-strokes of their look and shtick and the cartoon-like nature of their modus operandi go back to *The Archies* in the late sixties. Serious pop fans are not interested. In 2011, there was a mix-up with an award MTV bestowed on the US rock duo, critical darlings Black Keys. Instead of writing their name, MTV inscribed the trophy with the Black Eyed Peas instead. The Black Keys commented, "We figured that we should get proper ones made with our names on it, because in 20 years, nobody's going to know who the Black Eyed Peas are. We'd have this stupid award with Black Eyed Peas on it and nobody's going to get the joke." Time will tell...

The Black Eyed Peas' music is big, at times stupidly reductive, strewn with missteps (this writer may never come to terms with the sheer awfulness of 'My Humps') and glaringly obvious, but the heart, sincerity and sentiment behind it at times is overwhelming. Every generation gets the music it deserves, and frankly, alongside some of the over-produced confections grown in a laboratory that pass as mainstream pop in the 00s, thank heavens for will.i.am and the Black Eyed Peas.

# Black Eyed Peas UK
# Discography

**ALBUMS**

**BEHIND THE FRONT**
Fallin' Up / Clap Your Hands / Joints And Jam / The Way U Make Me Feel / Movement / Karma / Be Free / Say Goodbye / Duet / Communication / What It Is / ¿Que Dices? / A8 / Love Won't Wait / Head Bobs / Positivity
**Interscope/ will.i.am Music Group IND 90152**
**June 1998**

**BRIDGING THE GAP**
BEP Empire / Weekends / Get Original / Hot / Cali To New York / Lil' Lil' / On My Own / Release / Bridging The Gaps / Go Go / Rap Song / Bringing It Back / Tell Your Mama Come / Request + Line
CD BONUS TRACK: Magic
**Interscope/ will.i.am Music Group 490 781-2**
**September 2000**

**ELEPHUNK**
Hands Up / Labor Day (It's A Holiday) / Let's Get (It Started) / Hey Mama / Shut Up / Smells Like Funk / Latin Girls /Sexy / Fly Away / The Boogie That Be / The apl Song / Anxiety / Where Is The Love / Third Eye
CD BONUS TRACKS: Rock My Shit / What's Goin' Down
**A&M/will.i.am Music Group 9860692**
**June 2003**

**MONKEY BUSINESS**
Pump It / Don't Phunk With My Heart / My Style / Don't Lie / My Humps / Like That / Dum Diddly / Feel It / Gone Going / They Don't Want Music / Disco Club / Bebot / Ba Bump / Audio Delite At Low Fidelity / Union
**A&M/will.i.am Music Group 9882184**
**May 2005**

**THE E.N.D**
Boom Boom Pow / Rock That Body / Meet Me Halfway / Imma Be / I Gotta Feeling / Alive / Missing You / Ring-A-Ling / Party All The Time / Out Of My Head / Electric City / Showdown / Now Generation / One Tribe
CD BONUS TRACKS: Rockin' To The Beat / Mare
**Interscope   0602527081427**
**June 2009**

**THE BEGINNING**
The Time (Dirty Bit) / Light Up the Night / Love You Long Time / XOXOXO / Someday / Whenever / Fashion Beats / Don't Stop The Party / Do It Like This [The Situation] / [The Coming] /[Own It ] // The Best One Yet (The Boy) / Just Can't Get Enough / Play It Loud / [Everything Wonderful feat. David Guetta] / [Phenomenon / [Take It Off]
**Interscope 0602527574882**
**November 2010**

## ODDITIES

### RENEGOTIATIONS – THE REMIXES
Like That – Album Version / Ba Bump – Erick Sermon Remix / My Style (Feat. Justin Timberlake) – DJ Premier Remix / They Don't Want Music (Feat. James Brown) – Pete Rock Remix / Feel It – Jazzy Jeff Soulful Remix / Audio Delite – Album Version / Disco Club – Large Pro Peas Remix
**A&M /will.i.am Music Group 9838578-4 (US IMPORT)
March 2006**


## SINGLES

**1998**
Joints & Jam

**1999**
Karma

**2000**
Weekends

**2001**
Request + Line

**2003**
Where Is The Love
Shut Up

**2004**
Hey Mama
Let's Get It Started

**2005**
Don't Phunk With My Heart
Don't Lie
My Humps

**2006**
Pump It

**2009**
Boom Boom Pow
I Gotta Feeling
Meet Me Halfway
Imma Be

**2010**
Rock That Body
The Time (Dirty Bit)

**2011**
Just Can't Enough
Don't Stop The Party

**DVDS**

**BEHIND THE BRIDGE TO ELEPHUNK**
Let's Get Retarded (Live) / Hey Mama / Shut Up / Where Is The Love / B.E.P. Empire / Weekends / Get Original / Request + Line / Fallin' Up / Joints and Jam / Karma / What It Is / Head Bobs
**A&M /will.i.am Music Group 986 255-0**
**September 2004**

**LIVE FROM SYDNEY TO VEGAS**
Hey Mama / Smells Like Phunk / Dum Diddly / Don't Lie / Shut Up (Knee Deep Remix) Medley / Taboo Freestyle / apl. de. ap. Freestyle / will.i.am Freestyle / Fergie Freestyle / Labor Day (It's A Holiday) /

Pump It / Where Is The Love / Don't Phunk With My Heart / Let's Get It Started
**A&M /will.i.am Music Group 987 575 3**
**December 2006**

**FERGIE**

**ALBUM**

**THE DUTCHESS**
Fergalicious / Clumsy / All That I Got (The Make Up Song) / London Bridge / Pedestal /Voodoo Doll / Glamorous / Here I Come /Velvet / Big Girls Don't Cry / Mary Jane Shoes / Losing My Ground / Finally
**A&M /will.i.am Music Group 1707562**
**September 2006**

**SINGLES**

**2006**
London Bridge
Fergalicious

**2007**
Glamorous
Big Girls Don't Cry (Personal)
Clumsy
Impacto (Daddy Yankee ft. Fergie)

**2008**
Finally (ft. John Legend)
Party People (Nelly ft. Fergie)

**2010**
Getting' Over You (David Guetta and Chris Willis ft. Fergie and LMFAO)
Beautiful Dangerous (Slash ft. Fergie)

**will.i.am**

**ALBUMS**

**LOST CHANGE**
Ev Rebahdee / Lay Me Down / Possessions / Tai Arrive / If You Didn't
Know / Money / Lost Change / I Am / Hooda Hella U / Lost Change
In E Minor / Yadda Yadda / Em A Double Dee / Control Tower / Lost
Change In D Minor
**BBE BBEBGCD003**
**October 2001**

**MUST B 21 – Soundtrack To Get Things Started**
Take It (ft. KRS-One) / Nah Mean (ft. Phife) / B Boyz (ft. MC
Supernatural) / Here To Party (ft. Flii, Planet Asia and Kron Don) /
Bomb Bomb (Interlude) / Bomb Bomb (ft. MC Supernatural) / Swing
By My Way (ft. John Legend) / It's OK (ft. Triple Seven and Dante
Santiago) / Mash Out (Interlude) / Mash Out (ft. MC Lyte and Fergie)
/ Ride Ride (ft. John Legend) / Sumthin' Special (interlude) / Sumthin'
Special (ft. Niu, Dante Santiago and Taboo) / I'm Ready (Y'All Ain't
Ready For This) (ft. Tash and MC Supernatural) / We Got Chu (ft.
Planet Asia and Flii) / Go! (interlude) / Go!
**BBE BBEGCD005**
**September 2003**

**SONGS ABOUT GIRLS**
Over / Heartbreaker / I Got It From My Mama / She's A Star / Get
Your Money / The Donque Song (ft. Snoop Dogg) / Impatient / One
More Chance / Invisible / Fantastic / Fly Girl / Dynmaite (Interlude)
/ Ain't It Pretty / Make It Funky / S.O.S. (Mother Nature) / Spending
Money
**Interscope / will.i.am Music Group 1747675**
**September 2007**

# #WILLPOWER
Interscope / will.i.am Music Group
April 2012

## SINGLES

### 2005
CB (Sangue Born) (Marcello D2 ft. will.i.am)
La Patte (Saian Super Crew ft. will.i.am)
Beep (Pussycat Dolls ft. will.i.am)

### 2006
I Love My Chick (Busta Rhymes ft. Kelis and will.i.am)
Fergalicious (Fergie ft. will.i.am)
Hip Hop Is Dead (Nas ft. will.i.am)
A Dream (Common ft. will.i.am)

### 2007
I Got It From My Mama
Baby Love (Nicole Scherzinger ft. will.i.am)
Hot Thing (Talib Kweli ft. will.i.am)
Wait A Minute (Just A Touch) (Estelle ft. will.i.am)
I Want You (Common ft. will.i.am)

### 2008
In The Ayer (Flo Rida ft. will.i.am)
What's Your Name (Usher ft. will.i.am)
All My Life (In The Ghetto) (Jay Rock ft. Lil Wayne and will.i.am)
The Girl Is Mine 2008 (with Michael Jackson)
Yes We Can
We Are The Ones
Heartbreaker (ft. Cheryl Cole)
One More Chance
It's A New Day

**2009**
3 Words (Cheryl Cole ft. will.i.am)

**2010**
OMG (Usher ft. will.i.am)

**2011**
Forever (Wolfgang Gartner ft. will.i.am)
Free (Natalia Kills ft. will.i.am)
Check It Out (With Nicki Minaj)
T.H.E (The Hardest Ever) (ft. Mick Jagger and Jennifer Lopez)

**2012**
Nothing Really Matters (David Guetta ft. will.i.am)
Great Times

## KEY PRODUCTIONS
**2004**
John Legend – Get Lifted

**2005**
Pussycat Dolls – PCD
Mary J Blige – The Breakthrough
Shaggy – Clothes Drop
Earth Wind & Fire – Illumination

**2006**
Sergio Mendes – Timeless
Justin Timberlake – Future Sex/LoveSounds
Fergie – The Dutchess
Kelis – Kelis Was Here
John Legend – Once Again
Nas – Hip Hop Is Dead

**2007**
Bone Thugs-n-Harmony – Strength And Loyalty
Macy Gray – Big
Common – Finding Forever
Chris Brown – Exclusive

**2008**
Michael Jackson – Thriller 25
Mariah Carey – E=MC2
Sergio Mendes – Encanto
John legend – Evolver
Pussycat Dolls – Doll Domination

**2009**
U2 – No Line On the Horizon
Flo Rida – R.O.O.T.S
Cheryl Cole – 3 Words
Rhianna – Rated R

**2010**
Kelis – Flesh Tone
Usher – Raymond V. Raymond

**2011**
Britney Spears – Femme Fatale

# Black Eyed Peas Bibliography

Boyer, Paul S., Clifford E. Clark Jr., Joseph F. Kett, Neal Salisbury, Harvard Sitkoff and Nancy Woloch (Eds.). *The Enduring Vision: A History Of The American People*. DC Heath, Lexington, Toronto, 1996.

Bronson, Fred. *The Billboard Book Of Number 1 Hits*, Updated and Expanded 5th Edition. Billboard Books, 2003

Brown, Jake. *The Black Eyed Peas. An Unauthorised Biography*. Collossus Books, Phoenix, 2008.

Canfield, Jack, Mark Victor Hansen, Jo-Ann Geffen (eds.) *Chicken Soup For the Soul: The Story Behind The Son*. CSFTS, Cos Cob, CT, 2009

Carter, Shawn (Jay-Z). *Decoded*. Virgin Books, London, 2010

Dickson, Paul. *From Elvis To E-Mail: Trends Events And Trivia From The Postwar Era To The End Of The Century*. Federal Street Press, Springfield, MA, 1999.

Heller, Jerry with Gil Reavill. *Ruthless: A Memoir*. Simon Spotlight Entertainment, New York, 2006.

Keener, Rob and George Pitts. *VX: 10 Years Of Vibe Photography*. Vibe Books, New York, 2003.

Kutner, Jon and Spencer Leigh. *The 1000 UK Number One Hits*. Omnibus Press, London, 2005.

McIver, Joel. *Ice Cube: Attitude* Sanctuary, London, 2002

Sanna, EJ. *Hip-Hop: The Black Eyed Peas*. Mason Crest, Broomhall, Pennsylvania, 2008.

Shapiro, Peter. *The Rough Guide To Hip-Hop*. Rough Guides, London, 2001.

Sherman, Zachary, Kristopher Smith, Jaymes Reed, Darren G. Davis. *Fame: The Black Eyed Peas*. Bluewater Comics, Vancouver, Washington. Feb 11

Shea, Molly. *Hip Hop Headliners: The Black Eyed Peas*. Gareth Stevens Publishing, New York, 2011.

Southall, Brian. *The A-Z Of Record Labels*. Second Edition. Sanctuary Publishing, London, 2003.

Taboo with Steve Dennis. *Fallin' Up – My Story*. Touchstone, New York, 2011

Walker, John. *Halliwell's Film Video & DVD Guide 2006*. Harper Collins, London, 2006.

**Newspapers and Magazines:**

Many publications including Vibe; The Metro; The Times; The Sunday Express; Time Out New York; Muzik; The Independent; Billboard; The Mirror; Q; Mojo; New Musical Express; Clash Magazine; The Guardian; The LA Times; Uncut; Ebony, Newsweek; the Houston Chronicle; People Magazine; USA Today; Entertainment Weekly; Essence; News Of the World


**Internet:**
Allmusic, Discogs, Metacritic, Wikipedia

Key You Tube:
www.youtube.com/watch?v=Nrh7-fVtzwo&feature=related
www.youtube.com/watch?v=mV1kkvN05P4
www.youtube.com/watch?v=q3gHlOjV3dw&feature=related
Live 2010: www.youtube.com/watch?v=Mi5rKHWHO-M
You Tube: Eazy-E Funeral: www.youtube.com/watch?v=sdAMF--Fyec&feature=related


**Websites:**

**Adam.Intel**: iam-fan.com/?page_id=30

**Apl De Ap**:
www.asianjournal.com/aj-magazine/midweek-mgzn/678-the-apl-that-gave-back-to-the-tree.html?showall=1

People Magazine Ap. De. Ap: www.people.com/people/archive/article/0,,20460263,00.html

Apl De Ap – Azin Nightlife - www.jizo-entertainment.com/interviews/APL_DE_AP_black_eyed_peas_The_End_Interview.htm

Apl Brother: uk.eonline.com/news/black_eyed_peas_brother_
murdered/82289

**Alton Towers**: http://www.thisisstaffordshire.co.uk/Black-Eyed-Peas-
wow-crowds-Alton-Towers-extended/story-12898847-detail/story.
html

**Allure interview, July 2009**: brookehauser.com/?articles=dancing-
queen

**Avon perfume**: http://shop.avon.com/shop/product.aspx?pf_id=39692
www.avoncompany.com/aboutavon/history/mcconnell.html

**Bacardi**: /www.prnewswire.com/news-releases/bacardir-becomes-
official-spirit-of-the-black-eyed-peas-the-end-world-concert-
tour-2010-83479262

**Balistyx**: www.facebook.com/pages/BALISTYX/497375275353

**Bebot**: morecomplex.blogspot.com

morecomplex.blogspot.com/2006/08/open-letter-re-bebot-music-
vidoes.html

www.mtv.com/news/articles/1536408/black-eyed-peas-lowbudget-
bebot-shoot.jhtml

*The Beginning* www.hitquarters.com/index.php3?page=intrview/
opar/intrview_JFrost_interview.html

online.wsj.com/article/SB100014240527487047002045756427625286
80400.html

**Big Girls Don't Cry**: www.badboyblog.com/item/2006/9/21/
more-on-fergie-big-girls-don-t-cry

**Black Eyed Peas**: getting Retarded?: www.hiphopdx.com/index/
interviews/id.289/title.black-eyed-peas-getting-retarded

**Black Eyed Peas Experience:** sweetenyourwords.com/index.
php?option=com_content&view=article&id=446&Itemid=281

www.iol.co.za/scitech/technology/gaming/raving-rabbids-and-the-
black-eyed-peas-1.1213443

**Black Eyed Peas postpone solo albums:** www.mtv.com/news/
articles/1488181/black-eyed-peas-freeze-solo-lps.jhtml

**Boom Boom Box Interview**: iam-fan.com/?p=1084
www.billboard.com/#/features/video-will-i-am-on-making-hot-100-
history-1004004947.story

**Bridging The Gap**: www.hiphopdx.com/index/album-reviews/
id.21/title.black-eyed-peas-bridging-the-gap

**Bridging The Gap - MTV**: www.mtv.com/news/articles/1425922/
black-eyed-peas-talk-bridging-gaps.jhtml

**Bucky Jonson**: www.bbemusic.com/data.pl?release=BBECD083

**Cherry Lane:** www.thefreelibrary.com/
Cherry+Lane+Inks+Publishing+Deal+with+Black+Eyed+Peas.
-a0105730719

**Cracked. Com**: www.cracked.com/video_17618_black-eyed-peas-
have-officially-written-worst-song-ever.html

**Cheryl Cole** - www.guardian.co.uk/culture/2009/oct/22/cheryl-
cole-3-words-review

*The Dutchess*: www.ew.com/ew/article/0,,1535137,00.htm

www.mtv.com/news/articles/1539519/dutchess-meet-real-fergie.jhtml

www.mtv.com/news/articles/1538614/fergie-spices-up-lp-with-ludacris-breal.jhtml

www.theage.com.au/news/music/fergie-free-from-the-peas/2006/09/25/1159036445782.html?page=3

www.billboard.com/news/q-a-fergie-and-will-i-am-on-the-dutchess-1003157589.story#/news/q-a-fergie-and-will-i-am-on-the-dutchess-1003157589.story

www.contactmusic.com/news/mia-slams-fergie-for-copying-her-style_1044390

top40.about.com/od/singles/gr/fergielondonbr.htm

http://thephoenix.com/boston/music/24519-fergie-the-dutchess/#ixzz1kraUjFHJ

www.popmatters.com/pm/review/fergie-the-dutchess/

www.chartattack.com/reviews/61411/fergie-——-the-dutchess

buzzworthy.mtv.com/2007/10/16/fergies-new-clumsy-video/

**Dylan Dresdow**: www.soundonsound.com/sos/jul09/articles/it_0709.htm

**Eazy-E**: www.eazy-e.com

**Earth Wind and Fire:** www.contactmusic.com/pages/earthwindandfirex21x09x05

**Ed Magik TV**: zomobo.net/Fergie-Ferguson-Award

*Elephunk*: /www.mtv.com/news/articles/1455157/black-eyed-peas-funky-elephant.jhtml

http://drownedinsound.com/releases/3683/reviews/9600-

www.popmatters.com/pm/review/blackeyedpeas-elephunk

http://www.rollingstone.com/music/artists/black-eyed-peas#ixzz1f612xFpd

**The E.N.D World Tour**: www.billboard.biz/bbbiz/randb-hip-hop/black-eyed-peas-prep-for-high-tech-summer-1003984131.story

**The E.N.D World Tour Design**: Livedesignonline.com/concerts/0427-bep-end-world-tour/

**Sarah Ferguson** www.boston.com/ae/celebrity/articles/2006/11/16/clarke_takes_a_pass_on_game_plan_shot/

**Fergie woman of year**: www.billboard.com/#/news/fergie-q-a-billboard-s-woman-of-the-year-1004133607.story?page=2

**Stacy Ferguson**: www.papermag.com/arts_and_style/2005/07/fergie-solo-star.php

www.guardian.co.uk/music/2006/sep/08/urban.popandrock

Fergie Billboard interview: hpmusic.net/1365/fergie-interview-for-billboard-magazine

Ferguson Pregnant?: http://www.dailymail.co.uk/tvshowbiz/article-2061633/Fergie-makes-final-performances-Black-Eyed-Peas-Sao-Paulo.html#ixzz1k5cb9Bei

**Fergie and Duhamel wedding**: www.marieclaire.com/celebrity-lifestyle/celebrities/fergie-interview-black-eyed-peas

www.usmagazine.com/celebrity-news/news/fergie-and-josh-duhamel-celebrate-third-wedding-anniversary-2012101

www.elle.com/Pop-Culture/Cover-Shoots/Fergie/Fergie-is-ELLE-s-May-2010-Cover-Girl-Get-More-Cover-Shoots-on-ELLE.com

**Fazeteen**: www.fazeteen.com/issue17/black_eyed_peas.html

**David Guetta**: www.hiphopdx.com/index/news/id.10045/title.david-guetta-talks-producing-i-gotta-feeling-for-b-e-p-

**Hip Hop DX**: www.hiphopdx.com/index/interviews/id.874/title.william-i-am-hip-hopyou-arent

**David Faustino**: 215hiphop.ning.com/profiles/blogs/david-faustino-interview

**Dipdive** – Will.i.am. blog: dipdive.com/member/iamwill/

**Elle** - www.elle.com/Pop-Culture/Celebrity-Spotlight/will-i-am

**Fred Rister**: www.fredrister.com

**Glamorous**: hatgrapejuice.net/2011/07/vault-fergie-glamourou

**Hip Hop DX**: www.hiphopdx.com/index/news/id.17723/title.black-eyed-peas-to-take-indefinite-hiatus-post-miami-florida-show

**I Gotta Feeling** - www.youtube.com/watch?v=uSD4vsh1zDA

I gotta feeling sales stats: music.yahoo.com/blogs/chart-watch/week-ending-march-20-2011-songs-the-chris-brown-matter.html

http://www.independent.co.uk/arts-entertainment/music/news/black-eyed-peas-to-be-first-to-sell-million-downloads-in-uk-1999721.html

**Imma Be**:
www.radaronline.com/exclusives/2010/01/fergie-stuns-space-age-body-suit-sandstorm-delays-video-shoot

www.billboard.com/#/news/black-eyed-peas-back-on-top-of-hot-100-with-1004070968.story?tag=newstop1

**John Lennon Educational Tour Bus:** www.lennonbus.org/about_the_bus/press_releases/1450

**Just Can't Get Enough:** www.etonline.com/music/108772_Black_Eyed_Peas_Film_New_Video_in_Japan_a_Week_Before_Disaster/

**Losing My Ground**: www.hollywire.com/music/fergie-on-glamour-magazines-may-2008-issue

**Marie Claire**: www.marieclaire.com/world-reports/opinion/black-eyed-peas-interview

**Minot Rising**: www.minotrising.com

www.minotrising.com/wrap_up.pdf

**Nelly Furtado**: www.thehollywoodgossip.com/2007/04/random-celebrity-feud-of-the-day-fergie-vs-nelly-furtado/

**Madagascar numbers:** www.boxofficemojo.com/movies/?id=madagascar2.htm

latimesblogs.latimes.com/music_blog/2008/10/william-hans-zi.html

**Madagascar:** www.youtube.com/watch?v=tIEze2vYd3o

**Meet Me Halfway**: www.dailymail.co.uk/tvshowbiz/reviews/
article-1203304/The-Peas-mad-band--make-up.html

dipdive.com/member/iamwill/blog/4573/

**Sergio Mendes**: All Music.com/Timeless: www.allmusic.com/album/
timeless-r816381/review

*Monkey Business* **Reviews:**
Village Voice: www.villagevoice.com/2005-07-19/music/pop-your-
phunk/
www.guardian.co.uk/music/2005/may/27/popandrock.shopping5
www.metacritic.com/music/monkey-business/critic-reviews

*The E.N.D* **Reviews**:
Entertainment weekly: www.ew.com/ew/article/0,,20282707,00.html
The Guardian: www.guardian.co.uk/music/2009/jun/05/blac-eyed-
peas-end-album
http://www.prefixmag.com/reviews/black-eyed-peas/the-end/26153/
/latimesblogs.latimes.com/music_blog/2009/06/album-review-black-
eyed-peas-the-end.html
http://www.slantmagazine.com/music/review/the-black-eyed-peas-
the-e-n-d/1758
www.digitalspy.co.uk/music/singlesreviews/a206986/black-eyed-peas-
rock-that-body.html

*The Beginning* **Reviews:**
The Guardian: www.guardian.co.uk/music/2010/nov/25/black-eyed-
peas-begninning-review?INTCMP=ILCNETTXT3487

/www.independent.co.uk/arts-entertainment/music/reviews/album-
black-eyed-peas-the-beginning-interscopepolydor-2143857.html

**Miami:** www.theimproper.com/music/3986/fergie-black-eyed-peas-bid-farewell-in-miami-watch

**Toronto Sun Interview**: jam.canoe.ca/Music/Artists/B/Black_Eyed_Peas/2005/06/05/pf-1072398.html

**LATIMES:** latimesblogs.latimes.com/music_blog/2010/05/william-rave-dance-music-convergence-daisy.html

**The Guardian Interview**: www.guardian.co.uk/music/2009/may/22/black-eyed-peas-interview

**Karen's Kids**: karenskids.org

**Kim Hill interview** - /portalblackeyedpeas.com/2011/08/10/exclusive-interview-kim-hill-former-vocalist-of-black-eyed-peas/

**Let's Get It Started**: www.songfacts.com/detail.php?id=4532

**London Bridge**: www.mtv.com/news/articles/1536116/black-eyed-peas-fergie-first-solo-video.jhtml

http://www.rollingstone.com/music/news/fergie-dances-with-herself-20061019#ixzz1klGezgid

**Jim Deor**: www.jimdero.com/News%202006/May5Blackeyedpeas.htm

**Michael Jackson and will.i.am:**
http://today.msnbc.msn.com/id/15529981#.Tp8de2Bgpvl

**Macy Gray**: www.guardian.co.uk/music/2007/mar/30/urban.shopping
articles.latimes.com/2007/mar/25/entertainment/ca-rack25

www.slantmagazine.com/music/review/macy-gray-big/1072
gaylife.about.com/od/music/a/macygray.htm

**Sergio Mendes:** www.bluesandsoul.com/feature/303/bands_get_a_
brazilian/

**Metacritic**: www.metacritic.com/music/the-end

**Monkey Business**: allhiphop.com/2005/11/22/will-i-am-of-bep-
the-big-payback

**Monkey Business press release**: www.sing365.com/music/lyric.nsf/
Black-Eyed-Peas-Biography/6747F9726428AE2748256A17000B4062

**MTV**

MTV review of THE: www.mtv.com/news/articles/1674729/will-i-
am-jennifer-lopez-amas.jhtml

MTV review of Timeless: www.mtv.com/news/articles/1517301/
william-wants-pull-rubin-with-sergio.jhtml

MTV at Wiltern Theater: www.mtv.com/news/articles/1485991/
justin-upstages-nerd-black-eyed-peas.jhtml

MTV I Gotta Feeling. www.mtv.com/news/articles/1662489/black-
eyed-peas-prince-i-gotta-feeling.jhtml

MTV – Lost Change: www.mtv.com/news/articles/1519257/william-
im-battle-mc-dont-forget-it.jhtml

My Humps: http://pitchfork.com/features/staff-lists/6219-2005-
comments-lists-the-15-worst-releases-of-2005/

My Humps/Morrisette: www.spin.com/articles/alanis-morissette-my-humps-video

My Humps/Slate: /www.slate.com/articles/arts/music_box/2005/12/notes_on_humps.html

My Humps/Cake: www.people.com/people/article/0,,20034500,00.htm
My Humps/Alanis Morrissette: www.accesshollywood.com/_article_10455?&__source=rss%257Clatest_news

**Musicane**: top40-charts.com/news.php?nid=34752

**NME Jazz Café** 1998review: www.nme.com/reviews/artistKeyname/204

**New Year's Eve Luxor performance:** www.vegaschatter.com/tag/Black%20Eyed%20Peas

**New York Times:** www.nytimes.com/2011/01/23/magazine/23FOB-Q4-t.html

**Now 38 review**: www.avclub.com/articles/vol-38-may-2011,59077/

**Oprah interview**: www.oprah.com/oprahs-lifeclass/Black-Eyed-Peas-Singer-williams-Aha-Moment#ixzz1cSRQDWnX

www.oprah.com/oprahshow/williams-Childhood-Home-Video

**Pepsi**: www.bizcommunity.com/Article/157/82/17101.html

**Palm Beach Post**: www.pbpulse.com/music/concert-reviews/live-shows/2011/11/25/black-eyed-peas-show-a-long-night-with-some-great-moments/

**Papa Roach**: www.mtv.com/news/articles/1453368/papa-roach-team-with-black-eyed-peas.jhtml

**Party All The Time**: www.thedailyswarm.com/swarm/did-black-eyed-peas-steal-freelands-mancry/

www.timesofmalta.com/articles/view/20090708/local/black-eyed-peas-plan-tribute-to-michael-jackson.264193

**Peapod**: www.peapodfoundation.org/

**Polow Da Don**: www.futureproducers.com/forums/music-genres/rap-hip-hop-r-b/polow-da-don-interview-allhiphop-216210/

**Pop Matters**: www.popmatters.com/pm/review/blackeyedpeas-monkey

**Poseidon film**: www.mtv.com/news/articles/1506604/fergies-first-big-movie-disaster.jhtml

**Power To the People**: www.make-some-noise.org/noise.amnesty.org/atf/cf/%7BC1082DC5-B59B-4804-8F65-670576D6D430%7D/BLACK%20EYED%20PEAS%20ON%20RECORD%20OF%20THE%20YEAR%20051208.PDF

**PR Newswire**: www.prnewswire.com/news-releases/first-instant-def-digisode-starring-william-fergie-taboo-and-apldeap-now-live-at-instantdefcom-55909347.html

**Rap Reviews**: www.rapreviews.com/archive/2005_06_monkeyb.html

**Remix mag**: emusician.com/remixmag/artists_interviews/musicians/remix_direct_drive/

**RIME**: www.daveyd.com/williaminterview.html

**Robin Hood**: www.sting.com/news/article/4590

**Ron Fair:** www.mtv.com/news/articles/1484775/making-black-eyed-peas-where-love.jhtml

**Rolling Stone**: www.rollingstone.com/music/news/fergie-dances-with-herself-20061019

Rolling Stone THE: http://www.rollingstone.com/music/songreviews/t-h-e-the-hardest-ever-20111128#ixzz1gJNAlveR

www.rollingstone.com/music/news/exclusive-will-i-am-on-how-he-got-mick-jagger-and-jennifer-lopez-for-new-single-20111120#ixzz1gJOtY3D0

Rolling Stone review of *Monkey Business:* www.sting.com/news/article/988

Rolling Stone: Stevie Wonder - http://www.rollingstone.com/music/news/stevie-wonder-earth-wind-and-fire-to-rock-the-white-house-20090220#ixzz1ix35N8GY

**David Saltz**: www.pbpulse.com/music/concert-reviews/live-shows/2011/11/22/black-eyed-peas-had-right-guy-for-the-job-for-tour-ending-show

www.hitquarters.com/index.php3?page=intrview/opar/intrview_Ron_Fair_Interview.html

Setlist FM: www.setlist.fm/setlist/the-black-eyed-peas/2007/wembley-stadium-london-england-23d0fc03.html

**Sexual Harassment:** http://citinite.wordpress.com/2011/02/12/sexual-harrassment/

**David Sonenberg:** www.musicalive.com/adminImage/MA2004-11_1472-DSonnenberg.pdf

***Songs About Girls:*** www.billboard.com/bbcom/news/article_display.jsp?vnu_content_id=1003617523#/bbcom/news/article_display.jsp?vnu_content_id=1003617523

BBC review: www.bbc.co.uk/music/reviews/zfvr

www.contactmusic.com/news/william-learned-from-solo-failure_1187708

Entertainment Weekly www.ew.com/ew/article/0,,20057888,00.html

***Slant review:*** www.slantmagazine.com/music/review/will-i-am-songs-about-girls/1181

www.myspace.com/video/will-i-am/will-i-am-quot-songs-about-girls-quot-myspace-early-album-preview-part-1/17997469

**SOS:** www.rollingstone.com/music/lists/the-15-corniest-pro-environment-songs-20110422/will-i-am-s-o-s-mother-nature-19691231#ixzz1lQeGIMqm

**Spin:** www.spin.com/articles/black-keys-not-yet-done-insulting-black-eyed-peas

www.spin.com/articles/william-breaks-down-black-eyed-peas-new-disc

www.aceshowbiz.com/news/view/00017404.html

www.spin.com/reviews/black-eyed-peas-beginning-williaminterscope

www.guardian.co.uk/lifeandstyle/2008/aug/03/familyandrelationships.
whatiknowaboutwomen

**Streetfighter**: uk.bluray.ign.com/articles/100/1000408p1.html

**The Sun** – Willi I Am and Cheryl Cole: www.thesun.co.uk/sol/
homepage/showbiz/bizarre/2983422/WillIAm-talks-about-love-and-
friendship-with-Cheryl-Cole.html

**Sun Life Stadium**: http://www.miaminewtimes.com/2011-11-17/
music/black-eyed-peas-at-sun-life-stadium-november-23/

**Superbowl:** http://www.rollingstone.com/music/news/its-official-
the-black-eyed-peas-playing-super-bowl-20101125#ixzz1cdpdr4Z9

www.greatpersonalities.com/will.i.am/2.htm#ixzz1gskBGs6d

www.hollywoodreporter.com/news/super-bowl-halftime-show-
critics-97028

tvbythenumbers.zap2it.com/2011/02/07/super-bowl-xlv-poised-
to-break-viewing-records-ties-1987-with-highest-overnight-ratings-
ever/81684/

blastmagazine.com/the-magazine/entertainment/music/review-the-
super-bowl-xlv-halftime-show-super-sucked/

**Smokin' Grooves:** www.vh1.com/news/articles/500532/19980819/
index.jhtml

**Taboo:** www.ladybrillemag.com/2011/03/taboo-fallin-up-black-
eyed-peas'-rapper-ruminates-about-life-interview.html

Artist Direct: www.artistdirect.com/entertainment-news/article/
interview-taboo-of-the-black-eyed-peas/6070661

**The Tanning effect:**
tanningofamerica.com/blog/steve-stoute-interviews-will-i-am-on-the-tanning-effect

**Time Magazine:** http://www.time.com/time/magazine/article/0,9171,1870496,00.html#ixzz1iwxhWqS2

**Time Magazine**: www.time.com/time/magazine/article/0,9171,1870496,00.html#ixzz1d21IDj5M

**Top Of The Pops Magazine**: www.bbc.co.uk/totp/news/interviews/2005/05/20/19544.shtml

**Rocks Back Pages:** www.rocksbackpages.com/article.html?ArticleID=12643&SearchText=black+eyed+peas

Hammersmith review: www.rocksbackpages.com/article.html?ArticleID=8298

Mean Fiddler review: Black Eyed Peas/2001/Dele Fadele/NME/Black Eyed Peas: Mean Fiddler, London WC2 /19/11/2011 12:33:43/http://www.rocksbackpages.com/article.html?ArticleID=1921

**Sergio Mendes**: Sergio Mendes/2005/Bill DeMain/Performing Songwriter/Legends of Songwriting: Sergio Mendes/07/01/2012 10:16:25/http://www.rocksbackpages.com/article.html?ArticleID=14292

**Urban Smarts**: www.urbansmarts.com/interviews/bep.html

**U2 and will.i.am**: www.spin.com/articles/u2-and-william-collaborating-album

iam-fan.com/2011/07/will-i-am-talks-about-bono-from-u2/

/latimesblogs.latimes.com/music_blog/2009/10/rose-bowl-u2-attendance-will-be-venues-largest-ever.html

**The Voice UK:** www.starpulse.com/news/index.php/2011/12/02/william_joins_the_voice_uk1

**Videos**: top40.about.com/od/popmusicvideogalleries/tp/Top-10-Black-Eyed-Peas-Videos.htm

**Village Voice**: www.villagevoice.com/2001-04-24/music/haikus-and-atmospheres/2/

**X Men**: moviesblog.mtv.com/2008/02/21/william-sings-on-wolverine-becomes-teleporting-mutant

www.mtv.com/news/articles/1589665/william-reveals-xmen-origins-wolverine-details.jhtml

**X-Men Reviews**: www.metacritic.com/movie/x-men-origins-wolverine
www.guardian.co.uk/film/2009/may/01/x-men-origins-wolverine-review
www.empireonline.com/reviews/reviewcomplete.asp?FID=135356

**Wall Street Journal:** online.wsj.com/article/SB100014240527023037206045751699336 36121658.html

**World Cup**: news.bbc.co.uk/1/hi/8571893.stm

www.mtv.com/news/articles/1641300/black-eyed-peas-john-legend-alicia-keys-more-light-up-world-cup-concert.jhtml

http://www.dailymail.co.uk/tvshowbiz/article-1285648/World-Cup-2010-Black-Eyed-Peas-star-Fergie-sultry-Shakira-kick-party.html#ixzz1mdQym62uTaboo

**Yes We Can**: www.npr.org/templates/story/story.
php?storyId=99464506

★★★

**Official website:**
www.blackeyedpeas.com

**Unofficial**
www.portalblackeyedpeas.com

www.bepfanclub.com

# Acknowledgements

To Jules and Flora Easlea. Where is the love? Right here!

To the dear Easleas, Absaloms, Byfords, Batcocks, Cooks and Bushes

To Graham, Wendy, Nathan and Katy Brown

To Chris Charlesworth, David Barraclough, Jacqui Black and Charlie Harris

To 3 Flying Ducks Comedy Club. Leigh On Sea – Quack Quack Quack

The Middle Age Spread massive, Curly Dan, Grandmaster Adam, Dr Andrew B and Beardy Al

Chadders and Chandler

The Wolstanton Cultural Quarter and The Leigh On Sea Scene

To UMSM, Record Collector, Mojo and bbc.co.uk

Johnny Jazz and the Brighton Right-ons